THE NADIR & THE ZENITH

THE NADIR & THE ZENITH

TEMPERANCE & EXCESS IN THE EARLY AFRICAN AMERICAN NOVEL ◆ ANNA POCHMARA

THE UNIVERSITY OF GEORGIA PRESS
ATHENS

© 2021 by the University of Georgia Press
Athens, Georgia 30602
www.ugapress.org
All rights reserved
Designed by Kaelin Chappell Broaddus
Set in 11/13.5 Adobe Jenson Pro by Kaelin Chappell Broaddus

Most University of Georgia Press titles are
available from popular e-book vendors.

Printed digitally

Library of Congress Cataloging-in-Publication Data

Names: Pochmara, Anna, author.
Title: The nadir & the zenith : temperance & excess in the early African American novel / Anna Pochmara.
Other titles: The nadir and the zenith
Description: Athens : The University of Georgia Press, [2021] | Includes bibliographical references and index.
Identifiers: LCCN 2020041574 (print) | LCCN 2020041575 (ebook) | ISBN 9780820358918 (hardback) | ISBN 9780820359021 (paperback) | ISBN 9780820358925 (ebook)
Subjects: LCSH: American fiction—African American authors—History and criticism. | American fiction—19th century—History and criticism. | Temperance in literature. | Characters and characteristics in literature. | African Americans—Intellectual life—19th century.
Classification: LCC PS153.N5 P634 2020 (print) | LCC PS153.N5 (ebook) | DDC 813/.309896073—dc23
LC record available at https://lccn.loc.gov/2020041574
LC ebook record available at https://lccn.loc.gov/2020041575

CONTENTS

ACKNOWLEDGMENTS vii

Introduction ◉ The Zenith and the Nadir
THE EARLY AFRICAN AMERICAN NOVEL
1

Part 1. The Excess of Mulatta Melodrama

Chapter 1 ◉ Mulatta Melodrama
MIXED RACE AND THE MELODRAMATIC
MODE IN THE EARLY BLACK NOVEL
17

Chapter 2 ◉ The Apple Falls Far from the Tree
MATRILINEAL OPPOSITION IN
MULATTA MELODRAMA
31

Chapter 3 ◉ The Fall of Man
WHITE MASCULINITY ON TRIAL
59

Part 2. Black Tropes of Temperance

Chapter 4 ◉ The Genre Mergers of the Nadir
ANTIDRINK LITERATURE, SENTIMENTALISM,
AND NATURALISM IN BLACK
TEMPERANCE NARRATIVES
103

Chapter 5 ◉ Aesthetic Excess, Ethical Discipline,
and Racial Indeterminacy
FRANCES ELLEN WATKINS HARPER'S
SOWING AND REAPING
112

Chapter 6 ◉ Tropes of Temperance,
Specters of Naturalism
AMELIA E. JOHNSON'S
CLARENCE AND CORINNE
131

Chapter 7 ◉ Enslavement to Philanthropy,
Freedom from Heredity
PAUL LAURENCE DUNBAR'S
THE UNCALLED
147

Chapter 8 ◉ Metropolitan Possibilities and Compulsions
THE MULATTA AND THE DANDY IN
PAUL LAURENCE DUNBAR'S
THE SPORT OF THE GODS
165

Conclusion ◉ The Nadir and Beyond
ECHOES OF MULATTA MELODRAMA
AND THE BLACK TEMPERANCE NOVEL IN
THE EARLY TWENTIETH CENTURY
203

NOTES 211
WORKS CITED 225
INDEX 241

ACKNOWLEDGMENTS

✹ ✹ ✹

As with any academic project, this book could not have been written without assistance and encouragement from many people and institutions. I thank my friends and colleagues from the Institute of English Studies at my home university and from the Polish Association for American Studies for their continuing intellectual and emotional support. I am grateful in particular to Agnieszka Graff, Filip Lipiński, Zuzanna Ładyga, Ewa Łuczak, Łukasz Muniowski, Marek Paryż, Justyna Wierzchowska, Justyna Włodarczyk, and Joanna Ziarkowska. I also owe thanks to my friends and colleagues from the CAAR (Collegium for African American Research). I would especially like to thank M. Giulia Fabi, Tess Chakkalal, and Hanna Wallinger, who have encouraged and supported my interest in and research of the Nadir era and have generously shared their own expertise in the field. I'm truly grateful to P. Gabrielle Foreman and Hazel V. Carby, whose work has been an inspiration for my own writing, for their words of support and encouragement. I am indebted to Gene Jarrett for his help with archival sources on Paul Laurence Dunbar. I also consulted the Livesey Collection at the University of Central Lancashire, and I owe gratitude to Annemarie McAllister, the head of the *Demon Drink: Picturing Temperance* project, and to Bob Frost from the Special Collections & University Archives. For the help with my research of casta paintings, I thank Irma Méndez from the Museo de Historia Mexicana, Monterrey. A large part of this book was written during a residency at the Konvent art center in Cal Rosal, Spain, and I am deeply thankful to the local organizers for their warm welcome and to Alejandro Dorda, who initiated the 2018 residency project, as well as to the remaining fifty participants of the program, whose creative energy, intellectual stimulation, and kindness helped me finish. The book would take longer to write without help from my parents and my parents-in-law, to whom I am grateful for their understanding and financial support in cases of emergency and, primarily, for the time they lovingly devoted to taking care of my daughter when I was occupied with work. Finally, for his unswerving support and understanding, I thank my husband, Paweł Ryżko.

Earlier versions of parts of this study appeared as follows:

"Enslavement to Philanthropy, Freedom from Heredity: Amelia E. Johnson's and Paul Laurence Dunbar's Uses and Misuses of Sentimentalism and Naturalism," *Polish Journal for American Studies*, vol. 12, 2018, pp. 113–128.

"Tropes of Temperance, Specters of Naturalism: Amelia E. Johnson's *Clarence and Corinne*," *Atlantis: Journal of the Spanish Association for Anglo-American Studies*, vol. 38, no. 2, 2018, pp. 45–62.

"Like Mother Like Daughter? Matrilineal Opposition in African American Mulatta Melodrama," *Anglica: An International Journal of English Studies*, vol. 26, no. 1, 2017, pp. 165–192.

"Failed Patriarchs, Familial Villains, and Slaves to Rum: White Masculinity on Trial in African American Mulatta Melodrama," *NJES: Nordic Journal of English Studies*, vol. 15, no. 4, 2016, pp. 208–235.

THE
NADIR &
THE ZENITH

INTRODUCTION

❊ ❊ ❊

The Zenith & the Nadir

THE EARLY AFRICAN AMERICAN NOVEL

> The last decade of the nineteenth century and the
> opening of the twentieth century marked the nadir
> of the Negro's status in American society.
> —RAYFORD LOGAN, *The Negro in American Life and Thought*

The Nadir and the Zenith argues, both provocatively and seriously, that the historical moment when black people's status in American society reached its lowest point—famously labeled as the Nadir by Rayford Logan (xxi)—coincides with the zenith of black novelistic productivity in the pre–Civil Rights era.[1] The novels this book analyzes were released between 1876 and 1902, a time period that almost mirrors the one examined in Logan's study (1877–1901). In those years, at least thirteen African American authors published altogether not fewer than twenty-six novels.[2] The bulk of this corpus is magnified by the length of the narratives, written at a time when authors releasing installments were paid by the line. Additionally, because the data from the period is still fragmentary, the bibliography of early African American novels continues to be extended by newly rediscovered and reprinted works.[3] In contrast, during the 1920s—the pivotal decade of the New Negro Renaissance—only twelve African American novels were published.[4] Hence from the perspective of novelistic output, it turns out that the years of the historical Nadir during the Jim Crow era quantitatively overshadowed the oeuvres of the New Negro movement—traditionally represented as the high point of black literary history. The gradual improvement in the political situation of the black community after 1901 did not translate into an increase in novelistic production. Thus, paradoxically, the black novel's zenith coincides with the historical nadir of black people in the United States.

Being conscious of the imperfections of the quantitative method of comparing and evaluating bodies of literature, I do not intend to make claims about the aesthetic value of the writing produced in the periods referred to above. What I want to suggest, however, is that the fin-de-siècle black novel continues to be virtually absent from, or at least dramatically underrepresented in, critical accounts of African American literature, despite the volume of this corpus. As far as literary value is concerned, I will expose the aesthetic complexity and intricacy of black-on-black and black-on-white signifying practices employed by the "postbellum/pre-Harlem" authors, which have been either too frequently dismissed by scholars as an "aesthetic failure" (Bone 25; Tate 8; Bell 75) or have remained invisible due to their subtlety and their embeddedness in contemporaneous cultural practices.[5] Another central element of the novels analyzed in this work—one that critics perceived as problematic for many decades—is their rejection of racial realism. The expectation that black novelists represent African American life from the perspective of authentic (i.e., lower-class or folk and visibly black) characters has continued to be a key criterion in reading and evaluating African American literature at least since the turn of the twentieth century (Jarrett, *Deans and Truants* 1, 11–20).[6] This approach marginalized texts that either formally depart from literary realism or represent "inauthentic" (i.e., not unequivocally black) characters. In the case of nineteenth-century African American studies, this led to an almost exclusive focus on the slave narrative tradition and a corresponding neglect of a large body of fiction produced by black men and women before the so-called Harlem Renaissance (hereafter labeled the New Negro Renaissance). Instead of visibly black characters representing either the folk or the lower class, the selected novels by William Wells Brown, Charles W. Chesnutt, Paul Laurence Dunbar, Frances Ellen Watkins Harper, Pauline Elizabeth Hopkins, and Amelia E. Johnson center on racially indefinite protagonists or white-looking mulattas. Such dependence on racial ambiguity or indeterminacy directly led to their marginalization in the field of African American studies in the twentieth century.

The paradigm of racial authenticity is closely connected to black—as well as white—masculinist paradigms of militant heroism and brutal realism. Inasmuch as these critical lenses minimize the appeal of the melodramatic mode, the culture of sentiment, and other affect-based aesthetics, their long dominance further contributed to the marginalization of the works analyzed in this book. Due to these works' employment of stylistic excess and heightened emotionality, they were not treated as serious literature. Even though black feminist interventions have demonstrated the significance of black women's fin-de-siècle literature, culture, and activism at least since the late 1980s, women-authored novels from this corpus continue to be particularly absent from the canon or university curricula and are only marginally present in the critical discourse.[7]

In response to these critical exclusions and omissions, *The Nadir and the Zenith* sets out to analyze early black novels that subvert the traditional expectations set for African American texts. As Gene Jarrett argues, reading a cultural tradition through the lens of its anomalies has the potential to redefine it in a more radical way than a rereading of canonical works, as it brings about a readjustment of those monolithic, uncontestable paradigms of "cultural coherence and cohesiveness" imposed on literary productions (*Deans and Truants* 11, 15, 17). The anomalous corpus of early black novels implodes the monolithic myth of racial authenticity, masculinist resistance, and literary realism. Instead of phenotypically black characters representing the masses, the examined works focus either on racially indefinite protagonists, white-looking mulattas, or on "real Albinos," to use the slave auctioneer's taxonomy from *Clotel* (Brown 49). Instead of the dominant discourse of black authenticity, their aesthetics are distinguished by melodramatic excess and narrative implausibility. Instead of masculinist heroism and the publicly visible victories associated with it, the narratives represent the heroism of reform and local community activism, which is frequently invisible, exercised on the volatile boundaries of the private and the public, and mostly performed by women rather than men. Hence, over thirty years after Hazel Carby's *Reconstructing Womanhood*, which was considered "a cultural history and critique of the forms in which black women intellectuals made political as well as literary interventions in the social formations in which they lived" (7), the urgency of foregrounding and interrogating the complex intersections of gender and sexuality politics alongside race and class ideologies in this neglected corpus is all the more timely. In order to provide for the most comprehensive reading of these novels, I balance a mindful attention to their sociopolitical and cultural contexts with a close reading of the individual works. I also scrutinize the intertextual links between the primary sources and their signifying turn on hegemonic traditions, which notably include woman's fiction, the culture of sentiment, temperance discourse, and turn-of-the-twentieth-century naturalism.

Although the novels I discuss in *The Nadir and the Zenith* have often been either ignored or reductively misread by twentieth-century scholars, they exemplify several significant tendencies of black fiction in the period in general. Most notably, their aesthetic excess, unruly poetics, and undisciplined plots are contrasted with the ethics of temperance and self-discipline. In the disciplinary gospel of the novels, the new generation of protagonists serve as role models, which gives the narratives an orientation toward the future. Whereas Robert Bone argues that during this period the black novel was deeply classist, reactionary, and expressed the sentiment that the "bad Negro keeps the good Negro back" (18), such a conclusion misses the subtle ways in which the novels juxtapose the weak and servile "Old Negroes" of the slavery era with the independent, self-determined New Negroes, typically represented by black women exerting control over their private and communal bodies.

This futuristic direction is reinforced by the cult of temperance's consistency with the modern regime of self-discipline, and the divergence of such self-discipline from the ancient regime of masters and slaves, protectors and dependents (Foucault, *Discipline* 224–228). The novels' insistent praise of self-control and self-determination expresses a desire for self-governance, while their dysphoric subplots expose the dangers of dependency, feudalism, and slavery. As such, the African American corpus stands apart from the pastoral nostalgia for "the good old times" that characterized many strands of American literature after the Civil War. The late nineteenth-century canon perfectly exemplifies one of the central dialectics of US culture: "the contrast between the machine and the pastoral ideal" (Marx 353), which is frequently reconciled with "the idea of a redemptive journey away from society in the direction of nature" (Marx 69). In the Gilded Age of urbanization, industrialization, class strife, and new immigration, such genres as local-color fiction and westerns expressed and fulfilled a longing for an imaginary homogeneity of the rural past or the West before the end of the frontier.[8] Analogously, the plantation tradition and the dialect movement "fed nostalgia for a time when racial relationships had been simple and happy, at least for whites" (North 22–23). However, the disturbing injection of race politics is not limited to the plantation literature represented by Joel Chandler Harris and Thomas Nelson Page. As Jeffrey Louis Decker persuasively argues, US pastoralism, as well as its critical assessments, were inherently dependent on racial othering, whereby nonwhite "Calibans" are "apolitically positioned as the symbol of the 'dark, hostile forces' of nature" (Decker 289, 290). In contrast, the early African American novel, with its antipastoral and antinostalgic tone, avoids such incarceration in "the prison house of 'nature'" and the perpetuation of "a violent and historical civilizing mission" (Decker 287). As a result, whereas Bone was right to claim that the early black novelists were not influenced by "the regionalism of Harte, Twain, and Jewett" (21), *The Nadir and the Zenith* treats this lacuna as a politically significant evasion, a distancing from the traditions that "firmly establish in the minds of white readership a picture of the freed slaves as hapless, childlike, and eager for paternalistic protection" (North 22).

Apart from the problematic race politics of pastoral nostalgia, black fiction's challenge to create a redemptive character involved in a "journey away from society" is also meaningful from a gender studies perspective. According to Nina Baym, whereas in nineteenth-century fiction, life in the country was traditionally pictured as "the repository of virtue and decency," women authors "recognized country vices: brutalizing labor, mean minds, vicious gossip" and a constant "dread of drought and foreclosure" (45). Baym's observations are also valid for the fin-de-siècle black writers, for whom the unremitting toil in the fields triggered the specters of bondage and forced labor. For African American women in particular, rural isolation under the regime of slavery additionally signaled a threat from their abusive white, typically male, masters and later employers. As Harriet Jacobs, alias Linda Brent, claims, life on "a distant plantation" was much more dangerous than in a town, where it was easier to make slaveholders' "villainy ... public" (47; see also Fox-Genovese et al. 375). As a result, pastoral scenes in the corpus are either altogether absent or represented as short-lived and fatal in their consequences. Nor are there any idyllic rural feasts during which nature's wealth is offered for consumption, producing a community of consumers and masking human labor under the guise of natural abundance, a central feature of the pastoral according to Raymond Williams (30–33). To the contrary, the novels' temperance rhetoric is deeply suspicious of any "eating and drinking communion," "charity of the feast," and the frequently invisible, "insatiable exploitation" they are dependent on (R. Williams 31). As the narrator of Katherine Davis Chapman Tillman's *Clancy Street* laments,

"'Eat, drink, and be merry' too often became the motto of the black community after Emancipation," and she warns against perceiving "life as one continuous holiday" (252).

This does not mean, however, that the early black novel romanticized urban life. Significantly, whereas the early modern pastoral celebrated country life and its "absence of greed and calculation" in contrast to the city landscape of lawyers, politicians, and capitalists (R. Williams 28), African American writers approached the rural-urban dialectic in a more ambivalent way. They refrained from idealizing the country while relentlessly stigmatizing the greed, ambition, speculation, and calculation symbolic of the urban economy. Black novelists of the Nadir era position the unbridled passions of the marketplace as the antithesis of the ethics of temperance and advocate self-disciplinary practices as a moral and practical necessity. At the same time, however, modernity is presented as inevitable and definitely not worse than the past. In the last novel I examine in this book, *The Sport of the Gods*, Dunbar depicts the pitfalls of black urban migration without offering the rural South as a viable alternative to the metropolitan North. Overall, the future-oriented and antipastoral elements of the early African American novel form a complex nexus of subtle but definitively political meanings, which include a desire for self-governance, a rejection of pastoral plantation nostalgia, and a tentative embrace of modernity as unavoidable. In effect, decades before the New Negro Renaissance, the novels expressed hope for a better black future and called into being the modern era, in most cases embodied by the New Black Woman.

As has been mentioned, the *discipline* advocated by the novels is paradoxically complemented by sentimental, melodramatic, and, in the later years, also naturalist *excess*. While at first sight this might appear as a contradiction, a closer reading shows it to be a consistent and effective aesthetic whose key characteristic is an intense affective force that fosters a community of feeling. Lauren Berlant, one of the most vehement critics of the "business of sentimentality," claims that its defining feature is "affective universality" and that "what makes a thing sentimental is the presumption of emotional clarity and affective recognition" (*Female* 271–272). Even though Berlant is largely skeptical of a hegemonic culture of sentiment and its contradictory "bargains with pain, domination, terror, and exile" ("Poor" 663), she admits that the possibility of identification which forms the core of sentimental compassion not only constitutes a threat but also remains "the great promise of this affective aesthetic" ("Poor" 648). The affective edge of the heightened emotionality that characterizes the overlapping modes of sentimentalism and melodrama reduces the distance between the reader and the text, in effect producing what Berlant calls "an intimate public," a space of "emotional contact" and "mediation in which the personal is refracted through the general" (*The Female* viii).

These arguments also apply to the melodramatic mode. According to Peter Brooks, *melos*—the musical element that defines melodrama—intensifies the affective force of literary texts (14). Other critics also point to music's capacity to collectivize feelings (Frith 36) and "animate imagined communities" (Born 381). As Katrin Horn argues in her reading of excessive, highly affective styles, such works create communities of affective association. They have been historically significant, especially for minorities, and meet their need for a safe communal space (Horn 229). As will be demonstrated in the second part of this book, the excess of sentimentalism and melodrama is closely related to the naturalism that emerged precisely during the black Nadir (Howard 75). Although naturalism is frequently perceived as a documentary and objective aesthetic, in fact, its heightened photographic realism and focus on urban squalor, expressed in a yellow journalistic tone, are also excessive and sensational, whereas its reforming mission produces an analogous compassion in the other half to the "female complaints" of sentimentalism. As *The Nadir and the Zenith* shows, naturalism's affective force is as intense as that of sentimentalism and melodrama. Thus a striking combination of ethical temperance and aesthetic excess in the early black novel facilitates the emergence of a modern, self-governing black community that is not only public but also private, intimate, and cemented by affective attachments.

The first part of the book, "The Excess of Mulatta Melodrama," examines the most researched section of the early black novel corpus, which comprises mulatta narratives. Many critics have pointed out, even recently, a certain obsessive interest in those novels featuring mixed-race characters (Bost 11–16; Foreman, "Who's Your Mama?" 505–539).[9] Since the 1980s the figure of the mulatta has been reclaimed, primarily by black feminist critics, and presented as more subversive than tragic. More recently, analyses of the Nadir period's fiction began to reflect changing critical perspectives in the field of cultural studies. The millennial fascination with biracialism and people of color has been mirrored by the rise of mixed-race studies, which largely adopt a poststructuralist perspective of a decentered, performative subjectivity. At the turn of the twenty-first century, several critics have also used the lens of new materialism to scrutinize the mulatta's embodiment or engagement with affect theory and Berlant's readings of sentimentalism.[10] In the trope of the mulatta, these critical approaches have found an appealing object of analysis, and, in turn, they have productively reinvigorated the study of the racially anomalous texts of African American literature.

The Nadir and the Zenith builds on these findings and develops both the pioneering late twentieth-century readings and the more recent explorations of the period's black fiction. Yet, in contrast to most black feminist studies, this book explicitly adopts the premise that even though mulatta melodrama and gender ideologies are central to black women's fiction in this genre, they are also significantly present in the output of African American male writers.[11] Hence the corpus of the first part of this study will include works by Frances Ellen Watkins Harper and Pauline Elizabeth Hopkins as well as William Wells Brown and Charles W. Chesnutt, while in the second part I analyze works by Harper and Amelia E. Johnson as well as Paul Laurence Dunbar. The book also departs from many recent studies that conflate historical and literary figures in their corpora and, as a result, read the mulatta as an abstract, monolithic ideal, a fascinating epitome of hybridity. Many critics who aim to reconfigure the mulatta from the cliché of the tragic victim, "neither black nor white," nevertheless continue to treat the mixed-race figure as a homogeneous, transhistorical trope that functions in comparable ways in very different historical and geographical contexts, from the fin-de-siècle United States to the contemporary moment.[12] Atemporal or anachronistic readings tend to approach phenotypical mixed race as an illustration of postmodernist concepts such as ultimate aporia, free-floating signifiers, and cultural hybridity, or they use the literary trope to theorize about many later and nonliterary recastings of multiraciality (Bost 12; see also Doane 234). Even the most insightful of such analyses, frequently spanning more than a century—like Bost's sweeping survey (1850–2000), for example—run the risk of missing the sociohistorical changes in the significance of like representations across time. Whereas many scholars have creatively used queer studies, "theories of performance and performativity," or "mestiza theory" to read the mulatta as a figure "engaged in parodic performatives" or a "multiple, molten, fluid" identity (Zackodnik xxi–xxii; Bost 7–9), such is not the path I will take in this book.

Aware of the threats imbued in the millennial fascination with race mixing, the premature announcements of the postracial era, or simplified identification of fictions of passing as postmodernist narratives, "The Excess of

Mulatta Melodrama"—part 1 of this work—is determined to avoid such a frequently reductive atemporal approach. Not only does this book focus on a well-defined historical period—the black Nadir—but in my readings, I examine the difference between two dialectically opposite types of the mulatta. Moreover, my attention will be primarily devoted to the significance of the distinctive "albino" mulatta rather than the visible embodiments of hybridity, brownness, or biraciality. The white mulatta, I argue, performs a politically and aesthetically significant function in the melodramas analyzed in this work. Additionally, her invisible racial identity parallels the racially indefinite characters in the black temperance narratives. *The Nadir and the Zenith* maintains an ongoing awareness of the context in which it is written, and it will use the analytical tools offered by critical race theory, neo-Marxism, and intersectional feminism, at the same time balancing this early twenty-first-century perspective by focusing attention on the historical context of the Nadir, in which both mulatta melodramas and temperance narratives were published. As a result, the corpus of the study will be limited to works of African American fin-de-siècle fiction, which are synchronically positioned against hegemonic literary discourses and diachronically against their predecessors such as Brown's *Clotel* (1853) or Harriet Jacobs's *Incidents in the Life of a Slave Girl* (1861).

The primary sources examined in the first part of *The Nadir and the Zenith* represent the genre I refer to as *mulatta melodrama*. They consist of "black [or rather mulatto] female texts," defined in Claudia Tate's typology as works whose dominant "discourses and ... interpretations arise from woman-centered values, agency, indeed authority that seek distinctly female principles of narrative pleasure" (Tate 67).[13] The four novels—*Clotel; or, The President's Daughter*; *Iola Leroy; or, Shadows Uplifted*; *Hagar's Daughter*; and *The House behind the Cedars*—are authored by writers who identified as black even though their appearances ranged from the light-skinned Chesnutt to more visibly mixed-race Brown, Harper, and Hopkins. As the writers' critical commentaries demonstrate, they were well aware of the political significance of interracial characters and interracial relationships, which, especially during the Nadir, had a unique capacity to critique American race relations and to expose the absurdities of the color line.

The mulatta melodrama is characterized by a tripartite structure. At its center is a dialectical relationship between the antebellum mulatta mother and her daughter, the New Negro woman of the Woman's Era, and this female opposition is complemented by the figure of the failed white father.

All mulatta novels examined in chapter 2 are future-oriented and juxtapose the slavery era–mothers with their daughters, who embody the black community's hope. Chapter 3 uses the lens of masculinity studies to examine the figure of the white patriarch as well as other white men, whose gender performance is scathingly criticized in the analyzed works. Even though the texts' sympathy for the mother figures is much stronger than for the fathers, both parents are represented as less disciplined and weaker than their self-determined daughters. In that one of the charges that mulatta melodrama makes against white privileged men is their intemperance—manifested in different ways as indulgences for various appetites and passions, most frequently sexual and alcoholic—the third chapter will form a bridge between "The Excesses of Mulatta Melodrama" and "Black Tropes of Temperance" and will highlight the overlapping spaces between the two corpora examined in this book.

The analysis in the first part of *The Nadir and the Zenith* is largely synchronic, and the chapters study the same set of texts, which stems from the often-times uncannily close similarities among all the mulatta novels. Although the main focus of the study is the era of the Nadir, the first primary source is an antebellum classic, Brown's *Clotel; or, The President's Daughter* (1853). Apart from its canonical position as the founding text of African American fiction, I analyze its profound influence on later mulatta melodramas authored by other writers examined in this book. In addition, its relevance for a study of the postbellum era is also evidenced by the fact that Brown continued to rewrite his novel after the Civil War, and its last version, *Clotelle; or, The Colored Heroine; A Tale of the Southern States* was released in 1867. The following two novels, Harper's *Iola Leroy; or, Shadows Uplifted* (1893) and Hopkins's *Hagar's Daughter* (serialized in 1901–1902), represent the black Woman's Era. Both draw on Brown's text, frequently making direct intertextual allusions to his work. Harper's and Hopkins's novels focus, more centrally than *Clotel*, on a mixed-race female protagonist, yet the multigenerational family and relationality continue to be significant for their plots. These two black women's works are complemented by Chesnutt's *The House behind the Cedars* (1900), a novel that in the past has been studied much less widely than his more explicitly militant *The Marrow of Tradition* (1901), whose position in the canon is more central and better established.[14]

Whereas the mulatta narratives have attracted considerable critical attention (although they are still underrepresented in university curricula and literary anthologies), the second part of *The Nadir and the Zenith*, "Black Tropes of Temperance," enters the largely uncharted terrain of African American uses of US temperance discourse, which was one of the most powerful rhetorics of the nineteenth century. This book shows that an ethic of temperance, measure, and self-discipline is central to the early black novel. As has been mentioned, temperance is also a significant element in the mulatta melodrama, and although it is not always centrally important, it is nonetheless present in the works of virtually all writers of the era (see Bone 13–14).[15] The corpus selected for analysis is composed of works contemporarily distributed throughout the 1877–1901 Nadir era in a symmetrical way: Frances Ellen Watkins Harper's didactic drama *Sowing and Reaping* (serialized in 1876–1877) marks its beginning, Amelia E. Johnson's evangelical narrative *Clarence and Corinne; or, God's Way* (1890) falls in the middle, and Paul Laurence Dunbar's debut novel, *The Uncalled* (1900), was released at the very end of the era. Not only do these texts, published during the most difficult time in African American postbellum history, share an engagement with temperance literature, but they all feature racially indeterminate characters. As a result, like the mulatta melodramas, these novels have been marginalized by the authenticity regime and the dominance of the heroic/militant paradigm.

Part 2, "Black Tropes of Temperance," examines the significance of the paucity of references to racial difference at the height of racial segregation, thus confirming Kenneth Warren's argument that "concerns about 'race' may structure our American texts, even when those texts are not 'about race' in any substantive way" (*Black and White* 10). At the same time, I show that the racial indeterminacy in Harper's, A. E. Johnson's, and Dunbar's fin-de-siècle novels should not be reduced to a simplistic colorblind universalism. Such indeterminacy was complemented by a focus on economic conditions, which highlighted the power balance and social specificity of different characters. In these texts, race is connected to class representations in a complex way: class markers in the novels examined in "Black Tropes of Temperance" are deeply loaded with conflicting racial connotations. Like mulatta melodrama, the texts interrogate postbellum gender politics, yet their engagement with this issue is embedded in their use of temperance discourse. The three novels examined in part 2 illustrate that when adapting the conventions of reform literature to their own ends, black writers retained the tension between excessive style and the ethics of temperance that defined the hegemonic conventions of temperance discourse.

In contrast to mulatta melodramas, whose narratives are largely parallel and at some points virtually identical, the black temperance narratives evidence change and development as well as continuity. Hence the analytical approach to the corpus is different in "Black Tropes of Temperance" than in the first part of the book. Whereas in "The Excesses of Mulatta Melodrama" all chapters analyze the same primary sources, and the order of texts at times follows subject matter and relevance rather than chronology, in the second part of the book each chapter is devoted to a different novel, and the order is strictly chronological. Such a diachronic approach illustrates the change in the aesthetics that these novels employ, primarily visible in the growing dominance of naturalism and the gradual decline of sentimentalism. Significantly, however, all texts combine both aesthetic paradigms while at the same time gender-bending the traditional domestic narrative. *Sowing and Reaping*—the most faithful to the sentimental tradition—contains elements of naturalist logic, especially of social determinism; *Clarence and Corinne* intensifies its reliance on naturalism yet continues to rely deeply on the tactic of sentimental compassion; while *The Uncalled* draws from the cast of sentimental characters to evoke the reader's compassion. The intricate dialectic between sentimentalism and naturalism that is central to all these novels is one of the secondary yet significant issues investigated in part 2 of *The Nadir and the Zenith*. Rather than see them as opposites, I show that they share an extensive common ground. Finally, despite the variations in their combinations of sentimentalism and naturalism, all black novels that employ tropes of temperance do so with a firm reliance on the excessive chiaroscuro aesthetic of the melodramatic mode.

Due to the central presence of melodramatic oppositions and Manichean characters, I approach black temperance narratives through the lens of character typology in the same way as mulatta melodramas. This is further justified by the emerging use of naturalism by African American writers. As Richard Chase points out, classical naturalism in the United States strongly resembles the earlier romance tradition, in which characters were "abstract and ideal . . . two-dimensional types," and seemed "to be merely a function of plot" (13). Analogously, naturalism depicts flat, allegorical characters—"[t]he protagonist of a naturalistic novel . . . often seems to have no self. Psychologically, he is a simplified character compared even with the already simplified characters in the older romances" (199). In a similar vein, Donald Pizer—one of the most prolific and perceptive critics of late nineteenth-century naturalism in American literature (despite his traditionalist formalism)—contends that US naturalist novels do not focus on portraying psychological development and progression (*Realism* 40). Hence such representations of human experiences in black temperance narratives result in a static character construction, which parallels the rigid triangular structure of mulatta melodrama.

Although *Sowing and Reaping*, *Clarence and Corinne*, and *The Uncalled* cannot be classified as mulatta melodrama (inasmuch as their characters are not introduced as mulattas), the two corpora examined in this work share the theme of racial ambiguity. In black temperance fiction, however, it is produced in a different way and, as a result, has a different significance than in the texts discussed in part 1. Here the uncertainty regarding racial identity stems from an almost complete omission of bodily signifiers of race, whereas mulatta melodramas devote considerable space to painstakingly detailed depictions of mulatta protagonists' phenotypically white appearance. Apart from their parallel, though not identical, destabilization of the racial taxonomies of the day, both corpora employ the tactic of sentimental compassion and elements of melodramatic excess, similar to the recognition and family reunion scenes that drive the narratives of *Clotel*, *Iola Leroy*, *The House behind the Cedars*, and *Hagar's Daughter*. Such scenes are also significant in *Sowing and Reaping*, *Clarence and Corinne*, and *The Uncalled*. Hence mulatta melodrama, a well-established genre by the time black authors began to employ tropes of temperance in their fiction, shines through the façades of the palimpsest novels discussed in part 2 and adds to their affective and political force. A juxtaposition of these two seemingly quite different bodies of writing makes it possible to shed new light on both and produce new meanings in their readings. Mulatta melodrama highlights the significance of aesthetic excess in black temperance narratives, whereas the novels signifying anti-alcohol discourse bring to light the tropes of temperance present in black melodramas featuring albino protagonists.

Just as in mulatta melodrama, so too black temperance narratives are future-oriented and antinostalgic. They similarly contrast the reformers and self-disciplined persons of the younger generation with the older generation, especially those financially or socially privileged, who include such cliché temperance literature villains as saloon-owners driven by profit, drunkard fathers, and thoughtless parents who ruin their children with alcohol or do nothing to prevent their fall. Although one may find several drunkards and thoughtless young girls among the younger characters in the novels, overall their faults are by far overshadowed by the failures of their parents' generation. Similarly, there are also some true mentors and redeemers among the older generation, but they are outnumbered by the drunkard and absent fathers and helpless, or at best inept, mothers.

The Nadir and the Zenith concludes its analysis with a chapter devoted to Paul Laurence Dunbar's most renowned work of fiction, *The Sport of the Gods*. As argued by Jonathan Daigle, one of Dunbar's most perceptive readers, Dunbar "represents perhaps the best starting place for a reassessment of the black nadir" (633). This work demonstrates that, apart from its more general significance for the 1877–1901 period, Dunbar's last novel also meaningfully synthesizes the two corpora analyzed in this study: mulatta melodramas and temperance narratives. *The Sport of the Gods'* central connection to melodrama, vaudeville, and the emergent black musical theater tradition, as well as the mixed-race identities of its protagonists, makes it an ideal text to observe the changing influence and significance of mulatta melodrama at the dawn of the twentieth century. Most notably, the female protagonist, Kit Hamilton, is a *mulatta chorus girl* starring in *musical plays*—which are literally *mulatta melodramas*. Dunbar's last novel also enters into a direct dialogue with the novels examined in "Black Tropes of Temperance," including his own novelistic debut, a naturalist and melodramatic narrative of a drunkard's fall. While the significance of Joe Hamilton's fall is deeply embedded in the temperance tradition—most visibly through its use of the urban setting of New York and depictions of the black artistic and bohemian community—at the same time, it foreshadows the emergence of the black modernism of the New Negro Renaissance. *The Sport of the Gods* forms a germane bridge between the mulatta melodramas and black temperance narratives of the Nadir, on one hand, and the New Negro Renaissance with its bohemian "Niggerati" on the other. As a result, a careful reading of Dunbar's New York novel not only facilitates "a reassessment of the black nadir" (Daigle 633) but also a better understanding of the broader African American culture of the Jim Crow era.

PART 1

THE EXCESS OF MULATTA MELODRAMA

CHAPTER 1

✺ ✺ ✺

Mulatta Melodrama

MIXED RACE AND THE MELODRAMATIC MODE IN THE EARLY BLACK NOVEL

> There stood [Clotel], with a complexion as white as most of those who were waiting with a wish to become her purchasers.... "Real Albino, fit for a fancy girl for any one."
> —WILLIAM WELLS BROWN, *Clotel*

> They were all mulattoes,—all people of mixed blood were called "mulattoes" in North Carolina. There were dark mulattoes and bright mulattoes.
> —CHARLES W. CHESNUTT, *The House behind the Cedars*

> [A] closer inspection would have revealed that they were nearly all a little less than white.... From the few who were undistinguishable from pure white, the colors ran down the scale by minute gradations to the two or three brown faces at the other extremity.
> —CHARLES W. CHESNUTT, "Her Virginia Mammy"

Although frequently perceived as a cliché or a stereotype, mulatto figures in US literature can by no means be reduced to a single image. Not only do they form a wide visual spectrum, but this phenotypical diversity is also invested with many contradictory significations, from sterility to fecundity, from chastity to lasciviousness. In the context of such conflicting representations, I will begin the analysis of the Nadir's albino mulatta by positioning it against the critical corpus devoted to literary mixed-race characters in general. This will pave the way to define mulatta melodrama, a distinctive genre represented by William Wells Brown's *Clotel*, Frances Ellen Watkins Harper's *Iola Leroy*, Pauline Elizabeth Hopkins's *Hagar's Daughter*, and Charles W. Chesnutt's *The House behind the Cedars*. As I mentioned in the introduction, the excessive aesthetics and emotional intensity of melodrama are instrumental to the affective force of these texts, which in turn helps them form an intimate black community of writers, readers, activists, and characters—a self-governed and self-determined New Negro community that would respond to the limitations, or rather horrors, of the Nadir era.

At least since the emergence of black studies in the 1960s, and for many decades leading up to the turn of the twenty-first century, in the newly written histories of African American literature, the omnipresence of mulattas in postbellum fiction was regarded as shameful self-loathing. The character was labeled as "tragic," and its dominance in early black novels was indeed treated as a tragedy or, to use Houston Baker's words, as a "white-faced minstrelsy" (25). It was generally agreed that the texts featuring such characters were written under the influence of white standards and that the inauthentic light mulatta characters were designed to accommodate white readers' tastes.

Yet the thesis that African American fin-de-siècle mulatta novels were written to satisfy white demands or expectations has been disproved by historicist readings of the period. To the contrary, as critics have argued, they were intentionally loaded with political significance and intended for, as well as read by, black readers. For example, *The Colored American*, a magazine that published several mulatta narratives, including novels by Pauline Elizabeth Hopkins, declared that it was meant as a platform "*Of the Race, for the Race, by the Race*" (Ammons 3; emphasis in original). In *Domestic Allegories of Political Desire*, one of the earliest, most influential, and comprehensive studies of the era, Tate persuasively demonstrates that early black women's fiction was written for black readers, who must have "found pleasurable self-affirmation that reflected their racial and gender aspirations to live in a world where such stories were possible" (6). Embraced by black authors and readers at the turn of the twentieth century, the mulatta and the related theme of interracial love were, however, regarded as risqué by white readers. As literary historians point out, Hopkins's predilection for the theme was, for example, criticized by Cornelia A. Condict, who stated that "[t]he stories of these tragic mixed loves will not commend themselves to your white readers" and asked if the writer could not imagine "love beautiful and sublime within the range of the colored race, for each other?" ("Editorial" 398). In a frequently cited response to Condict's letter, Hopkins declared that her "stories are definitely planned to show the obstacles persistently placed in our paths by a dominant race to subjugate us spiritually. Marriage is made illegal between the races and the mulattoes increase. And then the hue and cry goes abroad of the immorality of the Negro and the disgrace that the mulattoes are to this nation. Amalgamation is an institution designed by God for some wise purpose, and mixed bloods have always exercised a great influence on the progress of human affairs" ("Editorial" 399).[1] She adds that her novels "expose the social life of Southerners and the wickedness of their caste prejudice" (400), and she "sing[s] of the *wrongs* of a race that ignorance of their pitiful condition may be changed to intelligence and must awaken compassion in the hearts of the just" (399). This short exchange of ideas demonstrates that not only were black writers conscious of their political uses of the mulatta figure but also that they pandered to black, rather than white, tastes.

The political significance of the mulatta is especially germane to the Nadir era. The period witnessed the rise and national embrace of Jim Crow segregation, upheld by the Supreme Court's infamous "separate but equal" doctrine set out in *Plessy v. Ferguson* (1896). It was a time of political disenfranchisement, with its necessary corollary of symbolic dehumanization and expulsion from the national body: "Between 1890 and 1907 every Southern and border state 'legally' disfranchised the vast majority of its African American voters" (Loewen 150). The Nadir was marked by unprecedented white-on-black violence. As James Loewen puts it, "It is almost unimaginable how racist the United States became during and just after the nadir. Mass attacks by whites wiped out or terrorized black communities in the Florida Keys, in Springfield, Illinois, and in the Arkansas Delta, and were an implicit, ever-present threat to every black neighborhood in the nation. Some small communities in the Midwest and West became 'sundown' towns, informally threatening African Americans with death if they remained overnight.... Lynchings offer evidence of how defenseless blacks were, for the defining characteristic of a lynching is that the murder takes place in public, so everyone knows who did it, yet the crime goes unpunished" (43). In such a context, representations of racial integration, interracial unions, and cross-race socialization constituted a direct attack on the political and social institutions of racial oppression. The mulatta protagonists in Frances Ellen Watkins Harper, Pauline Elizabeth Hopkins, and Charles W. Chesnutt's fin-de-siècle novels imploded the fragile, artificially defined boundary between white and black races that ideologically justified segregation and disfranchisement. Furthermore—especially in the novels set in the antebellum era—they manifested the history of interracial sexual violence: the omnipresent, routine, commonly accepted white men's exploitation of black female bodies.

Yet, as I have signaled, such an approach to mixed bloods in black literature has only recently been rediscovered, and for many decades the mulatta novels of the Nadir were virtually absent from black literary histories and canons. Apart from the regime of authenticity that limited the readings of African American fiction, from a black feminist perspective, the twentieth-century lack of critical attention to those texts stems from the fact that they were published during "the Woman's Era," an understudied period defined by "black women's autonomous organizations and a period of intense intellectual activity and productivity" (Carby, *Reconstructing* 7; see also Carby, "'On the Threshold'" 263). Since the late 1980s, a number of black feminist critics have continued to reclaim the (black) Woman's Era. Their studies have pointed out the subtle subversiveness of the period's white-looking female characters. In the black feminist readings, the mulattas, rather than helplessly tragic, were endowed with significant political meanings.[2] Whereas the inquiries from the 1980s and mid-1990s focus mainly on race and gender ideologies, more recent analyses of the period's fiction are driven by the dominance of poststructuralist and postcolonial approaches to identity (see Bost 12), which notably include intersectionality, hybridity, creolization, critical race theory, Ian Haney-López's race fabrication, Gloria E. Anzaldúa's mestizas, José Esteban Muñoz's brownness, Stanley Hall's "new ethnicities," and Butler's performative "subversion of identity"—all based on the notion of a decentered, de-essentialized subject.[3] As I mentioned in the introduction, I build on both twentieth- and twenty-first-century studies of the mulatta, yet unlike many of the comparative readings that span long periods, I specifically focus on the meaning of the black albino daughter and her mulatta mother in the melodramas of the Nadir.

The Nadir and the Zenith argues for a critical need to discriminate between the multivalent significances of the mulatta. A brief look at several accounts of the figure will suffice to demonstrate that it is a complex, overdetermined, and contradictory signifier, which cannot be conscientiously read without a detailed scrutiny of the context.[4] Charles White, referring to Edward Long's *The History of Jamaica* (1774), argued that scholars did not know "two mulattoes have any offspring" and "species were originally so created and constituted, so as to be kept apart from each other" (129). The residual traces of the sterility hypothesis continued well into the nineteenth century (Sollors 131–132). At the same time, an opposite approach emerged, contending that "Mulattoes ... insidiously pass the savage Ethiopian blood into the veins of the Anglo-Saxon or American" (Shufeldt 91); "steadily, albeit slowly and insidiously, the stream of dark blood has insinuated itself into the veins of the dominant" race (Chesnutt, "The Future" 124–133). Hence mulattoes were perceived as either sterile or, to the contrary, not only perfectly fertile but also intent on interbreeding. In a similar way, they were represented as color struck and condescending toward visibly black persons—they "draw certain lines," as a character from Chesnutt's "Her Virginia Mammy" puts it (86)—and, simultaneously, their family history was most likely related to "adultery" and illegitimacy, which made it unspeakable: "these things are not mentioned," a black woman responds in Nella Larsen's story of Helga Crane (37). In turn, mulattoes' elitist condescension toward blacker African Americans, sometimes bearing strong affinity to the white eugenic logic, was compensated for by the contempt they received from the black lower class. A black servant from *Clotel* ridicules the pretensions of the eponymous character: "Miss Clo needn't strut round so big, she got short nappy har well as. She tinks she white, when she come here wid dat long har of hers" (121). Hence, even before the Nadir, the anti-elitist critique mocks "white Negroes" who pretentiously mimic white ways and want to be "jes lak white fo'ks," to borrow a title from Dunbar's 1900 musical comedy.

In Brown, Harper, Hopkins, and Chesnutt's novels, the above contradictions take the form of the dialectic between the antebellum mulatta mother and the postbellum New Negro daughter. The mother is associated with the reproduction of biracial offspring and illegitimate relationships. The daughter, in contrast, represents a striving for respectability and self-discipline, and she remains childless in all mulatta narratives of the Nadir. The most significant cultural work in this corpus is not performed by the phenotypical embodiments of creolization, mestiza, or racial hybridity central to postmodernist critical discourse but by white-looking mulatta protagonists. The fact that these are specifically albino mulattas—figures that stand for "the absence of color," to quote Barbara Chase-Riboud ("Albino" 19)—who are at the center of the fin-de-siècle black melodramas parallels the anomalous racially indefinite characters that will be discussed in the second part of this book. In both cases, the protagonists are marked by an absence of racial bodily markers. Such literary constructions form a dialogue with the disembodied character of US citizenship that at the time excluded the subjects traditionally perceived as inescapably embodied, that is, women and African Americans. In the black melodramas that I examine, the predominantly postbellum "albino" New Negro heroines are juxtaposed with their antebellum "bright mulatta" unwedded mothers, whose mixed blood tends to be more discernible (Chesnutt, *The House* 370; Brown 47). Characteristically, despite their unmarried status, in their enslavement and passivity they vigorously oppose the "free(d) mulatta concubine" as discussed by Lisa Ze Winters who, referring to Saidiya Hartman, argues that this figure was inescapably perceived as seductive and endowed with "phantasmal ensnaring agency" (qtd. in Winters 5). Finally, rather than stand for an irreconcilable aporia and epistemological uncertainty, the dynamic of white and bright mulattas drives the early African American narratives of chiaroscuro oppositions, hidden identities, diegetic reversals, and revelations of secret knowledge, and thus it is instrumental for the work of the melodramatic mode, the elements of which, as will be shown, are discernible to different extents in all primary sources examined in *The Nadir and the Zenith*.

As many critics have pointed out, mulatta novels are involved in a complex dialogical relationship with the hegemonic "woman's fiction" as defined by Nina Baym, the sentimental domestic novel largely overlapping with it and theorized by Jane Tompkins (Tate 65–66; McDowell 29; duCille 4, 17; Raimon 8), and finally with the melodramatic mode as introduced by Peter Brooks (McCann 789–791; Gillman 3–6). The three literary aesthetics reimagine—in both similar and different ways—national politics as a family body (Tate 7–9; McCann 791, 808). As Philip Fisher puts it, in this body of writing "the central unit in which experience is recorded is not the individual, the class, or the society, but the family" (101). Melodrama is additionally motivated by a drive toward revelation and turns the secret and private into the public and generally acknowledged. Following Susan Gillman's and Sean McCann's reclamation of melodrama in the Woman's Era, this book analyzes the ways in which all the works that form the corpus studied here deploy "melodrama in the service of racial"—and I would add gender—"politics" (McCann 791). The melodramatic mode is not only central to the mulatta novels but also highly significant in the black temperance narratives.

The political dimension of private stories in mulatta melodrama and the intricate parallels between the family body and the national body are signaled in Hopkins's claim in *The Contending Forces* (1900) that "[r]aces are like families" (198). Analogously, in Harper's *Iola Leroy*, this connection is well exemplified by the reference to "being destined to pass through the crucible of disaster and defeat, till she was ready to clasp hands with the negro and march abreast with him to freedom and victory" (24). The sentence's feminine subject is "the Nation," yet it perfectly fits the eponymous character's story. After her own "crucible" of "pain and suffering," Iola is ready to "clasp hands with the negro"—in her case a representative of the rising black professional class, Doctor Latimer. The novel melodramatically privatizes the political: it "aggressively domesticates ... the public sphere" and foregrounds "an erotics of politics" (Hadley 535; Gillman 22). Such a melodramatic use of the intimate, sexually marked family body and romantic relations to talk about the abstract and dematerialized national body and political history is a critical edge of all the texts analyzed in this book.

The other driving force behind melodrama is to make the secret and private public. According to the most influential study of this aesthetic, Brooks's *Melodramatic Imagination* (1976), the "desire to express all seems to be a fundamental characteristic of the melodramatic mode" (4). Christine Gledhill, drawing on Brooks's findings, contends that melodrama "draws into a public arena desires, fears, values and identities which lie beneath the surface of the publicly acknowledged world" (33). This drive toward revelation is most conspicuously visible in the recognition scenes that propel all the mulatta melodrama narratives I analyze and are also used in A. E. Johnson's and Dunbar's temperance narratives. Terence Cave's monumental project *Recognitions: A Study in Poetics* (1990) posits a complex epistemological significance to such literary anagnorisis. Cave claims that recognition always evokes an epistemological crisis: "a disquieting sense ... that the commonly accepted co-ordinates of knowledge have gone awry" (2). Rather than stabilize and clarify, literary "recognitions" evoke "radical uncertainty" and the constant threat of "an imposture, the arrogation of a false identity and a false past" (240–241). Moreover, anagnorisis typically discloses sexual trysts and a threatening, buried past (241). The knowledge recovered in recognition scenes is "perverse," "improper," "dubious or disturbing," and it "reveals... the monstrous transgression of a taboo" (Cave 3, 7, 209). It is a *paradoxical* knowledge, a knowledge that transgresses a given *doxa* (203)—a knowledge that goes beyond, as Gledhill puts it, "the publicly acknowledged world" (33). Hence melodramatic recognition simultaneously makes the transgressive, private, and intimate past public and destabilizes the categories of truth and plausibility.

As Cave argues (referring to Brooks), the "dynamics of repression and the return of the repressed figure the plot of melodrama" (201). In postbellum African American fiction, the albino mulatta is the repressed that keeps returning, and the melodramatic desire for the revelation of transgressive, paradoxical knowledge primarily concerns the racial identities of the characters, whose mixed raciality is repeatedly revealed to themselves, to other characters, and to the reader. The obsessive repetitiveness of scenes of anagnorisis in the novels, with their references to the uncertain flows of "blood" in US society—"the drop of black blood" that might be hiding in every family; the inescapable "ties of blood"; the pride "of the old blood" versus monogenesis (according to which all humans are "of one blood")—insists on the recognition of the interracial sexual history of the illegitimacy, exploitation, and rape of black bodies. As far as their intraracial politics is concerned, in a dramatic contrast to Condict's objection that post-Reconstruction "novelists can imagine no love beautiful and sublime within the range of the colored race, for each other" ("Editorial" 398), all the texts promote a politicized erotics in which the female protagonist is rewarded with a happy ending only by choosing a black (though frequently mixed-race) suitor, thus having identified with the black community.

The combination of the mode of melodrama and the figure of the mulatta—which defines the structure of Brown, Harper, Hopkins, and Chesnutt's novels—produces interesting conceptual tensions. As Brooks argues, one of melodrama's defining features is its exclusion of "the middle ground," which stems from the polarization of opposites that characterizes the genre (18, 36). When this melodramatic aesthetic is paired with mulatta characters, who precisely constitute the racial "middle ground," it exposes the paradoxes inherent in what Frantz Fanon calls "Manich[ean] delirium" (183), namely, the American "melodramatic" imagination of irreducible race differences. The contrasts between the characters and ideas cease to be reducible to a polarized black-and-white opposition. The albino daughter is contrasted with her bright mulatta mother and not with phenotypically black characters, which distorts the typical melodramatic chiaroscuro. As Gillman claims, on one hand, the melodramatic mode fits the radicalism of turn-of-the-twentieth-century race relations and representations; on the other, the revelation frequently fails to result in a complete closure, and the novels' endings insist on the impossibility of resolution (6). Thus the fin-de-siècle mulatta melodrama further dramatizes the epistemological crisis pointed out by Cave as a central feature of melodramatic recognition scenes.

Another traditional element of melodrama complicated by the race factor is its relationship to the past. As David Grimsted states, melodrama tends to contrast the "degenerate present," most frequently urban, with the typically rural "immediate past as an epoch of great moral superiority" (224), which in the US context echoes Jeffersonian pastoralism. In contrast, as was pointed out in the introduction, all the novels of the Nadir examined in this study are antipastoral and antinostalgic. To put it simply, since the immediate rural past in mulatta melodrama is necessarily linked to plantation slavery, it cannot unproblematically connote virtue and bliss. Even though the selected novels depict moments of pastoral idyll, because of the looming shadow of slavery all such episodes are short-lived and fatal. This ambivalence in the representations of pastoral scenes, where the idyll is exposed as almost gothic isolation, is central to my reading of the mother figure as the foil of the white-looking mulatta daughter in chapter 2. Thus, in contrast to nostalgic melodramas that celebrate the lost innocence of the past and pastoral bliss, the fin-de-siècle mulatta melodrama is future-oriented and antinostalgic. Although it does represent urban modernity as fraught with obstacles that African Americans are forced to face in the era of the Nadir, the rural past is not romanticized in an escapist way. This is voiced not only in the narrative logic of the novels but also in the way they contrast the two generations of characters. They are unable to wholeheartedly empathize with the antebellum mulatta mothers, and they are critical of the failed white fathers, vesting all their hope for change and progress in the new generation of, predominantly postbellum, New Negro daughters.

The mulatta melodrama's triangular structure is formed by three characters: the white man, his bright mulatta partner, and their "albino" mulatta daughter. Although literary analysis based on character typology might seem quite basic or too closely related to the outdated "images of" method, which failed to account for the dynamic complexity of representations, its use here is justified by the melodramatic aesthetic of the novels that constitute the corpus. The stories of the characters in mulatta melodrama frequently function as allegories, which directly stems from the melodramatic "erotics of politics," namely, their projections of social and political phenomena onto the family body and individual, private relations. Moreover, as Brooks argues, melodrama uses its characters as symbolic oppositions that embody either unequivocal virtue or villainy, rather than as figures of psychological depth and complex development.

Another meaningful use of characters as tropes is the practice of *histotextuality*, that is, allusions to historical figures in the names and constructions of fictional characters, identified by Gabrielle Foreman as an important strategy of nineteenth-century black women's writing (*Activist* 10–14). Foreman's *Activist Sentiments* uses this tool to examine Harper's *Iola Leroy*, but as I demonstrate, it is also an effective tool to read other mulatta melodramas as well as the temperance-related texts analyzed in part 2. Michael Stancliff, another scholar of Harper, highlights the significance of her use of diverse but related meanings of the character—from literary, national, and racial to ethical—in a different yet complementary way to Foreman. He argues that "to analyze [Harper's] politics of subject formation with historical sensitivity, we need to begin with the most pervasive conceptual model of personhood in the nineteenth century, that is, character" (9). He adds that Harper's rhetorical pedagogy was premised "on a model of persuadable subjectivity, calling on a collective political will," and it "served to materially organize the African American character, which in turn became the engine of social reform and the germinating subjective ground of community" (9). He introduces the term *character talk* to analyze "the new disciplinary politics of character" and "to designate the pervasive conceptual reliance on cultural forms of characterological virtue in nearly all manner of social address, the communicative manner of ethical subjects negotiating general principles of ethical personhood" (9). Not only Harper's works but other mulatta novels as well apply such disciplinary politics of character to promote ethical virtue through their melodramatic oppositions of villainy and innocence, which are embodied by individual personalities but make gestures toward national characters, state bodies, and social politics.

On an anecdotal note, melodrama—originally understood as a theatrical performance accompanied by music (Brooks 14)—was important in the personal lives and outputs of all four black writers analyzed in the first part of this book. The black writers' engagement with different expressions of the melodramatic mode and its affective excess can be read as a reinforcement of their literary choices and their inclination for the affect-based genres that facilitate the emergence of intimate communities. As a reporter states, "In addition to her rare gifts as a vocalist, Miss Hopkins is the author of several successful musical comedies" (qtd. in Wallinger 43). In the late 1870s and 1880s, Hopkins performed in her family troupe, the Hopkins Colored Troubadours (Wallinger 42–43). As her biographer Hanna Wallinger claims, one of the immediate predecessors of her play *Peculiar Sam*—subtitled *A Musical Comedy in Three Acts* and staged under such titles as *Slaves' Escape*, *The Flight for Freedom*, and *The Underground Railroad*—was a drama titled *The Escape; or, A Leap for Freedom* (1858) authored by Brown, her "model as a writer, activist, and lecturer" (Wallinger 41). It was never performed by a cast of actors, but "there were numerous occasions when Brown gave a reading of it" (41). Harper, despite her multigeneric oeuvre, never authored or staged a drama, yet as Stancliff argues in regard to her rhetorical practice, we "can think of her stance as a performance" that assumed roles and positions not available to her in the social reality of the day (52). As evidenced in her letters, she was a self-aware performer; "[m]y voice," she wrote, "is not wanting in strength, as I am aware of, to reach pretty well over the house" (qtd. in Stancliff 2). Chesnutt, like Hopkins, had direct stage experience. In light of the many parallels between the excess of mulatta melodrama and tropes of temperance in the early African American novel that this book examines, it is highly significant that his engagement in performances includes a staging of the temperance drama *The First Glass*, an 1868 play by Nellie H. Bradky (Chesnutt, *Journals* 54–56). Those experiences with drama, stage, and performances link the authors of mulatta melodramas to Dunbar, the last writer analyzed in this book. Dunbar, mostly known for his poetry and only recently the subject of critics' attention as an author of three novels with racially indefinite characters, contributed to the rise of black musical theater in fin-de-siècle New York. This episode in his short life resonates with the depictions of the Tenderloin vaudeville and melodramatic mode in *The Sport of the Gods* (1902), which is discussed in chapter 8. As Dunbar himself suggests, although far from utopian, the communities of affective attachments produced in the black theater district had a considerable significance for the new immigrants from the South.

Another nonliterary reference that can facilitate a better understanding of mulatta melodrama is the tradition of *casta* paintings. These Latin American works of art powerfully echo mulatta melodrama's tripartite struc-

FIGURE 1. Miguel Cabrera, *From Spanish and Indian, Mestizo Is Born*, 1763, oil on canvas. Private collection.

ture, which in both cases is formed by the mixed-race family. Popular in the Spanish colonies in the eighteenth and nineteenth centuries, casta paintings "represent different racial mixtures that derived from the offspring of unions between Spaniards and Indians, Spaniards and Blacks, Blacks and Indians, and the subsequent mixtures of mestizos and mulattos" (Deans-Smith 171). In the works, interracial relations and their offspring, rather than denied or lamented, form the basis of "an orderly colonial society composed of idealized casta subjects" (175). The paintings record and celebrate the complex taxonomy of America's racially mixed inhabitants. Despite the considerable contextual distance between the Latin American art genre and the US black novel of the Nadir, mulatta melodrama and casta paintings share a common ground, which is aptly exemplified in Miguel Cabrera's *From Spaniard and Indian, Mestiza* (fig. 1). I selected a painting in which the offspring is a mestiza, not a mulatta, because it downplays the visibility of racial differences in an analogous way to the figures of albinos in Brown, Harper, Hopkins, and Chesnutt's novels. The Indian woman and her mestiza daughter are more similar to literary white and bright mulattas than mulattos from casta paintings because of their more racially ambiguous look. The image perfectly illustrates the structure of the fin-de-siècle mulatta melodrama. The focus falls on the female family members: the faces of the mother and the daughter are depicted en face and in great detail, in contrast to the male figure, whose face remains invisible. The only information we get about the father comes from his clothes, which, typically for the casta tradition, clearly indicate his upper-class status. The mother casts a sideways, flirtatious look at the man. The daughter's expression, in contrast, seems more ambiguous and might be read as critical.

In many respects, casta paintings are completely alien to US culture. In the nineteenth century, US citizens with enough cultural and financial capital to commission paintings did not want to recognize, let alone celebrate, miscegenation. The repressive and ideological state apparatuses of Jim Crow segregation promulgated a belief in rigid boundaries between the white and black races (Saks 39–69).[5] At the same time, a largely parallel structure to the casta paintings was expressed in literature, a medium more easily available to the underprivileged and minorities. Thus the recognition of interracial relations, absent from painting, found its expression in African American reform fiction, with mulatta melodrama at its center. As the two following chapters will show, the triad in Cabrera's painting accurately portrays the typology of mulatta melodrama: the failed upper-class white father, the easily courted mother, and their self-determined New Negro daughter. Thanks to its visual form, the image expresses the essence of mulatta melodrama's structure at a glance, thus providing a synthesized representation of the genre and serving as an apt introduction to the several hundred pages of the novels analyzed in the following chapters.

CHAPTER 2

※ ※ ※

The Apple Falls Far from the Tree
MATRILINEAL OPPOSITION IN MULATTA MELODRAMA

> The loveliness of Negro women of mixed blood is very often marvellous, and their condition deplorable; ... their mothers were like themselves; their fathers they never knew; debauched white men are ever ready to take advantage of their destitution, and after living a short life of shame, they sink into early graves.
> —PAULINE ELIZABETH HOPKINS, *Hagar's Daughter*

This chapter analyzes literary representations of matrilineal relationships and their correlation with race politics and the melodramatic aesthetic. Though the main focus is on African American fiction of the Nadir, my analysis begins with William Wells Brown's *Clotel; or, The President's Daughter* (1853), the incontestable ur-text for the African American mulatta tradition, without which it is difficult to understand the intertextual complexity of the later works. The novel interweaves the abolitionist polemic and slave narrative with a complex and highly melodramatic plot revolving around three generations of heroic mixed-race women: Currer, Clotel, and Mary. Both euphoric and dysphoric coincidences are complemented with multiple, fragmentary, and simultaneous plotlines, all delivered at a frenetic narrative pace that sometimes introduces characters and forgets them on the following page. The result of such a combination is chaotic excess, which highlights both the traumatic experience of slavery and the relational and vulnerable identities of the novel's characters. J. Noel Heermance, in one of the first comprehensive analyses of *Clotel*, finds the work flawed and inconsistent due to its borrowings and heteroglot structure; in his words, it contains "enough material ... for a dozen novels" (165). Although more recent critics have been much more generous about Brown's aesthetic,[1] Heermance's assessment is correct in the sense that at least "a dozen novels" have been written by the recasting of *Clotel*'s plots. Among them are several subsequent versions of the novel published by Brown. The last, a postbellum rewriting—*Clotelle; or, The Colored Heroine: A Tale of the Southern States* (1867)—enables the daughter, now renamed as Clotelle, to purchase the farm on which she used to work as a slave. Such closure, in which the protagonist makes a "free voluntary choice of belonging to the African American community," bears a very close resemblance to the political dynamics of the works of the post-Reconstruction period (Fabi, *Passing* 28–29). Seen in such a light, *Clotel/Clotelle* emerges not only as the ur-text of the African American mulatta melodrama tradition but also as a representative of the genre in the postbellum period, which further justifies its place in any analysis focused on fin-de-siècle African American literature.

The three postbellum texts explored here—Frances Ellen Watkins Harper's *Iola Leroy* (1892), Charles W. Chesnutt's *The House behind the Cedars* (1900), and Pauline Elizabeth Hopkins's *Hagar's Daughter* (1902)—form a complex network of intertextual connections to *Clotel*. The melodramas of the Nadir era rewrite Brown's excessive material in diverse ways. Harper's and Chesnutt's novels contain subtle though meaningful allusions to the 1853 narrative, whereas Hopkins quotes it extensively without even changing the names of the characters. All these intertextualities are further intensified by resonances among the turn-of-the-century works themselves. Both the intertextual reverberations among the novels and intratextual reiterations of melodramatic recognitions in the selected texts exemplify a repetition compulsion and thus, as I argue, help manage the ideological anxieties and fantasies central for the period of the Nadir, indelibly marked by the rise of racial segregation and interracial violence.

From the thematic perspective of this chapter, the most important diegetic similarity is the novels' retelling of a story of a mulatto mother and daughter. Using the notion of mulatta melodrama, with its triangular structure as outlined in chapter 1, I complicate the traditionally overgeneralized perception of female mixed-race characters, which dates back at least to Maria Lydia Child's "The Quadroons" (1842), with its analogously tragic mulatta mother and daughter (Rosalie and Xarifa), yet which—as I signaled in the introduction—is also present in contemporary academic discourse. As will be demonstrated, despite many apparent similarities, there is a significant difference between the two generations of mulattas, which is exemplified by the problematic mother-daughter relationship as represented in the selected novels. Notwithstanding their empathy and understanding for all mixed-race characters, due to the future-oriented and antinostalgic character of African American mulatta melodramas, the genre invests its hope in the younger generation of New Negro women and subtly, or in some cases more explicitly, contrasts them with their antebellum mothers. In the novels of the Nadir and its ur-text, *Clotel*, these two figures respectively embody slavery, which gives way to the black Woman's Era.

Most critics in the field have acknowledged that the mulatta narratives clearly center on the black family and privilege the matrilineal line, and they have exploited the multifarious meanings of the "child following the condition of the mother" rule and pointed out "the centrality of Black maternity" or the "mother's law" (Zackodnik 89–90; Foreman, *Activist* 99, 104).² The excessive, repetitive poetics of the texts precisely stem from the intergenerational similarities between mulatta characters in each novel. As one of the very few white female characters of *Hagar's Daughter* claims in the utterance cited in the epigraph (159), the mulatta literally and tragically follows the condition of her mother. Although a similar statement is later repeated by the intrusive narrator (238), the level of the plot in Hopkins's work—as well as other texts analyzed here—disproves the thesis that the mulatta daughters are just like their mothers. Focusing especially on the narrative construction of courtship, romantic choices, and the settings, I argue that the figure of the light-skinned antebellum mother functions as the foil for her free, or freed, daughter. All four novels correlate the mother with slavery and reconstruct the formulaic seduction plot with a white lover as the suitor to represent her victimhood. The daughter, on the other hand, epitomizes freedom, self-reliance, and romantic self-control, whereas her ability to pass for white, as a "real Albino," underscores her self-determined choice of a black identity (*Clotel* 49). In the postbellum novels, she performatively calls into being, embodies, and eventually interpellates the New Negro woman of the black Woman's Era.

The need for disidentification with the mother figure and the significance of her passive character have been examined by critics of hegemonic "woman's fiction." Nina Baym argues that the mother often represents "the passive woman," who serves as a foil for the protagonist and highlights her independence (28). Another insightful scholar of popular fiction for women, Tania Modleski, also analyzes the role of the passive mother figure and claims that, in particular, the gothic novel's depictions of women's isolation and victimhood express "separation anxieties" and further the necessary separation from the mother: "Gothics in part serve to convince women that they will not be victims the way their mothers were" (73–83). Modleski's claim, at first blush, fits all too neatly into the representation of African American filial bonds in mulatta melodrama. Since the mothers are either literally slaves or are metonymically marked by the condition of slavery, their powerlessness is not simply a hyperbolic metaphor. The postbellum daughters' identification with their mothers is necessarily wrought by fears of reliving their mothers' victimhood and is driven by a need for individuation and separation. Hence the mulatta victim-mother can be explained as a trope that illuminates these post-Emancipation "separation anxieties" of black women.

On the other hand, this augmented need to disidentify with the mother figure is problematized by the repetitive images of family separations, both in the analyzed novels and in the collective imagination fueled by strategies of compassion in nineteenth-century reform discourse.[3] Whereas Modleski's woman reader and heroine need to disidentify from their mothers in order to gain autonomy, the black heroine is frequently traumatized by a premature separation from her mother. The mulatta narratives are driven by a desire for a multigenerational family reunion, which complicates the need for filial separation. Furthermore, since, as many critics have pointed out, African American narratives tend to challenge the helplessness of the tragic mulatta stereotype (Carby, *Reconstructing* 73),[4] the mulatta mothers are necessarily less passive or immature than their white counterparts in "woman's" or gothic fiction. They do not fully fit Baym's depiction of the passive woman as "incompetent, ignorant, cowed, and emotionally and intellectually undeveloped" (28). Hence the contrast between the mother and the daughter in African American narratives, though it is dramatized by the opposition of slavery and freedom, is not as pronounced as in white hegemonic fiction. The relationship could be aptly described by the phrase Deborah McDowell uses to talk about different generations of black women writers: "the changing same" (xi). The change and the difference are nevertheless visible and significant; as will be demonstrated, they are intricately related to the aesthetic of mulatta melodrama.

In melodrama's drive to simultaneously make the private political and to project national politics onto the family body, the historical past of slavery and the present era of freedom are reconstructed as an intergenerational matrilineal conflict. The polarization of the mother and the daughter occurs on several levels: from romantic, geographical, and historical to economic, all mutually informing one another. The mothers are represented as easily courted concubines, eager to either cohabitate with or get married to a white man. There is hardly any representation of their decision-making processes, self-awareness, or desires.[5] Significantly, the setting of the quickly terminated idyll is rural or suburban, always isolated and private. The pastoral setting, on one hand, serves as an argument by analogy for the natural character of the interracial union, while, on the other hand, its secluded character and lack of integration with the social texture expose the myopic and fatal character of the relationships. The antebellum mothers remain in most cases marginal figures and serve as foils to the New Negro protagonists, whose courtships are extensively prolonged by the narrative and interpolated with numerous obstacles. The novels' closures range from the excessively happy ending in *Iola Leroy*, tragedy in *The House behind the Cedars*, to an intermixture of the two in *Hagar's Daughter* and *Clotel*. Despite these differences, all these texts are infused with the melodramatic poetics of coincidence, which either artificially fix what seems irreconcilable and thus "draw attention to themselves—and to literary form as a whole—as artifice" (Cave 2; exemplified by *Clotel* and *Iola Leroy*) or, on the contrary, emphasize the improbability of legal interracial relationships after emancipation (as in *Hagar's Daughter* and *The House behind the Cedars*). As Hazel Carby claims in reference to the ending of *Hagar's Daughter*, their excessive, forced, or failed closures enable the texts to shift "the attention of [the] reader from individual to nation, from acts of particular characters to systemic oppression" (*Reconstructing* 152).

Apart from the explicit criticism of racism and social segregation, the novels—partly through their rewriting of hegemonic woman's fiction and women's reform discourse—voice many gender-oriented criticisms. The fact that the mother always lives in seclusion can be read, for example, as a hyperbolic relegation of nineteenth-century hegemonic femininity to the private sphere and the gothic isolation that is its predetermined result (Epstein 83–87; cf. Sánchez-Eppler, "Bodily" 28–59). Yet the introduction of black characters also exposes the limitations of hegemonic fiction's logic and highlights the specificity of black women's condition. Apart from the mother-daughter dyad, the narratives feature the white father, whose irresponsibility is solely or partially to blame for the "ordeals," "trials," and "sufferings" of women (the role of the white fathers is the focus of chapter 3). As a result, through their triangular structure, mulatta melodramas criticize the systemic dependence of women on men and expose the tenuous and illusory character of the protection offered by the ideology of domesticity. The guarantees of the domestic sanctuary are especially unreliable for black women, whose isolation in the private sphere may easily turn them into private property. This is conspicuous in the figures of mulatta mothers, who perfectly embody the domestic ideals of true womanhood yet are not rewarded for their proper performance of gender ideology in accordance with the holy grail of nineteenth-century woman-centric fiction: namely, the euphoric ending of marriage (DuPlessis 4; Dannenberg 7–8).

Mulatta in the Secret Garden:
Idylls & Sorrows in the Olden Days

Historically, all mothers in the novels—Molly in *The House behind the Cedars*, Marie in *Iola Leroy*, the eponymous Clotel and Hopkins's explicit rewriting of her as Hagar—are correlated with the condition of slavery, and their storylines formally parallel the temptation plot dating back to the eighteenth-century novel (Baym 26). They exhibit moral weakness, which is parallel to both the white male's lack of self-control (discussed in the following chapter) and to the self-indulgence and shortsightedness of the older generation in black temperance narratives. Characteristically, in all novels of the Nadir era, the mother's story is either revealed in fragmented retrospection rather than chronologically or, as in Hopkins's work, represented in separate or minor parts of the text. Such a narrative positioning highlights the distance between the mother's antebellum subplot and the central plot of the New Negro daughter. In the first version of Brown's work, this marginalization is marked by the fact that the mother, despite being the eponymous character, dies in the middle of the narrative, and it is the daughter's storyline that closes the novel.[6] Overall, the mother figures tend to be relegated to the peripheries of the texts; accordingly, they have attracted less scholarly attention than their heroic daughters. This work is aimed at uncovering their stories and examining the ambivalences inherent in them to show how they serve to foster the individuation of the next generation of female characters endowed with self-determined agency and thus performatively call into being the New Negro woman.

In Brown's *Clotel*, the eponymous heroine meets her white lover, Horatio, at a quadroon ball, and even though he is introduced as her "conquest,"[7] the affair is narrated only through her mother's thoughts and Horatio's desire "for the most beautiful girl, coloured or white, in the city" (48). At the frantic narrative pace of hypercondensed action, which characterizes many chapters of the novel, it takes Brown just one paragraph to place the young couple at a secluded cottage, where they pass "their time as happily as circumstances would permit," to announce the birth of their daughter, and to introduce Horatio's political ambitions, which consequently destroy the "quadroon's home" (65–66). The next chapter of the heteroglot text devoted to Clotel's subplot is entitled "Separation." The diegetic tempo of this section accurately exemplifies what Gérard Genette dubs a *summary* in his typology of narrative movements (94–106). Its pacing is further highlighted by contrast with a narrative pause: the description of the couple's home. The passage depicting the cottage is long, elaborate, detailed, and hence worth closer scrutiny. To a careful reader, the tenuous character of the couple's relationship is already foreshadowed by the fact that the cottage is "hired" rather than bought (64). The description highlights the seclusion of the house, which is located far from the city center, "scarcely to be seen," "retired from the public roads," and "almost hidden among the trees." Such isolation mimics and reinforces the "social wall of separation" that "the edicts of society had built up" between Clotel's home and Horatio's public life. The abundance of vines—clematis and passionflower—suggests Clotel's dependence and lack of autonomy, which foreshadows the way that Paul Laurence Dunbar will imbue creepers—most notably in the title of his first volume of poetry, *Oak and Ivy* (1893), and in the imagery in *The Sport of the Gods*—with the tragic political significance of dependence in the black community half a century later.

Overall, Clotel's position at her cottage is a hyperbolic image of nineteenth-century hegemonic femininity, confined to the private sphere and relegated to the obligations of maternity. The novel dramatizes the helplessness of such a position, which is possibly one of the factors that made *Clotel* an attractive text for a white female audience. The politics behind the white female empathy for black bondwomen has been recently criticized as objectifying by a number of scholars (Sánchez-Eppler, "Bodily Bonds" 29).[8] Yet in the melodramatic title of one of the chapters, "Today a Mistress, Tomorrow a Slave," Brown problematizes the easy analogies and identifications employed in the nineteenth-century suffrage movement. As the story unfolds, Clotel is sold down the river, and it turns out that for a black woman, forced mobility, separation, and displacement are far worse a fate than confined domesticity. Faced with the choice between death and slavery, Clotel jumps into the Potomac and dies. As Teresa Zackodnik argues, referring to Philip Brian Harper's analysis of *Iola Leroy*, the black woman may not "appeal to the rhetoric of separate spheres" in the same way that white women do. Paradoxically, when the "private" bliss ends, she becomes "the private property of [a] white man" (P. Harper 17; Zackodnik 108). Hence the isolated setting of the idyll both criticizes the hegemonic separate spheres ideology and, by racializing the narrative, exposes the specific systemic oppression of black women.

Apart from this critical dimension of the description of the cottage, the long paragraph celebrates in an evocative way nature's hybridity and the productive coexistence of different plant species: "The *pride of China mixed* its *oriental* looking foliage with the *majestic magnolia*, and the air was redolent with the fragrance of flowers, peeping out of every nook and nodding upon you with a most unexpected welcome. The tasteful hand of art had not learned to imitate the lavish beauty and *harmonious disorder of nature*" (64; emphasis added). While pointing out its lack of originality and its indebtedness to Child's "The Quadroons," Ann duCille claims that the passage is a "metaphor for racial and marital accord" (26). Beyond stating that Brown improves the description, however, she does not go into detail, arguing that his "highly appropriative style makes such a formalist reading difficult." Yet when compared to the original sentence, in which "[m]agnificent Magnolias, and the superb Pride of India, threw shadows around [the cottage], and filled the air with fragrance" (Child 61), Brown's passage is slightly, albeit significantly, changed. It makes the trees "mix" and emphasizes the "oriental" character of the pride of China. Hence the juxtaposition of the two trees is racially charged in a more explicit way: the "oriental" metonymically stands for the racially marked blackness (Harper uses "the luxuriance of the Orient" in *Iola Leroy* to point to the African American presence in American culture [282])—and "magnolia" for southern whiteness and plantation magnanimity. Other details in the description, taken verbatim from Child's short story, further emphasize the diversity and fertility of the garden. The reader may imagine how the two species of vines covering the piazzas—clematis and passionflower—must have beautifully and inseparably intermingled. The profusion of different flowers results in the "lavish beauty" and "harmonious disorder" of the garden. Since the passage celebrates the coexistence of different genera, it can be seen as alluding to racial hybridity.[9]

The figurative similarities between floral and racial interbreeding are also used by Hopkins in her novel *The Contending Forces* (1900), whose intrusive narrator explicitly postulates such an analogy: "Combinations of plants, or trees, or of any productive living thing, sometimes generate rare specimens of the plant or tree; why not, then, of the genus homo?" (87). As Gillman convincingly argues, Hopkins here strategically uses the nineteenth-century language of evolution, extending its logic and pointing out its contradictions, arguing for the possible profits of the presence of racially mixed people in the African American community (68).[10] Hence, apart from the fact that the natural setting, "a perfect model of rural beauty," naturalizes the union of Clotel and Horatio, the specific images aestheticize racial diversity and the hybridity of nature and present it as productive and harmonious.

A strikingly similar setting is introduced in Chesnutt's *The House behind the Cedars*. John Warwick, having passed for white for many years, decides to visit his mother and sister during a visit to his hometown. Unknowingly, he follows his sister Rena back to their family house.[11] The reader follows Warwick and recognizes the eponymous "house behind the cedars." Chesnutt, analogously to Brown, highlights the isolation of the place, yet—as the novel is partly grounded in the realist tradition—here the distance from the town center is made visible by the length of the walk narrated by Warwick's internal monologue, which takes up seven descriptive paragraphs and points to the subsequent changes in the surroundings. Following Rena, Warwick "passed a factory, a warehouse or two, and then, leaving the brick pavement, walked on mother earth, under a leafy arcade of spreading oaks and elms" (273). The movement is away from the urban and industrial and toward the rural and natural. Since the male protagonist comes back to his childhood home, the direction is also temporarily regressive and potentially nostalgic. The walk reverses industrialization and seemingly recovers the romanticized pastoral ideal of "the mother earth" with its disturbing racial othering (273). As Warwick moves away from town, he notices that the pastoral images are accompanied by "the decline of respectability" of the neighborhood and its racialization—Rena on the way helps an old black woman "lift a large basket" and place it on "the cushion of her handkerchief" and "pull[s] a half-naked negro child out of a mudhole" (274). The houses grow "scattering and the quarter of the town more neglected," and finally as they reach their destination, the protagonist realizes that he is following his own sister to a "yard shut off from the street by a row of dwarf cedars." As he peeps though "narrow gap in the cedar hedge" (275), he sees a garden, in which

> walks were bordered by long rows of jonquils, pinks, and carnations, enclosing clumps of fragrant shrubs, lilies, and roses already in bloom. Toward the middle of the garden stood *two fine magnolia trees*, with heavy, dark green, glistening leaves, while nearer the house two mighty elms shaded a wide piazza, at the one end of which *a honey-suckle vine, and at the other a Virginia creeper, running over a wooden lattice*, furnished additional shade and seclusion.... The house stood on a corner, around which the cedar hedge turned, continuing along the side of the garden until it reached the line of the front of the house. The piazza to a rear wing, at right angles to the front of the house, was open to inspection from the side street, which, to judge from its deserted look, seemed to be but little used.... [T]he back yard ... was only slightly screened from the street by *a china-tree*. (275; emphasis added)

The privacy of the house, already announced in the novel's title, is emphasized by the details: the thick "dwarf cedar hedge" with only "narrow gaps"; a "china-tree" concealing the house from the street; "a honey-suckle vine ... and a Virginia creeper." The trailing plants provide "additional shade and seclusion" but may also signify the inhabitants' vinelike dependence, like the clematis and passionflower in *Clotel*. Different flower species are not separated but intermingled and listed in a long and specific catalog: "jonquils, pinks, and carnations, enclosing clumps of fragrant shrubs, lilies, and roses already in bloom" form a "bright carpet of flowers" (275). Just as in Brown's text, both the magnolia and china-tree—with their racialized significance—are present. All this makes the representation of the setting strikingly similar to Clotel's cottage—secluded, isolated from the rest of the neighborhood, far from the town center, and marked by dependence. The combination of the natural setting and seclusion is further underlined through the last name of the house's proprietor. Rena's mother, who owns the house, is called Molly Walden, which triggers associations with Thoreau's famous experiment and resultant memoir. However, even though both Molly Walden's and Thoreau's reclusive lives were largely contemporaneous, their meanings were quite opposite. Thoreau's gesture signified transcendentalist self-reliance, freedom, and volition, whereas Molly's was naturalistically due to "circumstances, some beyond her control" (289).

Still, this does not mean that Molly's seclusion is totally devoid of emancipatory potential. As evidenced by the extensive quotation, both in *Clotel* and in *The House behind the Cedars*, considerable space, unparalleled in descriptions of other places, is devoted to depictions of the amazingly fertile flower gardens. The sheltered garden signifies secrecy but also potentially constitutes a heterotopian space that challenges the boundaries between races and species. Michel Foucault, in his very short, very sketchy, and very influential essay "Of Other Spaces: Utopias and Heterotopias," claims that the garden is the oldest example of "contradictory heterotopias," which are able to "juxtapos[e] in a single real place several spaces, several sites that are in themselves incompatible" (25). Interestingly, in the text, he refers to Persian gardens and their affinity with carpets, which "were originally reproductions of gardens (the garden is a rug onto which the whole world comes to enact its symbolic perfection, and the rug is a sort of garden that can move across space)." Hence Chesnutt's use of the by-now-worn-out simile of "the bright carpet of flowers" can be read as a celebration of harmonized differences, where "foreign" or otherwise "incompatible" elements harmoniously interact.

The garden is the buffer zone between the public street and the private house of Molly Walden, a former mistress of a nameless white man, father to her two children, John and Rena. Its long description, just like in *Clotel*, is in stark contrast to the scarce space devoted to Molly's relationship. This imbalance further emphasizes the lack of her agency, since as György Lukács claims in his seminal "Narrate or Describe?," heavy descriptiveness, which characterizes naturalist fiction, precludes the characters' development of subjectivity (110–148). Since the narrative begins many years after Molly's lover's death, their relationship is mentioned in a few fragmented asides that at first keep the reader in the dark about its interracial character, suggesting that she might be a white "fallen woman," at the time a highly popular figure in melodramas, dime novels, and naturalist narratives. In the introductory pages of *The House behind the Cedars*, the reader is informed that she "accepted less than marriage" and, "if she had sinned, she had been more sinned against than sinning" (347, 286). Only several chapters into the book is the secret racialized, and not until the beginning of the second part of the text is the entire story explicitly revealed.

Just like Brown in the case of Clotel and Horatio, so too Chesnutt does not go into detail about the relationship. Molly's perspective is completely absent from the diegetic analepses that summarize her love life, which precludes the reader's sympathy for or identification with Rena's mother. We are told she was a young beautiful mulatta, playing next to a well, which through biblical associations with the Samaritan woman possibly foreshadows Molly's position as the social outcast. "A gentleman drove by one day, stopped at the well, smiled upon the girl, and said kind words. He came again, more than once, and soon, while scarcely more than a child in years, Molly was living in her own house" (371). The narrative plays into the ethnic difference between Jesus and the Samaritan woman of the biblical scenario and the illegitimacy of her relationships with men. Here, however, the well is the beginning of Molly's moral decline rather than the salvation suggested in the Bible. Despite this reversal, the association with the biblical character may serve to partially cast off the specter of the illegitimacy of Molly's situation. Mirroring the pace of Brown's narrative, in the next paragraph the white father dies and leaves the family without the legal protection of a will. Thus an analysis of depictions of gardens and the relationships between mothers and their white lovers demonstrates that both novels underplay the romance and courtship, simultaneously focusing on description of the setting that is provided for their short-lived relationships.

It must be emphasized, however, that the house is owned by Molly, and though her interracial relationship begins before emancipation, in contrast to all other mulatta mothers, she is not a slave. Despite the significant difference in her condition—"she yet had freedom of choice, and therefore could not wholly escape blame"—Molly's plot closely parallels the remaining narratives (372). This resemblance is plainly visible in the similarity between two passages of intrusive narration from Brown's and Chesnutt's novels. Justifying Clotel's illicit relationship, the narrator explains that "amongst the slave population no *safeguard* is thrown around virtue, and no *inducement* held out to slave women to be chaste" (Brown 46; emphasis added). Similarly, the narrative voice in *The House behind the Cedars* excuses Molly, who "with every *inducement* to do evil and few *incentives* to do well" is "entitled to charitable judgment" (372; emphasis added). More generally, as Winters argues, free(d) black women experienced an "inescapable connection to slavery": "[t]o write these women as 'free(d)' is to underscore the precariousness of their freedom" (6). Hence Molly's position differs but nominally from that of Clotel.

The promptly entered-into illicit unions of Clotel and Molly in many ways parallel the marriages of mothers to white gentlemen in Harper's and Hopkins's novels. Most importantly, both are declared illegal when it comes to light that the women are not white. Despite the initial lawful character of the relationship in *Iola Leroy*, the courtship proceeds in the one- or two-paragraph pace that was used by Brown and Chesnutt. Fresh from school, not having seen her owner Eugene Leroy for years, Marie immediately responds to his proposal: "she bow[s] her beautiful head and softly repeat[s]: 'Until death do us apart.'" An immediate "strictly private" wedding follows, and "Marie return[s] as mistress to the plantation from which she ha[s] gone as a slave" (74, 65, 76). The reader, however, is informed of Eugene's intentions before Marie, as the male character takes up one entire chapter to tell his part of the story, which is constructed as a narrative of a decadent aristocrat ultimately saved from overindulgence and death by his octoroon nurse. The addressee of this confession is his cousin Alfred Lorraine, the melodramatic villain of the text, rather than the object of his affections. Marie's focalization of the courtship is completely absent from the novel.

What follows is the familiar state of idyll, although Harper's text emphasizes the utopian and escapist seclusion rather than the natural beauty of a heterotopic garden. "In a quiet and beautiful home," on a "lonely plantation," Marie is "sheltered in the warm clasp of loving arms," and "her life" seems "like a joyous dream" (76). Like Clotel, who lives behind a "social wall of separation," Marie is also "shut out from the busy world, its social cares and anxieties" (86). The end of the bliss is quickly foreshadowed with the visits of Alfred. For her husband, Alfred is "the only relative who ever darkens [their] doors" (90); and for Marie, "with his coming a shadow [falls] upon her home, hushing its music and darkening its sunshine" (89). The narrative confirms Marie's premonitions. Alfred, after Eugene's sudden death from yellow fever, takes over their fortune, challenges his wife's manumission and their marriage license, and consequently remands her and her children to slavery. The narrative highlights the idyllic natural setting—"birds ... singing their sweetest songs, [and] flowers breathing their fragrance on the air"—only to contrast it with the family tragedy (93). Just as in *Clotel*, the seclusion of the place is unable to protect the family bliss. To the contrary, after the wife becomes a slave, the isolation of the sheltered space is a key factor that reinforces its dangerous character. As Harriet Jacobs, alias Linda Brent, memorably argues, for female slaves especially, life on "a distant plantation" was much more dangerous than in town where it was easier to make slaveholders'"villainy... public" (47). Her statement is supported by historians who likewise claim that "the rural isolation of plantations shielded many offenders from the eyes of the community" (Fox-Genovese et al. 375). Thus the remoteness and social separation of the Leroys' home facilitate the ease with which Alfred turns the women in the private sphere into his private property. Putting an end to the pastoral idyll in the novel, Harper recasts the narrative device of the husband's sudden death, which was frequently used in hegemonic woman's fiction. This diegetic turn leaves the woman powerless and thus exposes the fatal consequences of the absolute financial dependence of women on men.[12] Marie's predicament is further dramatized by the fact that her helplessness is a result of a literal rather than metaphorical slavery. Hence, like *Clotel*, Harper's rewriting of the popular narrative twist makes the novel appealing to all women anxious about their dependence on men, yet simultaneously the literal slavery of her characters problematizes the straightforwardness of the popular nineteenth-century "woman as a slave" metaphor.[13]

In Hopkins's novel, the setting of Hagar and Ellis's love affair is reminiscent of the extensively described Jamesian mansions, and the narrative implicitly acknowledges this association: Enson Hall "remind[s] one of English residences with their immense extent of private grounds" (31). Again, the desiring and courting are narrated from Ellis's perspective, and the scene of engagement resembles the natural idyll from the previous works, as the place is "closed to the public." The scene also epitomizes the romantic view of transcendence through nature. In complete isolation from social reality, Hagar rests suspended in a handmade hammock. "Lying there, with nothing in sight but the leafy branches of the trees high above her head, through which gleams of the deep blue sky came softly, she felt as if she had left the world and was floating, Ariel-like in midair" (36). When Ellis comes and disturbs her, she falls out of the hammock; he catches her, asks her to marry him, and she succumbs to his "passionate kisses" (38). Thus are they betrothed and get married in the next paragraph, even though the narrative needs to give an account of Hagar's mother's death before the wedding takes place.[14] In the compulsive repetitiveness of the novel's poetics, this pace of courtship is duplicated when Hagar gets engaged to her second husband. The narrative evocatively points out "her eager acceptance" of the proposal (81). Ultimately, as in the other works discussed in this chapter, Ellis's engagement promise to Hagar that she will be "so loved and shielded that sorrow" will never touch her is not fulfilled (38). Like Marie, she is remanded to slavery after her husband is pronounced dead.

Thus the novels repeatedly represent the rural idyll undercut with an imminent ending looming over it. The dialectical descriptions of the cottages, plantations, and gardens are at once pastorally beautiful and gothically threatening. Just as Mary Wollstonecraft, criticizing gender politics and submissive women in Rousseau's *Emile* (1762), points to the risky appeal of the image in which "the graceful ivy, clasping the oak that supported it," forms "a whole in which strength and beauty [are] equally conspicuous," so too the vines in Clotel's and Molly's gardens are, on one hand, remarkably beautiful and thus metaphorically represent interracial romance as natural, and on the other portray the fatal consequences of servile dependence, which, according to Rousseau (and not only Rousseau), was "a state natural to women" black or white (269).

Analogously, as the charm of romantically secluded settings turns into the threat of gothic spaces when the family idyll is prematurely terminated, the novels posit the necessity of social integration and insist that the private should be made public. The private/public binary in the texts functions in two different but interrelated ways. Since all the novels rely on the melodramatic aesthetic and its will toward revelation, through repeated moments of anagnorisis they insist that the private secret is always made public. When, for example, a white lady asks Molly's daughter about her race, she asks her "something very *personal*" and then adds that Rena "must have a *romantic history*" (427; emphasis added). The personal secret is Rena's race, which, when revealed, publicizes the *history* of southern interracial "*romantic*" relations. Even though the works I analyze do not portray women's lack of consent, as for example Jacobs's *Incidents in the Life of a Slave Girl* or Hopkins's *Contending Forces*, their representations of mothers' uncritical and prompt acceptance of the proposals made to them bear the traits of a seduction novel, especially since all the women enter into relationships that essentially turn out to be "less than marriage" and all the unions result in pregnancies. The obsessive repetitiveness of anagnorisis—mostly of the daughters' true identities—may be a way to insist on the *recognition* of the interracial sexual history of the illegitimacy of their mothers. Apart from the relentless drive for private stories to be exposed as national history, the public-private boundary is challenged in yet another way. Through the contrast between mothers and daughters, the texts insist that women's seclusion in the private is dangerous, myopic, and impossible in the modern times; accordingly, the daughter's presence in the public sphere—though frequently perilous—is represented as inevitable.

In the Public Eye:
The New Mulatta's Freedoms & Discontents

The enslaved, victimized, domestically confined mothers, all too eager to enter into interracial relationships, serve as foils that highlight the self-determination and independence of their New Negro daughters. Contrary to the abolitionist feminist mulatta as analyzed by Sánchez-Eppler, whose "body displays not only a history of past miscegenation but also a promise of future mixings" ("Bodily Bonds" 41), the new generation of protagonists recasts the significance of the availability of the mixed-race body to white males. In contrast to their antebellum mothers, the emancipated daughters showcase self-restraint and do not get married to attractive white suitors. The narratives devote a lot of space to their decision-making process, ethical development, and growing self-awareness. Two of them—Iola and Mary—after extended trials are rewarded with respectable black husbands. In contrast to the antebellum, premodern, rural context of their mothers' subplots, the daughters' storylines are predominantly positioned in the postbellum public sphere. The women enter the workforce as nurses, teachers, and office workers or at least engage in some traveling. The novels either embrace the newly gained self-determination or at least represent dynamic modernity as inescapable and the rural idyll of secluded cottages as utopian and myopic. Even though they do depict the threats of the public sphere and feature scenes of a lonely woman in danger, they tend to challenge the familiar scenario of a damsel in distress saved by a knight in shining armor. Just as in the hegemonic woman's fiction analyzed by Baym, "the traditional rescuing function of the novel is denied" to the male protagonist in mulatta melodrama (40).

The contrast between Clotel and her daughter, Mary, is primarily visible on the level of plot resolution. Mary's storyline exemplifies Brown's signature poetics of narrative chaos and excessive coincidence. Her choice of a husband is introduced in a passing remark that artificially stitches together different plots yoked together in the space of a single paragraph. The fragment, whose logic borders on stream of consciousness, begins with a retelling of Clotel's arrest and death, moves on to the concurrent slave revolt, introduces its last insurgent, George, and narrates his entire life story, including a summary of his trial and a full record of his impassioned abolitionist defense speech. Despite his references to the American Revolution, which are meant to move both the audience in court and the intended reader, George is pronounced guilty. Such tragic yet logical closure of his story is quite unexpectedly disrupted, and the last sentence in this several-pages-long paragraph moves back from the trial to George's earlier spousal choice: "[H]e was sentenced. Being employed in the same house with Mary, the daughter of Clotel, George had become attached to her, and the young lovers fondly looked forward to the time when they should be husband and wife" (191).[15] The dramatic arbitrariness in the narrative logic of the paragraph reflects the lack of coherence and absurdity of slavery as experienced by the characters and points out the ways in which the political and the private are interconnected in the narrative. It forcefully illustrates M. Giulia Fabi's claim that Brown "obliges the reader to experience the incoherence and displacement that he sees [as] central to [a] slave's life" (*Passing* 9).

Reversing the sentimental damsel-in-distress plot, it is Mary who saves her lover by changing clothes with him. Unlike her mother, she does not experience even a moment of rural idyll, and the wedding is postponed until the very end of the novel—by three chapters and by ten years. George, continuing the reversal of gender roles, dresses up as a woman and manages to escape to Canada. Then, unable to find Mary, he moves to Europe, where the two are finally reunited by an improbable, coincidental anagnorisis, which is delayed and complicated by Mary's dark veil and in turn facilitated by George's lost book. In contrast to the illusorily safe, secluded setting of Clotel's cottage, the scene of the wonderful recognition of George and Mary takes place at a public spot, a cemetery in Dunkirk. After two meetings, her and his fainting, and his "bursting into a flood of tears," the extensive two-chapter anagnorisis is complete (202). The narrative makes their meeting possible through the introduction of a Frenchman, who helps Mary escape and takes her to France. The text insists on the platonic character of their relationship as Mr. Devenant only "transfers" his brotherly love onto Mary, who closely resembles his dead sister (204). Additionally, the reader is informed that George has continued to be at the center of Mary's life since her only son with Devenant is named after him. Furthermore, the narrative follows George rather than Mary, and thus the French husband is present only in Mary's reminiscences and is conveniently dead when the near-white lovers reunite (a scenario that Dunbar's *The Sport of the Gods* will signify on over half a century later). This complex stratagem allows for the preservation of Mary's respectability and the final happy family reunion. At the same time, both its narrative and chronological postponement and its radically coincidental character suggest the unlikelihood of such reunions for black families in general. Significantly, the final happy ending in *Clotel*, a text with plots "enough ... for a dozen novels" (Heermance 165), is reserved for the only mulatta who chooses a black husband, even though he is light-skinned and does not openly identify with his African origins or slave heritage.

In the four chapters that Brown adds to his novel in the postbellum edition, Mary, renamed Clotelle, comes back to the United States, performs heroic deeds during the Civil War, and then becomes a teacher in a school for freedmen. In this version, not only does the protagonist choose a black husband but Jerome is dark-skinned, and she also heroically decides to embrace her blackness, which even further underlines her self-determined character. At the outbreak of the white southern "rebellion," Mary/Clotelle and George/Jerome go to New Orleans to assist their kin in "a state of starvation and sickness" (105). George/Jerome joins the army, and after just one paragraph the reader is informed in a graphically excessive way that his head is "entirely torn off by a shell" when he tries to save the body of a deceased white officer (106). Mary/Clotelle also takes part in military action, and, just as in the past, she tries to assist men to escape from bondage: she "secretly aid[s]" "ragged, emaciated Union prisoners" "in their escape" from prison in Andersonville, Georgia (107). After the men's plan to build a tunnel ends in failure, Mary/Clotelle begins to "interest herself in another mode of escape for the men thus so heavily ironed" (110). This one succeeds, and as a result, she has to flee yet another time. Once more she is imprisoned, and once more she escapes. At the novel's end, "to [the freedmen's] education and welfare she resolved to devote the remainder of her life, and for this purpose went to the State of Mississippi, and opened a school for the freedmen; hired teachers, paying them out of her own purse" (114). The purse—inherited from her white father—enables her also to buy the plantation on which she lived as a slave. Finally, as duCille notes, her independence is all-encompassing; she is "unencumbered by child, man, or marital obligations" (28), which makes her the first postbellum New Negro woman in African American fiction.

Harper's 1892 character to a large extent follows in the footsteps of Mary/Clotelle. Iola represents self-determination, self-restraint, and devotion to social work more intensely than any other mulatta in African American literature. Her story to a large extent parallels the "trial and triumph" trajectory—the central plot of hegemonic woman's fiction according to Baym (40, 104). The narrative similarity is further reinforced on the lexical level as the words "trial" and "tried" are used eleven times in the novel to refer to hardships experienced by Iola and other black female characters (54, 104, 106, 115, 118, 210, 227, 247, 250, 272). Yet the diegetic expectations raised by woman's fiction do not prepare the reader for the inordinately delayed triumph of Iola. It does not immediately follow the trial, and the trial itself is narrated with many narrative gaps and silences. Because of legal flaws in the documents, her father's death triggers the central mulatta melodrama peripeteia: Iola's social status suddenly changes from white to black and from free to enslaved, which begins what the narrative repeatedly and vaguely refers to as the abovementioned "hour of trial" as well as the "fiery ordeal," "siege of suffering," "ministry of suffering," and "crucibles" (106, 114, 195, 196, 256). Her story is not narrated in chronological order, and Iola herself is introduced only in the fifth chapter of the novel. Such narrative absences and gaps formally highlight the unspeakable character of her experiences.[16]

The shock of being remanded to slavery and resisting more or less explicitly described attempts at seduction are followed by two legitimate marriage proposals from a young white doctor, whom Iola seems to be in love with but whose offers she rejects out of racial loyalty and ethical responsibility. The fragmented story of her past is communicated in passing mentions in dialogues and through extradiegetic narration, abounding in words such as "self-respect," "resolve," "pledge," "duty," and "purpose" (57, 117; 112, 118, 208, 209, 211; 118; 56; 60, 200, 205, 219, 263, 271; 114, 144, 235, 236). In one such conversation, her husband-to-be, Dr. Latimer, thus summarizes Iola's story: "I know a young lady who could have cast her lot with the favored race, yet *chose* to take her place with the freed people, as their teacher, friend, and adviser. This young lady was *alone* in the world. She had been fearfully wronged, and to her stricken heart came a brilliant offer of love, home, and social position. But she *bound her heart to the mast of duty*, closed her ears to the *syren song*, and could not be *lured* from her purpose" (263; emphasis added). The "syren song" of the marriage proposal and "love, home, and social position" rejected by Iola accurately describes Eugene Leroy's offer, so promptly accepted by her mother. Volition and solitude highlight Iola's self-reliance, whereas the "lure" accentuates the necessarily relational character of her position. Harper's narrative contains one significant element that is absent from the novels analyzed by Baym: namely, race politics. In the text, Iola's white looks serve to further underline her self-determination. The invisibility of black racial markers enables her to choose her identity and to make the ethical choice to be black. As the reader learns from one of Iola's strong declarations, she is "resolved that nothing shall tempt [her] to deny [her color]," and "[t]he best blood in [her] veins is African blood" (208). Thus her near-whiteness helps emphasize her moral development and exercise of volition.

The reference to the "syren song" and the comparison of Iola to Odysseus, "bound to the mast," foreshadows the way in which the novel's happy ending is postponed. Whereas "an episode of financial reversal and an interlude of self-support became virtually obligatory in woman's fiction," and the typical heroine becomes temporarily financially independent and frequently works as a teacher (Baym 71), in Harper's text Iola's professional endeavors are significantly extended. As the narrative opens, freed Iola becomes a devoted nurse during the war. As soon as the "hospital [is] closed, ... Iola obtain[s] a position as a teacher" (145). Then, after her school is burnt, one entire long chapter is devoted to her attempts to find different jobs in two cities in the North. Subsequently, Iola decides to go back to teaching, and her fiancé encourages her to become a writer (262). At the end of the novel, Iola, having gotten married, works at a Sunday school in the South. Her narrative trajectory comes full circle—she settles down in the same town in the South from which she was rescued in the fifth chapter when she enters the narrative. What makes Iola's work-related episodes seem even more prolonged and to some extent anticlimactic is the fact that many come after the key climax in the story, the moment of family reunion—which takes place exactly two-thirds of the way through the text (i.e., in the twenty-second out of thirty-three chapters). Harper thus rewrites and intensifies the hegemonic "trial and triumph" formula, making Iola's trials more extended and her newly gained independence more heroic. Such a delayed construction of the romantic narrative is also instrumental in the race politics of the novel: it helps balance the text's post-Emancipation optimism with attention to the dramatic racial discrimination of the Nadir.

When, finally, the respectable black Dr. Latimer is positioned in Iola's path, their relationship is introduced in stark contrast to the conversation between Eugene Leroy and Alfred Lorraine that announces the planned marriage of Eugene and Marie. This time it is Iola who takes up most of the chapter, which is entitled "Dawning Affections," to eulogize the "high, heroic manhood" of Dr. Latimer in a conversation with her uncle. In addition, the marriage itself is neither secret nor immediate and takes place only a year after the proposal. In contrast to Marie's isolation in the private sphere, both Iola and Frank Latimer actively take part in the life of their community. Although Claudia Tate convincingly points to the limitations of Iola's "commitment to public service" at the end of the novel, it should be emphasized that she does not remain completely insulated within the private sphere (98). Depictions of her home challenge the very private-public boundary: "[H]er doors are freely opened for the instruction of the children before their feet have wandered and gone far astray. She has no carpets too fine for the tread of their little feet" (279). She metaphorically makes her home a school for freed children. The permeability of private-sphere boundaries is also visible in Iola's public service. Not only is Iola's home open for children, but in "lowly homes and windowless cabins her visits are always welcome." This affectionate, rather than forced or top-down, flexibility of the border between the private and the public in Harper's text is the foundation of the emancipated black community. Characteristically, even though the narrative ends with a detailed report on the fates of its main characters, Iola—just like the last incarnation of Brown's heroine as well as other mulatta daughters analyzed in *The Nadir and the Zenith*—is still childless at the end of the novel. This absence of children can be read as a further refusal to relegate Iola to the private sphere. Overall, in contrast to her mother, Iola refuses to pass as white, rejects a comfortable life in the private sphere, and throughout the narrative supports herself. She chooses a black husband but does not have children. While represented in a variety of public spaces, she is also socially embedded within the black community.

Whereas in *Clotel* and *Iola Leroy* the contrast between mothers and daughters primarily stems from the plot construction, in *The House behind the Cedars* this difference is reinforced with shifting perspectives between different focalizers and the extradiegetic narrator. In contrast to the complete absence of her mother's focalization from the summary passages depicting Molly Walden's interracial relationship, Rena's consciousness and her decisions are at the center of the novel's attention. Her relationship is interchangeably narrated from the perspective of her fiancé and through her own internal monologues. Chesnutt's narrative is more intensely melodramatic than Harper's, with even more coincidences and peripeteias, which in turn feed Rena's extended introspections. Unlike the self-sacrificing Iola, Rena initially agrees to leave her mother, Molly, and to share her brother's life of passing as white. She engages in a relationship with a white southern gentleman, George Tryon, and the courtship lasts for four long chapters. Because of her sense of guilt regarding both the racial secret and the abandonment of her mother, she dreams of Molly's illness, returns to visit her, and by an improbable coincidence her black identity is discovered by her white fiancé. After this anagnorisis he rejects her, and she decides she will "never marry any man" (387). Instead, in "service to her rediscovered people" (396–397) she becomes the model black female reformer—a teacher. In contrast to *Clotel* and *Iola Leroy*, whose female protagonists are rewarded with a near-white professional husband, Chesnutt's narrative interestingly revises this optimistic scenario. Jeff Wain, a mulatto who courts Rena in the latter part of the novel, is a scheming, impoverished, and immoral villain who masquerades as a responsible bourgeois reformer. Fortunately, Rena mirrors the Baym heroine, who "is canny in her judgment of men and generally immune to the appeal of a dissolute suitor" and easily sees through his plans (Baym 41). Molly's explicit championing of Wain as Rena's future husband further emphasizes the contrast between the daughter's heroic self-restraint and the mother's myopic indulgence and/or materialist opportunism. In contrast to the triumph that closes hegemonic woman's fiction, *The House behind the Cedars* closes with Rena's lonely death. Rather than enter a bad marriage, she eventually dies as a result of her panicked flight from two admirers.

Unlike Molly, who is confined to the house and garden throughout the course of the entire novel, Rena from the very beginning (when her brother follows her from the town center to her house) is predominantly positioned in public. Her errand to town directly leads to the most critical of the novel's many anagnorises, the discovery of her mixed-race identity by George. After the broken engagement, she leaves the secluded, private house behind the cedars for the public sphere of school and a rented room. Her ordeals in the public are not rewarded at the end of the narrative, and as Fabi points out, the novel "dramatizes the lack of safe space for women like Rena" (*Passing* 84). The final climactic scene in the text graphically illustrates the dangerous position of a single woman outdoors. Just before a storm, on her way home from school Rena faces the stalking advances of both the dishonest mulatto, Jeff, and her former white fiancé, George. Morally heroic, the mulatta protagonist does not run to the "white knight" as could be expected, but "[s]he turn[s] and flees" (302–304, 449). Moreover, since this coincidence positions the villain alongside the white lover, it highlights the similarities between the two characters and thus exposes the latter as a failed hero, a point analyzed in detail in chapter 3. Rena's vulnerable position is accentuated by the dramatic setting of the scene: the violent storm, wild swamp, and finally a phallic "huge black snake, ... frightful in appearance" (448). Additionally, the swamp potentially positions the two suitors as slave catchers following fugitive bondmen with bloodhounds, which is later reinforced in the case of Tryon, who follows "the false scent" (459). Tellingly, in his representation of the pursuit, Chesnutt juxtaposes Rena with another lonely woman in public. When searching for his former fiancée, George follows clues that lead him to a woman whose "sandhill sallowness" represents both her complexion and her class. Her lack of self-control is visible in her drunken condition as well as in the resulting "tipsy cordiality" toward George (453). The woman's appearance, intemperance, and lack of refinement make her an additional foil for Rena's fairness, moral self-control, and respectability. This marginal figure also interestingly resonates with images of white or racially ambiguous intemperance that are discussed later in this book. As George concludes, she is "not fair, and she [i]s not Rena." With these melodramatic juxtapositions in the novel's finale—of Rena and the nameless drunk woman and of Jeff and George—Chesnutt implicitly challenges both the absurdity of racial boundaries in the Jim Crow regime and the narrative of white heroism.

Hopkins's novel, as critics have pointed out, bears a close resemblance to Chesnutt's (Tate 198), which is most conspicuously visible in their closures. In both texts, the death of the near-white female protagonist prevents her from an interracial union. Both end with the white suitor overcoming his racial prejudice and returning to the heroine's home only to find her dead. In *Hagar's Daughter*, in contrast to the suburban and idyllic Enson Hall that has provided the setting for her parents' brief courtship, Jewel's romantic relationship with white lawyer Cuthbert Sumner is predominantly located in public spaces of Washington, D.C. As we find out in an analepsis, Cuthbert meets Jewel as a debutante at her "coming-out" ball, yet the narrative introduces them in the streets of Washington through the eyes of the novel's villain who, like many others "in the stream of well-dressed pedestrians ... watch[es] with interest ... the occupants of the handsome carriages" going down Pennsylvania Avenue and scrutinizes the couple sitting in "a sumptuous Russian sleigh" (75). The visual control that is exercised by the villainous General Benson over the protagonists is repeated in other scenes, which take place in a theater, in prison, and in court, where the setting of the couple's encounters is marked by analogous panopticism. The *publicity* of the couple's relationship is visible also in the attention devoted to it by the press. When reporting the murder for which Sumner is framed, the papers include profuse and alleged information of the romantic relations of the protagonists (181–184, 266–267). This public character of Jewel and Sumner's turbulent relationship is contrasted with several secrets: the villains' false identities and their conspiracy against the couple, Hagar's passing, and Jewel's hidden black identity. As melodrama, *Hagar's Daughter* is driven by a desire to make the private public and to reveal the true identities of all its characters. In its narrative closure, however, the ultimate revelation does not result in the complete reconciliation that characterizes many popular melodramatic plots.[17]

Even though, as Tate convincingly points out, in contrast to the female characters in *Contending Forces*, Hopkins silences Jewel's voice, limits her agency, and makes her actions centered on Sumner rather than on the black community and reform activities (207), nevertheless the protagonist still exhibits exceptional courage and independence, and it is suggested that if it were not for her premature death she might have become a model New Negro woman reformer. Even before she finds out about her mixed-race ancestry, she engages in philanthropic activities to support the black community. She asks her millionaire father to help the family of their servants: Venus and her brother. "He is a genius," she argues, "and Venus has given up her hopes of becoming a school teacher among her people to earn money to help develop his talents. Can't we do something for them, papa?" (89). His response clearly suggests that this is not a solitary gesture or a passing whim on her part and that she is especially interested in uplifting the black community: "You're always picking up lame animals, Blossom; from a little shaver it's been the same. If you keep it up in Washington, you'll have all *the black beggars in the city* ringing the area bell" (89; emphasis added). Despite his mocking tone, Senator Bowen promises to "look the matter up," and hence "Blossom" uses her race and class privilege as well as her father's love for his only child to aid a black family that—as will be shown in the next chapter—is centrally significant in the novel's narrative twists and turns.

Another episode that demonstrates Jewel's departure from the passive and tragic mulatta cliché narrates how, like Mary in *Clotel*, she saves her fiancé from imprisonment by hiring a detective who helps her solve the case, and subsequently she is punished with captivity—though, due to the postbellum context, in her case it is kidnapping rather than relegation to slavery.[18] In her depiction of Jewel's abduction, Hopkins recasts the popular postbellum image of the unprotected woman in public. Yet, even though the narrator points out that "the Washington streets [are] famous for their loneliness and seclusion, stretching like immense parks in all directions" (210), the kidnapping passage presents the dangers of the public sphere as analogous to Enson Hall and its "long dim stretch of woods" and "immense extent of private grounds," rather than to the expected metropolitan commotion. Even though "the streets" represent "terror for the lone female pedestrian," Jewel is kidnapped only after she enters her well-protected private sphere. The "thick underwood," "full and dense foliage," and "the gloomy shade of the trees" shielding her house prevent the kidnappers from being seen by her escort—Chief Henson. Moreover, the capturers are not strangers but are close relatives and loyal servants. Thus, even though the chapter opens with a threat that foreshadows Jewel's abduction and that merges together "terror," the metropolis, and "lone female pedestrians," subsequent paragraphs undermine this association. Jewel is kidnapped within "the great entrance gates" to her residence, "in the close proximity of the house," by people hired by her uncle (210). Following in the footsteps of other mulattas resisting entrapment and true to her upbringing in the West—she "had been brought up on a ranch; . . . and even in Washington she was never unarmed when without male escort"—Jewel draws "her revolver with intent to fire" and exhibits "unnatural strength in her frantic struggle for freedom" (210–211). The episode—with skillfully built suspense—nevertheless ends with the failure of her resistance. Eventually, she is rescued by her maid cross-dressed as a boy, in contrast to her mother, who after her jump into the Potomac is saved by a man, a local oyster-digger, and then married by the wealthy miner Bowen (266).

Apart from the difference in the settings of Jewel's and Hagar's courtships, the contrast between the mother and the daughter is also visible in the narrative pace and resolution of their romantic relationships. The engagement of Jewel and Sumner is much more extended than that of her parents, although the narrative states that it is "a desperate case on both sides" (85). Whereas Hagar and Ellis's first meeting, courtship, engagement, and wedding are all summarized within six pages, the novel devotes the entire second part, taking up twenty-nine out of thirty-seven chapters, to the relationship between Jewel and Sumner. The couple is twice separated, and both moments serve to showcase the mulatta's romantic self-restraint. When she is led to believe that Sumner loves another woman, Jewel, like Rena, decides she will "never love—never marry" (144). The second separation comes after the couple's secret wedding and results from Sumner's hesitation about

Jewel's mixed-race identity. In a way that reminds one of Brown's reticent representation of Mary's marriage to Devenant, the novel implicitly preserves the protagonist's virginity and respectability. Since Jewel and Sumner get married in prison, and their final separation happens just after he is finally released, before nightfall, the couple is not given a single night in the nuptial bedroom. Before the final resolution occurs, however, the reader follows numerous and turbulent peripeteias. The accidental meetings, recognitions, and misrecognitions result both from the melodramatic coincidences of the narrative and from the villainous conspiracy of its characters. Sumner becomes "[t]he victim of a *plot*," "a *plot* for ten millions" hatched by General Benson, Jewel's evil uncle (93; emphasis added). Simultaneously, the lovers are at the mercy of the highly melodramatic *plotting* of the novel. Jewel is separated from her lover by means of Benson's plot, Sumner coincidentally finds out about the plot from his female colleague, and he is subsequently framed by Benson for her murder. Meanwhile, Jewel receives help from an experienced detective, who subconsciously feels an urge to assist her and, as it turns out, is coincidentally her biological father. The solution of the murder mystery and the uncovering of Benson's conspiracy reunite the lovers and lead to their secret marriage.

The revelation of Jewel's racial identity brings about the final separation of the spouses. The closing peripeteia occurs in the next-to-last chapter of the novel, at the moment when the two couples—Hagar/Ellis and Jewel/Sumner—have already reunited, and the reader does not expect any new revelations. Hagar, in an extended scene, inspects the contents of her late husband's secret box. The narrative pace is relatively slow and abounds in pauses with digressive observations, such as "she undid the knot with the feeling of pride which attends the operation of succeeding in untying a string without cutting it" (276). Having closely examined the numerous memorabilia of Senator Bowen, at the very bottom of the trunk Hagar finds "something vaguely familiar," which turns out to be baby attire "her own hands had fashioned twenty years before," and her mother's locket that was about her baby's neck when she jumped with her into the Potomac (277–278). The use of such material evidence was already recognized by Aristotle, who classifies it as a "recognition by signs," more particularly by "acquired" signs, such as necklaces, and criticizes it as "the least artful" form of anagnorisis, resulting from a "lack of resourcefulness" (21).

Hopkins's text, however, is certainly not deficient in resourcefulness. The sophistication of the trunk inspection scene, apart from the masterful building of suspense, is notable in the way that the complex construction of the discovered signs parallels the convolution of numerous interrelated hidden identities in the novel. The representation of Hagar's husband's private trunk, which contains a locket with "the intricate ... triple case" and a hidden spring that opens its secret compartments, accurately mirrors the interrelatedness and profusion of secrets in this novel, in particular, and the triangle that structures mulatta melodrama in general (277). The evidence from the trunk reveals that Hagar's foster daughter is actually her biological daughter, hence she is of mixed race. Whereas until this moment the melodramatic drive to disclose the secret has contributed to the fortunate reconciliation and exemplifies what Hillary P. Dannenberg labels as a euphoric family reunion (95), the introduction of the race secret complicates the closure. Jewel is reunited with her mother and father but at the same time is separated from her lover, whose race prejudice makes him hesitate for a moment too long. The novel's ending challenges the binary opposition of euphoric and dysphoric closures postulated by Dannenberg and clearly illustrates the tension discussed in the introduction—the tension between the racial ambiguity of the mulatto and melodramatic Manichaeism. Furthermore, Jewel's death, similar to Rena's, prevents her from an interracial union. Hence, although all the works expose the inescapable, though frequently invisible, *paradoxical* historical interrelatedness of black and white communities and families through their use of the mulatta figure, they simultaneously insist on the self-determined emergence of the black community through the "erotics of politics" and reward only endogenous spousal choices of the mixed-race daughters. Both the revelation of interracial history and the politicized erotics that are defining for mulatta melodrama have a deeply significant political critique when read in the historical context of the Nadir period of Jim Crow segregation and interracial violence.

There can be yet one more reading of the political import of the melodramatic elements of the narratives. Like the earlier texts, the two early twentieth-century novels—*The House behind the Cedars* and *Hagar's Daughter*—excessively use the melodramatic narrative devices of coincidences and peripeteias. Yet whereas Brown and Harper employ them in *Clotel* and *Iola Leroy* primarily to highlight the improbability of a black family reunion and to compensate for it with poetic justice, Chesnutt's and Hopkins's use of negative coincidences in the novels' closures—both white suitors arrive a moment too late—underscores the improbability of interracial unions after emancipation. In the logic of their narratives, an interracial marriage at the beginning of the twentieth century seems less probable than the whole series of implausibly coincidental meetings of Rena and Tryon in *The House behind the Cedars* and a mother and child's survival of a jump into the Potomac and their eventual reunion in *Hagar's Daughter*. Finally, even though all the texts analyzed here employ the conventional endings of death and marriage—rather than the open endings that Rachel DuPlessis has labeled "writing beyond the ending" (4)—their melodramatic excess denaturalizes the narrative closures. The endings seem either "too neat to be real," artificial due to the surplus of coincidence (Cave 2), or superfluous as they follow earlier plot resolutions and frequently stop short of an ideal reconciliation. Thus, despite the seeming conventionality of mulatta melodrama closures, their artifice and excess suggest that it is impossible to tell the story of American interracial relations within the narrative options offered by the "cultural legacy [of] nineteenth-century life and letters" (DuPlessis 4).

Though the closures and marital choices of the protagonists further highlight the divergence from their mothers, which I have tried to outline throughout this chapter, it must be underlined that the daughters' ethical development and resultant choices of race and husband stem precisely from their devotion to the matrilineal heritage. While the novels disapprove of the mothers' lack of self-restraint and eagerness to enter into relations with white men, they are definitely written as a protest against the "white and male fantasies of the lascivious, predatory jezebel" that served to cover sexual violence against black female bodies (Winters 5). In the triangular structure of mulatta melodrama, it is the white father figure on whom self-indulgence, intemperance, irresponsibility, and the shame connected with them are ultimately projected, a stratagem that will be the focal point of the next chapter. The fathers and other white men, whose portrayals frequently border on a melodramatic embodiment of evil and villainy, are the ultimate figures of distancing.

CHAPTER 3

The Fall of Man

WHITE MASCULINITY ON TRIAL

> I became acquainted with death, the death of *true manliness* and self-respect.... [T]here is many a poor clod-hopper, on whom are the dust and grime of unremitting toil, who feels more self-respect and true manliness than many of us with our family prestige, social position, and proud ancestral halls.
> —FRANCES ELLEN WATKINS HARPER, *Iola Leroy*

> [Cuthbert Sumner from New England] looks very different from most of the men one meets in Washington.... More *manly*. Chivalrous, generous-hearted—a manly man in the fullest meaning of the term.
> —PAULINE ELIZABETH HOPKINS, *Hagar's Daughter*

> [T]hat strange, ridiculous something which we misname Southern honor, that honor which strains at the gnat and swallows a camel, withheld me, and I preferred to do worse. So I lied to you.... I am a liar and a thief.
> —PAUL LAURENCE DUNBAR, *The Sport of the Gods*

Whereas chapter 1 problematized the critical generalizations about the mulatta figure in African American fiction, this one shifts focus onto a subject that has been left almost unexplored. I conclude part 1 with an analysis of the triangular structure of mulatta melodrama from a masculinity studies perspective. Using tools and theoretical concepts from narratology and gender studies, I will show how the mulatta narratives and their focus on interracial relations engage with specific nineteenth-century ideologies of southern masculinity, northern "marketplace manhood," and reformed manliness.

As one of the key figures in masculinity studies, Michael S. Kimmel, argues, the dominant ideology of manhood in the South was defined by "property ownership and a benevolent patriarchal authority at home," and its central archetype, the Genteel Patriarch, "embodied love, kindness, duty, and compassion, exhibited through philanthropic work, church activities, and deep involvement with his family" (16). Alternatively, David Leverenz labels this gender paradigm as "patrician masculinity," founded on "property, patriarchy, and citizenship" (78). Patriarchy, in this ideology, was closely related to ownership since male power was rationalized as necessary for the protection of all chattels and dependents. Elizabeth Fox-Genovese and Eugene D. Genovese, in their study of slaveholders' self-representations, underline that "virtually all members of southern society shared a fundamental attachment to independent rural households anchored in absolute private property" (6). In contrast to the contemporaneous ideology of hegemonic masculinity in the North—that is, an emergent marketplace manhood with its stress on productivity, individualism, and self-reliance or even "self-interest" (Dorsey 105)—the patrician did not engage in productive endeavors but assumed a much wider responsibility and authority over his dependents. He pledged to support and defend not only the white nuclear family but the families of slaves as well—every "southern slaveholder, according to the model, was supposed to treat his slaves as part of his 'family, white and black'" (Fox-Genovese et al. 369). The southern patrician paradigm contained strong residues of the late eighteenth-century definition of a gentleman as "a man not only independent of employer or landlord, but also a man who possessed dependents. The greater the number of those dependent on him, of course, the greater the independence and hence manliness of the man.... White men proved that they were men by asserting that they were not boys, slaves, or women, all of whom they considered to be dependents" (Dorsey 35). Southern rhetoric frequently celebrated such a relationship in images of a pastoral idyll: as one Justice Johnson argued,

"Surrounded by his family, his dependents, his flocks and his herds, with all around him looking to him for food, for comfort, for protection or instruction, [the planter] cannot but form a high estimate of his own importance in the scale of creation" (qtd. in Fox-Genovese et al. 119).

These broader definitions of southern upper-class manhood need to be complemented with the significance of a man's word of honor and oath-taking, which is especially relevant in the plot of mulatta melodrama. As Bertram Wyatt-Brown argues, although its import was marginal in America in general, in the South "the sacerdotal nature of the oath was something impressive, particularly to ... whites" (55; see also Fox-Genovese et al. 631n38). The critical significance of the word of honor can be illustrated by the fact that an "oral pledge of a gentleman was thought to be the equivalent of the signed oath" (Wyatt-Brown 56). As an unidentified citizen of South Carolina declared, a "man's word must be better than his bond, because unguaranteed.... [A] promise, however foolish, must be kept" (qtd. in Fox-Genovese et al. 119). The values of honor and chivalry were deeply imbued in the ideology of protection and dependents, and it is in their light that the white men's promises in the novels need to be examined.[1]

Because of its visible Eurocentric, feudal, antidemocratic residue and the postcolonial anxieties of the early republic, the patrician ideology of masculinity was soon challenged by the celebrations of all-American self-reliance, autonomy, democracy, productivity, and competitiveness. Furthermore, as a result of the reorganization of the private and public spheres after the Industrial Revolution, philanthropy and compassion, connotatively linked to "Genteel Patriarchy," began to be correlated with hegemonic femininity. Accordingly, as John Mayfield claims, already by the outbreak of the Civil War, "the gentleman had become a quaint, cartoonish thing in literature" of the region (*Counterfeit Gentlemen* 125–126; see also Fox-Genovese et al. 114–116).

Yet although the patrician paradigm occupied a precarious position in antebellum America, it actually reinforced its currency as a reaction to and compensation for the defeat of the Confederacy. Its continued appeal remained visible at least until the early twentieth century, as Thomas Nelson Page's works, Thomas Dixon's novels, and D. W. Griffith's *The Birth of a Nation* evidence. The glorification of a patrician South with a cavalier at the center is best exemplified in Page's first collection of short stories, *In Ole Virginia* (1887). The gentlemen heroes in his works are defined by their land ownership and their honor (MacKethan 49; see also Bailey 110–121). The stories offer an idyllic representation of gentlemanly paternalism and depict many melodramatic instances of masters protecting their dependents. The cavaliers prevent the disintegration of black families or save their slaves from fire ("Marse Chan") and drowning ("Unc' Edinburg's Drownin': A Plantation Echo"). They die defending the southern honor, and their eulogies are delivered in dialect by the grateful former bondmen.

This postbellum literary revival of the patrician paradigm explains the insistence with which mulatta melodrama launched its attack on white southern gentlemen at the turn of the twentieth century. In their critiques, African American authors were able to trigger the already existing "cartoonish" associations between the southern gentleman and feudalism, effeminacy, or foreignness discussed by Mayfield. More significantly, their narratives dramatize these connotations and demonstrate that the glorious southern lifestyle resulted in violence and tragedy. Simultaneously, they celebrate the northern reform ideal of self-discipline and compassionate manliness. The novels also exploit the popular association between southern gentlemen and effeminacy that was used already in antebellum reform discourse. Since most reform movements defined masculinity through self-restraint and in opposition to indulgence and passion, the abolitionist movement used such assumptions to attack southern slaveholders as "emasculate by indulgence" or "luxurious and effeminate" (qtd. in Dorsey 144; see also 190–191). As a result, in *Hagar's Daughter* Senator Bowen, a newcomer from the West, sounds very convincing in his explicit critique of southern patricians and eastern elites. The former are completely incompatible with the modern market economy: "[T]hese dumb-headed aristocrats are worse to steer into a good paying bit of business for the benefit of the government treasury than a bucking bronco" (87), whereas the latter are accused of dishonesty: "Talk about deceit in women! Women ain't in it compared with these Eastern raised gents they call men!" (135). Even though Senator Bowen—as an entrepreneur and a politician with a weak spot for gambling—does not readily fit the compassionate manhood ideal of the contemporaneous reform movements, his rugged western perspective provides a vivid contrast that highlights the unmanly characteristics of Washington's political elites depicted in the novel.

The African American mulatta novels' offensive against mainly southern gentlemen primarily assumes three forms. Their implicit and less trenchant critique is targeted at the white father of the interracial family and his next-generation equivalent—the white hero that fails the new mulatta. This first form of offensive fundamentally concerns the men's failure to protect their dependents, which in the narrative structure is typically communicated through what Nina Baym calls the "termination of male control" (40)—that is, the father's death, the results of which expose the weakness of the ideology of patriarchal protection. In the second form of criticism, the postbellum character is initially introduced as a model hero—attractive, compassionate, financially stable, and intelligent—and yet his failure to stand by the woman he loves due to her mixed-race origin results in her death. The third front of the novels' attack is much more explicit and in most cases is directed against the white melodramatic villain in the novel. Characteristically, in all cases, the villain is not a stranger and is closely related to the interracial family. The father's and lover's moral failing and the villain's scheming are represented as systemically related to "idolatry of the Moloch of Slavery" as well as the ideology of southern masculinity and the cultural practices of southern gentlemen, such as gambling and drinking, which, when judged by the standards of northern manliness, are unmanly and barbarous (283). The representations of white males' uncivilized behavior indirectly enter into a dialogue with the contemporary ideology of retrogressionism that presented newly emancipated black men as reverting to savagery (Tate 10). Black authors expose the barbarous elements of the southern masculine performance. Overall, they reflect the fin-de-siècle discontent over or crisis of US masculinity and participate in its remaking. The images of male moral weakness and immoderation also strongly resonate with the images of male intemperance, whose significance for these novels I will discuss at the end of this chapter. The indulgence and lack of self-discipline that define male characters in the mulatta novels are parallel to the images of drunkenness that are used by black writers of the Nadir. The male weakness and lack of self-control in the novels also illustrate the overlap between melodrama and naturalism, which is discussed in part 2 of this study, "Black Tropes of Temperance." The melodramatic excess and dysphoric trajectories of those characters are marked with the emergent determinist ideology and the central role that chance plays in US literary naturalism.

Sins of the Fathers

Mulatta melodrama reconstructs one of the essential kernels—to use Seymour Chatman's term—of woman's fiction, in which the "death of the father [... plunges] a comfortable and unprepared family into poverty" (Baym 39). Baym convincingly argues that in white woman's fiction, the plot that "terminates male control" simultaneously exposes the market economy as unpredictable and "profoundly irrational" (40). African American mulatta melodrama expresses analogous anxieties related to the financial instabilities of the market, yet the addition of the race difference to the conventional plot device modifies its significance. The novels use this narrative kernel to challenge the ideology of patriarchal protection that in the southern imagination was supposed to defend women, children, and slaves. The way in which the novels recast the death of the father exposes the dramatic disparity between the social conditions of white and black women, between poverty and chattel slavery, and between the North and the South. Whereas white heroines in woman's fiction are left without financial support and property rights, in Brown's, Harper's, and Hopkins's narratives the mulatta protagonists become private property (i.e., mistresses become chattels). In Chesnutt's novel, this construct is less explicit, yet free mulattas are left without male protection and are barred from the opportunities open to their white peers.

As was analyzed in detail in the previous chapter, short-lived interracial unions are a defining element of mulatta melodrama, and in all cases, the white father is presented as responsible for the tragic end of the romantic idyll. The narratives expose his moral weaknesses and broken guarantees of protection. As a character from *Iola Leroy* comments, "I could never understand how a cultured white man could have his own children enslaved.... [H]ow a civilized man could drag his own children, bone of his bone, flesh of his flesh, down to the position of social outcasts, abject slaves, and political pariahs" (63).

Ann duCille points out that "[t]he failure of southern 'gentlemen' to provide for and protect either their legal white wives or their 'black' slave families" drives the plot of *Clotel* (19). This is clearly visible in the case of the most developed white male character in the novel, Horatio Green. Having formed an acquaintance at a quadroon ball, Horatio buys the eponymous Clotel, and they enter "a marriage sanctioned by heaven, although unrecognised on earth" (65). Though he initially agrees to manumit Clotel and her family and move to France or England, none of these promises are fulfilled. The narrative assesses him as "an *ardent* young man *weakened* in moral principle, and unfettered by laws of the land" (66; emphasis added). Since "ardor," especially when accompanied with "weakness," is frequently criticized in the sexual politics of female passionlessness and male continence central for both hegemonic woman's fiction and mulatta narratives intertextually related to it (Cott),² the reader trained in these contemporaneous conventions already at the beginning of the text expects Horatio to fail as a protector of the family. Ultimate self-control, celebrated in the nineteenth-century female tradition, stands in dramatic contrast to the narrative of Horatio's actions. All his moves are determined by his desires, "unfettered by laws of the land": first for Clotel's beauty, then for a political career, and finally for "that insidious enemy of man, the intoxicating cup" (66, 120).³ Having experienced "a change [of] the spirit of his dreams," he leaves Clotel and their daughter, Mary, without any protection and later sells the mother and accepts the presence of the daughter as a slave in his new white family, where she is mistreated by his legal wife (66). Horatio represents the ways in which southern culture encourages self-indulgence and fickleness rather than self-discipline and steadiness among white men, and thus exposes the limitations of the patrician paradigm. At the same time, Horatio does not meet the standards of "Genteel Patriarchy" as he breaks oaths and fails to protect his partner and daughter time and again. "Defeated in politics, forsaken in love by his wife, he seemed to have lost all principle of honour" (120). By turning Horatio's relatives into his slaves, Brown rewrites and challenges the apologetic image of the slave-owning system as modeled on a family structure. Whereas the popular southern rationalization compared slaves to dependent family members, *Clotel* conflates the two groups and demonstrates that chattel slavery is radically different from family protection, even for the actual slave children and life companions of the owner. Horatio's failures trigger the dramatic peripeteia of women sheltered in the private sphere, who, due to male fickleness, become private property.⁴

Horatio is not the only man represented as a failed patriarch in the novel. Already in the title, the text alludes to the American president, and it opens with Thomas Jefferson's leaving of Clotel, her mother, and sister without any protection. The president is meaningfully alluded to again in the novel's climactic scene: Clotel's death. Ultimately, the protagonist escapes from the "prison stand[ing] midway between the capitol at Washington and the *President's house*" and jumps into the Potomac (183; emphasis added). The narrator concludes the episode with another reference to Jefferson: "Thus died Clotel, *the daughter of Thomas Jefferson*, a president of the United States; a man distinguished as the author of the Declaration of American Independence, and one of the first statesmen of that country" (185; emphasis added). As critics have pointed out, this symbolically charged setting serves to politicize Clotel's death (Berthold 19–29). On the other hand, however, the passage also serves to melodramatically domesticate American public institutions since Jefferson is presented as a father, and the president's house is exposed as a home. The allusions to American political institutions through the setting and the figures of Jefferson and Horatio quite radically politicize the failures of patriarchy in the novel. The failed patriarch ceases to be a marginal, individual character—he transcends the regional realm and gains national significance.

Whereas in *Clotel* men primarily fail through absence or withdrawal, in the remaining texts the fathers are dead or at least assumed dead for the main part of the plot, and thus their patriarchal authority is terminated as in the woman's fiction discussed by Baym. This narrative kernel of a patriarch's sudden death is also marginally present in *Clotel* in a chapter entitled "Truth Stranger Than Fiction." Clotel's sister Althesa and her white husband, Henry Morton, unexpectedly die in an epidemic of yellow fever, leaving their daughters without protection. The two girls, brought up as white and free, suddenly learn that they are officially classified as enslaved and black, which leads to their imminent deaths. This is one of the very few instances in which Brown closely embraces the tragic mulatta stereotype and heavily borrows from Lydia Maria Child's "The Quadroons."

Harper's novel, published forty years after *Clotel*, vehemently challenges the tragic mulatta figure. In the text, the mulatta protagonists are heroic survivors even though a sudden death of the patriarch signifies on the Child/Brown story and results in the central peripeteia of the protagonists. Iola's father, Eugene Leroy, dies of yellow fever just like Henry Morton, and a clerical mistake relegates his wife, Marie, and their children to slavery. But before moving on to an analysis of Eugene's death and its consequences, a brief exploration of his character will shed additional light on the narrative's representation of southern manhood. Eugene shares Horatio's passion and lack of self-discipline, and thus he is positioned as unmanly when judged according to the standards of northern self-restrained manliness. "Young, vivacious, impulsive, undisciplined," Eugene is placed "in the dangerous position of a young man with vast possessions, abundant leisure, unsettled principles, and uncontrolled desires. He [had] no other object than to extract from life its most seductive draughts of ease and pleasure" (61). Even after he is saved by Marie from overindulgence, and his "every base and unholy passion die[s]" (70), the narrative still accentuates "the feebleness of ... [his] moral resistance" and the detrimental influence of "his environment" (86). "Instead of being an *athlete*, armed for a glorious *strife*, he ha[s] learned to drift where he should have *steered*, to float with the current instead of nobly *breasting the tide*" (86; emphasis added). Again, the southern context is represented as encouraging indulgence instead of manly self-determination. His lack of independence is contrasted with the agency and muscularity of the athletic fighter, rower, or swimmer, which further emasculates Leroy and undermines his mastery.

Moreover, in Harper's earlier novel, the temperance narrative *Sowing and Reaping*, the discussion of which opens the second part of this book, almost the exact same description—"drifting where he ought to steer" and "floating down the stream" rather than "holding the helm and rudder of his own life" (101–102)—is used to describe a gentleman drunkard who, in many ways, resembles Iola's father. Thus Eugene is intertextually marked with intemperance, which additionally highlights his similarity to the intemperate Horatio. Just as temperance narratives conventionally position former drunkards as powerful temperance advocates, the novel's most explicit critique of the indulgence of southern patricians is expressed in Eugene's description of his decadent juvenile adventures. Eugene acknowledges that "unwarned and unarmed against the seductions of vice," he grew "wayward, self-indulgent, proud, and imperious," "ignorant of the value of money," "never having been forced to earn it" (67–68). The narrative, in his monologue, recasts the popular reform trope of a young man without proper ethical guidance (Parsons 110–111). Possibly alluding to the un-Americanness of the southern gentleman, Harper locates Eugene's devotion to "debasing pleasures" in "the capitals of the old world" (68). As the character openly admits, his lifestyle results in "the death of true *manliness* and self-respect" (68; emphasis added). Furthermore, Eugene makes his case representative of southern patricians in general: "[T]here is many a poor clod-hopper ... who feels more self-respect and true manliness than many of us with our family prestige, social position, and proud ancestral halls." He explains that the institutions of slavery "sap [the] strength" and "undermine [the] character" of gentlemen (61). Since "manliness" was the dominant contemporary term referring to the hegemonic ideology of masculinity in the North (Bederman 1–44), its very use here can be read as a challenge to southern masculinity.

Despite his own critique of the corruptions of southern patriarchy—strongly endorsed in the narrative—Eugene's own manhood is also questioned in the novel. After their wedding, he promises Marie that "all that human foresight can do shall be done for you and our children" and that he "will make arrangements either to live North or go to France" (81–82). Just before

Eugene's death and the consequent tragic peripeteia, Marie tells her husband again that she wishes they "could leave the country" and that she is afraid of his cousin Alfred Lorraine. In the conversation, he dismisses her as "growing nervous" (89). They go on vacation to the North to soothe her nerves, and on the way, they contract the yellow fever. Eugene "trie[s] to brace himself against the infection which [i]s creeping slowly but insidiously into his life, dulling his brain, fevering his blood, and prostrating his strength. But vain [a]re all his efforts" (92). There is "no armor strong enough to repel the invasion of death." Even though he dies assured that he has left his family "well provided for" (93), his evil cousin Alfred annuls the will and Marie's manumission, eventually turning the Leroys' *private sphere* into his own *private property*. The incident exposes Eugene's supposedly sober and sensible attitude as irresponsible, whereas Marie's "fearful forebodings" and "intuitive feelings" turn out to be judicious and true (93, 89), which reverses the reader's gender expectations regarding rationality. Harper also uses an analogous reversal in *Sowing and Reaping*, where the main character's fears about the dangers of liquor are dismissed as irrational. In addition, in contrast to the traditional expectations about feminine weakness, it is not the "nervous" Marie but her protector Eugene who succumbs to the virus.

Moreover, Eugene's individual precautions and legal actions are not enough when confronted with the forces of slavery or the unpredictability of fate. The children, far from being protected by the Genteel Patriarch and "well provided for," are instead hunted as slaves, and his daughter, Iola, goes through a "fiery ordeal of suffering" (114, 195), which refers generally to enslavement and more specifically to sexual violation. The ideology of patriarchal protection is an illusion, and in its context children may be enslaved, sold, and raped after the death of their father. The system of slavery also undercuts "the sacerdotal nature of the oath" and word of honor as Eugene's repeated promises of protection are broken as a result of his cousin's actions. Since Harper's novel blends melodramatic and documentary sensationalism, this sudden reversal of fortune is presented as statistically representative. Referring to Iola's story, a southern gentleman underlines his familiarity with many similar incidents, which suggests that they were not a marginal phenomenon (99).

Eugene's character can also be read as a recasting of the mythical chivalric and humane slave owner. Through his actions, Harper demonstrates that the combination of "property ownership" and "benevolence" celebrated in the patrician paradigm was impossible in the antebellum South (Kimmel

16). Eugene "conduct[s] his plantation with as much lenity as it [is] possible," yet it results from his "feebleness" rather than volition and self-determined action (86). Evoking the forces of habit and environment, the narrative positions him as a naturalist "character victimized by determinism" (Howard 104). Harper's skepticism regarding benign slave owners is reinforced by two episodic characters. The villainous Alfred's father, "easy and indulgent," is too humane to sell his slaves and thus ends up losing the "property" (64). His emasculated power is fatal in its consequences and effectively as cruel as overt oppression. Another "kind master" in Harper's novel problematizes the notion of benevolent authority in a different way. "Mighty good" Marse Robert is represented as reliant on the authority of his black slave, who has "great 'sponsibilities on [his] shoulders" (25). Thus Marse Robert's benevolence is inherently linked with a lack of mastery and role reversal: he is the one who assumes the position of the dependent in relation to his slave. Such portrayal dramatically diverges from the images of benevolent but dependable and protective masters in the works of Page that I mentioned at the beginning of the chapter. Harper's representations also speak to the anxieties present in southern antebellum rhetoric. As Fox-Genovese and Genovese explain, the southern slaveholder was faced with a number of contradictory expectations: "[H]e was simultaneously to be gentle, forbearing, and kind—but stern, even severe, when duty, dignity, and preservation of authority required" (Fox-Genovese et al. 369). Harper's kind-hearted gentlemen—Marse Robert, old Lorraine, and Eugene—expose and highlight the inescapable contradiction between mastery and benevolence, philanthropy and authority, located at the very center of the patrician paradigm.

Ellis Enson, the father of Jewel in *Hagar's Daughter*, in many ways parallels Eugene. In that Hopkins's novel is even more melodramatic than *Iola Leroy* and secret knowledge thoroughly permeates its twisted plots, neither Ellis nor his wife Hagar is aware that their marriage is miscegenational, and both are introduced as representatives of white patrician families. Hopkins, drawing strongly on Brown's character without even changing his name, introduces a slave trader, Walker, who claims Hagar as his property. Ellis, after some hesitation, pledges to remarry Hagar and to "sail from a Northern port for Europe" (61). Yet his brother—closely akin to Eugene's evil cousin Alfred—decides to murder his sibling to take over the entire family property. Thus Ellis's promise to Hagar that she will "be so loved and shielded that sorrow shall never touch her" is broken one chapter after it is given (38). Moreover, he is murdered before he manumits her, which the family's lawyer judges as "a great oversight—a great mistake" (73). Twenty years after her husband's death, Hagar still feels that "he had failed her" (276). Thus, similar to Horatio's and Eugene's stories, the termination of Ellis's control challenges the ideology of patriarchal protection and the safety of dependents it is supposed to guarantee.

Additionally, since the protagonists are introduced as the white aristocracy of the South, the novel suggests that due to the interracial history of the region no one could feel completely protected from the mark of slavery. The presence of white mulattos threatens every member of southern society with the specter of racial indeterminacy and, in the antebellum context, with the condition of the slave. Having said that, most of the narrative of *Hagar's Daughter* does not place the issue of racial difference in the foreground: its melodramatic plots juxtapose villainy with victimhood in a universalist way. Thus, from the perspective of the characters' race, the novel largely—with the very meaningful exception of its closure—parallels the temperance narratives with racially unmarked characters, which are discussed in the following part of this book.

The failed patriarch in *The House behind the Cedars* is scarcely present. He dies many years before the narrative begins, and his relationship with Molly—as was mentioned in chapter 2—is depicted in a very summary way. Nevertheless, the fragmented information about Rena's father ideally matches the above-discussed portrayals and their challenges to the patrician paradigm. He is introduced as Molly's "protector," "rich and liberal" (371); his patrician features indicate blue-blooded origins (373). The courtship between him and Molly is described in two sentences; "scarcely more than a child in years," Molly becomes his concubine (371). The idyll in the house behind the cedars, "the good old days" from Molly's uncritical and clearly materialistic perspective, also comes to an end in a typical way: "seven years before the war, ... death suddenly removed the source of their prosperity" (372). Though the house—unlike in the case of slave mulatta mothers—is owned by Molly, "larger expectations were dependent upon the discovery of a *promised* will, which never came to light" (372; emphasis added). According to the most reliable of the novel's characters, aptly named Judge Straight, the patrician gentleman simply "did not make a will" (290). Hence the nameless white patrician repeats the all-too-familiar scenario of passionate love, lenient benevolence, and broken promises, a fatal combination that leaves his children without protection.

Overall, the impulsive changes of heart, broken promises, and sudden deaths in the four novels reveal the irresponsibility and recklessness of white patriarchs. Even though the white fathers are not represented as villainous—actually, they are portrayed as rather sympathetic—their moral failures are strongly criticized. The novels unremittingly point to the tragic consequences of these men's weaknesses, feebleness, leniency, or even supposed benevolence. Their vices, however, are largely attributed to the southern environment, and the texts advocate northern manliness based on self-restraint, which makes southern gentlemen seem unmanly. On the other hand, the patriarchs' recurrent broken oaths and the images of family members/slaves left unprotected expose them as emasculated even when measured against their own patrician paradigm of patriarchal protection and honor. Their immoderation and indulgence—as a result of which they fail as protectors of their dependents—strongly parallel the images of drunkards both in the hegemonic anti-alcohol discourse and in the black temperance novels, which illustrates the similarity between the two corpora analyzed in this book.

The failed fathers, in contrast to their New Negro daughters, highlight the future-oriented, antinostalgic character of mulatta melodrama. Similarly, the inebriates are contrasted with their temperate children, who exhibit self-control and express hope for change and reform. Thus both corpora are structured by analogous oppositions of characters: the weak parents are juxtaposed with stronger children.

The narrative kernel of the patriarch's death and terminated male control gains more significance in African American mulatta melodrama than in the predominantly northern context of hegemonic woman's fiction, and hence the black authors not only echo but meaningfully signify on the narrative as defined by Baym. Whereas hegemonic woman's fiction primarily targeted northern "marketplace manhood," an ideology mostly defined by success in the public sphere rather than by its relationship to the private, the depictions of the patriarch's failure to protect his family in the mulatta novels attack the very basis of the southern patrician paradigm, rooted in the benign power to shield his dependents. Moreover, the slave owner's death results not only in the loss of financial stability and property by his dependents (similar to the case of white narratives), but the unprotected family members become private property, which shows the difference between black and white women's situations. Such a complete reversal also illustrates the increased significance of melodrama in the black rewritings of hegemonic woman's fiction.

Failed Heroes

The white fathers find their foils in the white gentlemen that court their daughters. As was argued in the second chapter, the race of the chosen husband is one of the key differences between the antebellum mulatta mother and her New Negro daughter. Whereas the former eagerly entered into unions with white gentlemen who would later fail as patriarchs, the latter either proudly and self-determinedly rejected white men's courtship—like Iola Leroy—or the interracial romance is melodramatically undercut by the narrative's plotting, which is the case in *Clotel*, *The House behind the Cedars*, and *Hagar's Daughter*. Brown's *Clotel* is the only text that actually presents a white—though European—man, Mr. Devenant, who helps the mulatta escape slavery. Yet he is only marginally present in the novel and conveniently killed off by the end of the narrative. Ultimately, just like *Iola Leroy*, *Clotel* promotes the erotics of politics celebrating black intermarriage, especially visible in the later versions of Brown's narrative, which marry Mary/Clotelle to a perceptibly black man rather than a white mulatto. Yet the novels' intraracial erotics is signaled in all editions, as the only mulatta that survives in the end is Mary/Clotelle—the single black female character who marries within the African American demographic. As a result of Iola's rejection of Dr. Gresham's repeated proposals and Brown's relegation of Mr. Devenant to the margins of the novel, the most interesting, elaborate, and significant images of white suitors are represented in the uncannily parallel plots of the two novels published almost simultaneously: Chesnutt's *The House behind the Cedars* (1900) and Hopkins's *Hagar's Daughter* (1901–1902). The narratives initially present these white suitors as heroes and invest them with romantic desire for the female protagonist, only to represent their moral failure after the albino mulattas are recognized as black. In both novels, the white suitors are correlated with the imagery of snakes, which—when read in the context of similar images in reform discourse—emphasizes the failures of their manliness.

George Tryon's moral integrity is, as his name suggests, tried throughout the twisted, melodramatic plots of Chesnutt's novel. Otherwise kindhearted and intelligent, aesthetically sensitive and physically fit, he nevertheless toasts the Anglo-Saxon race—"may it reign forever"—with "all his heart" and "a thrill of that pleasure which accompanies conscious superiority" (357–358). Characteristically, it is one of only three mentions of drinking in the postbellum novel, subtly imbued with temperance rhetoric, which in itself makes George a suspicious figure. The subject of white supremacy in "the fair Southland," which is toasted, and postbellum retrogressionist ideology—which argues that there is "a special tendency of the negro blood, however diluted, to revert to the African type"—reappears several times in the novel as an idea that the average southerner, even one liberally minded, takes for granted (338, see also 435). Such a southern sense of superiority is directly linked with its aristocratic pretensions and the inclinations for Walter Scott and the chivalric romance. In a way that recalls Mark Twain's *Life on the Mississippi* (1883) and *Huck Finn* (1884), *The House behind the Cedars* implicitly but consistently mocks all manifestations of the courtly mind of the South.[5]

The subtle character of Chesnutt's derisions and his incorporation of chivalric discourse into the novel's plots enable a more critically inclined reader to realize the seductive character of such romantic ideologies. Just as it is easy to root for Cinderella-like Rena—an upstart from nowhere (305)—to become the "Queen of Love and Beauty," the narrative seems to encourage the reader to cheer for George during a Scott-inspired tournament. As the narration focalized by Rena informs, when "he rode down the lists, more than one woman found him pleasant to look upon. He was a tall, fair young man, with gray eyes, and a frank open face" (303). His performance "barely escap[es] perfection," and as a result, "Sir George Tryon" is "proclaimed victor in the tournament and entitled to the flowery chaplet of victory" (303–304). His name also invests the passage with allusions to the legend of St. George and the dragon. In its most popular *Golden Legend* version (from the 1260s), the English knight defeats the snake-shaped and venom-spewing monster with a lance. In the legend, with this deed he impresses a racially marked North African princess (either Libyan or Egyptian, depending on the version), which additionally fits the context of Chesnutt's novel, where George Tryon, with his British ancestry, performs a similar feat in order to win the mulatta's favor. The Freudian imagery in the passage—the lance held by George, mentioned eight times, and the wreath of flowers that he wins and gives to Rena—further serves to emphasize the sexual differences that drive the hegemonic romantic narrative.

Additionally, Tryon's horse-mounted masculinity, emphasized with his "lance, held truly and at the right angle," is contrasted with what seems to be at first a comic-relief character—a visibly black, dialect-speaking Frank Fowler. Rena's neighbor and faithful friend comes to the tournament just to make sure she is fine and is injured in minstrellike fashion:

> As the troop passed the lower end of the grand stand, a horse, excited by the crowd, became somewhat unmanageable, and in the effort to curb him, the rider dropped his lance. The prancing animal reared, brought one of his hoofs down upon the fallen lance with considerable force, and sent a broken piece of it flying over the railing opposite the grand stand, into the middle of a group of spectators standing there. The flying fragment was dodged by those who saw it coming, but brought up with a resounding thwack against the head of a colored man in the second row, who stood watching the grand stand with an eager and curious gaze. He rubbed his head ruefully, and made a good-natured response to the chaffing of his neighbors, who, seeing no great harm done, made witty and original remarks about the advantage of being black upon occasions where one's skull was exposed to danger. Finding that the blow had drawn blood, the young man took out a red bandana handkerchief and tied it around his head. (300)

This long passage is instrumental in highlighting George's aristocratic prowess: Frank is not on horseback but is hurt by a "prancing" horse; he is not holding a lance but is injured by its broken piece; and finally, after he puts the bandana on his head, he begins to closely resemble the stereotypical black mammy and provides a grotesque contrast to George, "the knight of the crimson sash" (304). Yet the series of these melodramatic oppositions is overturned at the end of the novel, which also juxtaposes Frank and George, but in a way that only serves to deride the meaninglessness and buffoonery of southern aristocratic aspirations and romantic longings. Not only does Sir George Tryon fail to defeat any real-life serpent-shaped dragons, but toward the end of the narrative, he is paired with and thus metonymically likened to a "huge black snake"—a thinly veiled metaphor of male sexual aggression that petrifies Rena (448).

While out looking for Rena, who is suffering from brain fever and additionally weakened by the whiskey she is given instead of a doctor's visit, Tryon—again mounted—fails to find her, and it is his mounted position that contributes to his failure: the "splashing of his horse's hoofs in the water prevented him from hearing a low groan that came from the woods by the roadside" (452). As a result, he follows a "false scent" (459)—which resonates with the classic abolitionist image of the slave catcher armed with bloodhounds—and instead of Rena, he finds a drunken sallow-complexioned, "sandhill poor white" woman, whose "incoherency of speech" has been taken for a sign of mental distress. The scene is a reversal of the initial anagnorisis that triggers the dysphoric peripeteia, in which Rena is recognized as black and rejected as a fiancée. Whereas in Patesville, George was forced to recognize his white fiancée in a mulatta woman, here he sees a "white enough" woman in whom he has hoped to recognize his former mulatta fiancée. "With tipsy cordiality," the woman offers him a "bottle, the contents of which had never paid any revenue tax," which ironically contrasts with and derides the toast to the superiority of the white race at the beginning of the novel.

Just as Rena is melodramatically paired with the inebriated sallow sandhill woman, in George's pursuit of the lost girl her former fiancé is contrasted with Frank. Rena's faithful neighbor again travels the region to make sure she is all right. At the beginning of the novel, he promises that if Rena should need it, he will "take [his] mule an' [his] kyart an' fetch [her] back, ef it's from de een' er de worl'" (294), and true to his word, he uses his mule and cart to bring Rena back home. His "beast" and "a load of buckets and tubs and piggins" provide a neat foil to Tryon's water-splashing horse. While patiently waiting for the animal to drink from a stream, Frank hears a female voice in the bushes, and at first he thinks it belongs to a white woman, which evokes a feeling of terror in him, but then recognizes Rena's voice with a thrill that is compared to "an electric shock" (457). He selflessly leaves his cargo on the road and turns his mule-driven cart into a jessamine-canopied bed. Thus while "Sir George Tryon," "the knight of the crimson sash," has failed and broken his oaths, Frank keeps his promises and escorts Rena back home in the vehicle ornamented with the fruits of "the grand triumphal sweep of nature's onward march" that—like the shockingly indifferent natural forces in Crane's classic "The Open Boat"—"reck[] nothing of life's little tragedies" (458). Although the narrative fails to incorporate the euphoric ending of a marriage between the aristocratic white mulatta and the lower-class black man,[6] his heroism and sacrifice are recognized by Rena. "Frank, ... you loved me best of them all," are her last words before she dies (461).

While the irony in *The House behind the Cedars* is subtle, it becomes more conspicuous when read along with other works by Chesnutt. For example, in the frequently anthologized and clearly satirical story "The Passing of Grandison," published a year before *The House*, he also juxtaposes a failed white hero—"extremely indolent" Dick Owens, who is reduced almost to a minstrel sambo stereotype and "needs some one to look after him" (533, 542)—with the heroic black Grandison. The true hero not only manages to escape to Canada but—successfully tricking southern aristocrats lulled by their deep belief in slavery as a "blissful relationship of kindly protection on the one hand, and of wise subordination and loyal dependence on the other"—takes his entire extended family with him (536, 544). Chesnutt explicitly mocks the "feudal heart" of southern slave owners, thrilled by what they read as "appreciative homage," while in fact being fooled by a clever performance of submissiveness that enables Grandison to implement his melodramatically excessive rescue plan: not only does he flee, "but his wife, Betty the maid; his mother, aunt Eunice; his father, uncle Ike; his brothers, Tom and John, and his little sister Elsie, [are] likewise absent from the plantation"; "the wholesale nature of the transaction carried consternation to the hearts of those whose ledgers were chiefly bound in black" (544). *The House behind the Cedars* is melodramatic and sentimental, whereas the short story is light-toned and satirical, but they both juxtapose the failed white hero—George/Dick—with the true and visibly black one—Frank/Grandison—in parallel ways. The explicit mockery of Dick's Sambo-like recklessness and laziness thus casts a satirical light over the melodramatic figure of George and highlights the subtly ironic tone of the novel's representation of the southern mind, illustrated, for example, by the following passage: the "influence of Walter Scott was strong upon the old South. The South before the war was essentially feudal, and Scott's novels of chivalry appealed forcefully to the *feudal heart*. During the month preceding the Clarence tournament, the local bookseller had closed out his entire stock of 'Ivanhoe,' consisting of five copies, and had taken orders for seven copies more. The tournament scene in this popular novel furnished the model after which these bloodless imitations of the ancient passages-at-arms were conducted, with such variations as were required to adapt them to a different age and civilization" (298; emphasis added). The "feudal heart" in the fragment, which echoes the mocked slave owners from "The Passing of Grandison" (536), belongs to southern patricians, in general, and to George, the winner of the tournament, in particular.

His feudal mind-set, with strong residual traces of the ideologies of slavery, is also manifested in his attitude toward Rena. As has been mentioned, Chesnutt suggests that George, pursuing his mentally distressed former fiancée, resembles a slave-catching bloodhound following a "false scent"; additionally, in his letters and his thoughts, he imagines a relationship that at best could repeat the myopic scenario of Clotel and Horatio's "marriage sanctioned by heaven, although unrecognised on earth" (65), and at worst Iola's nameless "fiery ordeals" and "crucibles" (106, 256). Interestingly, however, such a feudal attitude toward Rena is visible also in the opening chapters of the novel, when she is a white woman. When inviting her to join him as the Queen of Love and Beauty, he first makes sure that she is not "*bound to some one else*" (305), to which her brother tellingly replies, "[s]he is entirely *free*" (306). The images of bondage and ownership—which powerfully resonate with abolitionist discourse—are also repeated when George insists on their prompt wedding, because what he first and foremost desires is "the certainty of possession" (317). Such clichéd tropes of romantic love as slavery demonstrate the gender inequality of such scenarios, but when put in the context of nineteenth-century US race relations and slavery-related discourses, they need to be read as impregnated by the actual ownership of black bodies by privileged white males.

An analogous claim of possession is declared by Cuthbert Sumner. When he reunites with his wife, Jewel, he folds "her in his arms with a passion and strength that [are] resistless" and says, "Mine at last!" (267). This is not, however, the only analogy between the two characters, as will shortly be demonstrated. At the same time, Cuthbert also resembles Eugene Leroy, with his youthful sowing of wild oats. As his attorney explains, in his younger days Cuthbert was "wild" (250). His indulgence is explained as a result of both his temperament—"proud, passionate, high-spirited"—and the environment—as a half-orphaned child, without his mother's moral suasion, he was "uncontrolled personally and in the expenditure of money" (250). Yet the lack of discipline during his youth also shows in his later years. It does not take a lot of effort for Aurelia, "flashing her jewels," to seduce him with her "siren charms" (117, 104),[7] even though he is madly in love with another "Jewel": "Cuthbert Sumner (blind and foolish) was not the kind of man to let the memory of little Blossom prevent him from holding a beautiful, yielding form closely clasped in his arms, and returning clinging kisses with interest when such a rare opportunity offered" (102). The narrator then makes an attempt to justify Cuthbert's morality as well as the narrative plausibility of the twist with a reference to men's general lack of control over their sexual urges: "I question if there are many men that would." Later, when Cuthbert is rejected by Jewel, he immediately begins to spend "his nights in search of *excitement* that is supposed to *drown care*," which is a euphemistic description of inebriety (125; emphasis added). As a result, "[d]ays of insane recklessness" follow (125). His attitude to alcoholic drinks does not meet the standards of temperance activists: not only does he drink wine (though, much like Tryon, mostly at upper-class social gatherings), but most damningly he offers a glass of wine to a woman in distress, a stenographer at his office, Elise Bradford. Ironically, this wine cup turns into an actual glass of poison after the novel's villain, St. Clair, adds arsenic to it when Cuthbert leaves Elise alone (183).

Moreover, once Cuthbert realizes that he has been the victim of a conspiracy, he has a nightmare about a dark snake's den, which strongly resonates with the use of snake imagery in both abolitionist and temperance discourse.[8] Its significance is illustrated in the title of the first anthology on temperance in American literature, *The Serpent in the Cup*. As the authors explain, the title alludes to Walt Whitman's *Franklin Evans; or, The Inebriate*, in which "a stinging serpent unseen, sleeps" and "within that cup there lurks a curse" (Reynolds and Rosenthal 6). The snake images are also present in the oeuvre of the most active African American temperance activist, Frances Ellen Watkins Harper. In many texts, Harper draws on the meanings that the snake bore in the temperance and antislavery movements: an allegory of temptation and seduction but also of bondage and entrapment. She repeatedly quotes the biblical passage warning against wine that "will bite like a serpent and sting like an adder" (*Iola Leroy* 185). She also recasts it in different contexts, investing it with slightly different significances. For example, in her poem "A Double Standard," a woman becomes a social outcast after she is seduced by a male tempter, who is endowed with the "serpent's wiles," and she does not "even hear / The deadly adder hiss" (*Brighter* 345). And finally, though certainly no less importantly, fifteen-year-old Hopkins in her first published work, "Evils of Intemperance and Their Remedies," writes about "the many headed serpent, whose poison fangs none can escape if once they become entangled" (5; see also Wallinger 26–27), whereas in a text published just a year before *Hagar's Daughter* began to be serialized, she states that "[t]o-day we have again *the rise of the slave-power*, for the old spirit is not dead; the *serpent was scorched, not killed*; so we have lynch-law and ... the Convict-lease system and the word of influential Southerners that in it they have a better thing than *slavery*, for them'" ("Famous Men" 30).

When read in the context of the above-listed sources, the snakes in Cuthbert's dream become densely overdetermined metaphors that stand for a family of meanings such as intemperance, bondage, seduction, conspiracy, deception, and snares: "[H]e dreamed that he was in a deep, dark pit. Darkness blacker than the blackest night was all about him; but as he lay there, for he dreamed that he was reclining on the floor of the pit, suddenly beneath his body he felt a movement as of a monstrous body—a regular undulating movement. Then it seemed borne in upon his mind that the pit was a snake's den; the monsters—*three in number*—*pythons of immense size to whom human victims were offered as sacrifices.* He had been thrown to these sacred reptiles as their next victim. In his dream, horror and terror paralyzed both thought and action for a time.... As he calculated his chances of escape, he heard the dragging and sweeping of a long ponderous body in motion moving toward him" (165–166). The three pythons in Cuthbert's dream uncannily resemble popular temperance images featuring snakes, such as "The Worm of the Still" (fig. 2). This 1887 image, authored by Jessie Shepherd, comes from *Harper's Weekly*, and the gigantic serpent closely parallels the monstrous pythons from above as well as Hopkins's 1874 "many headed serpent" with "poison fangs." Thus Cuthbert tries to escape not only the snares of the inveterate drinkers from St. Clair and Walker's gambling den but also serpents of his own: inclinations toward indulgence, intemperance, and other sensual appetites and urges that threaten his disciplined manliness. The uncontrolled sexual desire represented by snakes is especially visible when, in the dream, he feels dominated by a phallic symbol that rises from beneath him: under "his body he felt a movement as of a monstrous body—a regular undulating movement." That the snakes also signify Cuthbert's own sexual urges resonates with the image of Rena's pursuit in *The House behind the Cedars*, in which masculine sexual advances are paired with the image of a frightful "huge black snake" (448). Such phallic innuendo is present in many temperance images such as Shepherd's (fig. 2). The tension between good and evil is expressed through the sexual difference: religion, temperance, and youth are represented as realistic, white-robed female figures, and they are dramatically contrasted with the grotesque, large-headed, gaping-mouthed, gigantic black serpents. The phallic shapes of aggressive reptiles are loaded with the undertones of male sexual aggression and threat. Overall, snake images in the reform discourse reinforce the critique of uncontrolled male sexual desires and other appetites.

However, in the context of the twisted plots of *Hagar's Daughter*, the clichéd snake image gains yet one more meaning. Foreshadowing Zora Neale Hurston's masterpiece "Sweat," Hopkins blends biblical and African religious tropes and dialectically opposes the satanic serpent with the power of snake charmers and the use of snakes in the African American conjure tradition.[9] In the novel, a black conjure man (whose magic, as will shortly be shown, is directly related to the birth and villainy of St. Clair), "put[s] a snake skin 'roun' he neck" for protection and "den he pray[s] to de debbil" to "help [him] to conquer [his] enemies" (64). Similarly, Aunt Henny, the black mother figure "born wif a veil," uses "de skin ob a rattlesnake" and "er sarpint's toof" to shield her mistress from evil (43, 41). Moreover, in the gothic images that liken Hagar, after she is dysphorically recognized as a descendant of black slaves, to a ghostly figure of madness and revenge in the first part of the novel, snakes are also evoked:

> There, too, the wrongs that you have done this day
> To Hagar and your first-born,
> Shall waken and uncoil themselves, and hiss
> Like adders at the name of Abraham. (58)

These lines come from an abolitionist poem recalled by Hagar (and written by Hopkins for the novel) that uses the story of the biblical Hagar, Abraham's racially marked Egyptian concubine.[10] Yet, since at this point in the novel she becomes a markedly gothic persona, the poem can also be read as magic art performed by a female snake charmer against her oppressors (preceding Hurston's Delia from "Sweat" by twenty-five years). Overall, as this digression shows, the phallic, biblically symbolic snakes that signify, among others, Cuthbert's sexual appetites are opposed by the black and, in the case of Aunt Henny and Hagar, female snake charming powers. Unlike the hegemonic female allegory of temperance that combats the python in Shepherd's image, the African American conjure women have the power to control the snakes and employ them to defeat their evil enemies.

Cuthbert's encounter with the snakes is also parallel to the earlier-analyzed knightly figures, George Tryon and St. George, and their defeat of, or failure to defeat, the dragon. Similarly, despite his northern origins, Cuthbert's romantically inclined attitude is also presented as evidence that "chivalry" has not "died out of our practical world" (126). "[H]aving no taste for a commercial life," he chooses not to follow in his father's footsteps and does not become "a wealthy manufacturer," but instead goes down south to follow several of the failed white patriarchs discussed in the previous section and enters both "[t]he world of fashion" and "a career of politics" (83–84).

FIGURE 2. Jessie Shepherd, *The Worm of the Still*, from *Harper's Weekly*, 1887.

Admired by all the society belles, Cuthbert is perceived by Jewel as "a result of generations of culture and wealth combined" (84). Hence, in her eyes, he embodies both cultural and financial capital, and his northern origins make him "very different from most of the men one meets in Washington" or, as she explains, "[m]ore manly" (85). Yet his premodern chivalric inclinations are out of place in the "practical world" of the late nineteenth century, and his lack of entrepreneurial proclivity actually makes him strongly resemble the southern patricians.

In a strikingly similar way to George Tryon, Cuthbert becomes mulatta melodrama's failed hero. In both cases, if it were not for the race difference, the recognition of the heroines' illegitimate origins in both novels would not preclude a euphoric ending. Just as George's flaw is rooted in his upbringing and manifests itself in his toast to white supremacy, "Cuthbert Sumner was born with a noble nature," and "his faults were those caused by environment and tradition. Chivalrous, generous-hearted—a manly man in the fullest meaning of the term—yet born and bred in an atmosphere which approved of freedom and qualified equality for the Negro, he had never considered for one moment the remote contingency of actual social contact with this unfortunate people" (265). Hence, on one hand, he is praised for his manliness in distress. "A buzz of admiration" passes as he takes the defendant's seat. "Erect, easy, dignified, Sumner took his place with the same grace that had marked his entrance into the crowded halls of pleasure. He met the steady stare of those thousand eyes coolly, steadily" (243). And later, as the trial progresses, he remains "cool" and "motionless as a statue" (250), thus evidencing manly self-control. He also exhibits traits of the compassionate manhood promoted by the reform movements: having heard Elise Bradford's story of seduction, his "eyes filled with tears which were no shame to his manhood" (162).

Yet whereas he is moved by and empathizes with the story of the fallen girl seduced by the evil St. Clair, he has much less empathy for the predicament of the mulattas in the novel. Despite her earlier support for him, after Cuthbert finds out about her origins he feels "thankful that Mrs. Bowen is only [Jewel's] step-mother" and decides that "with all sympathy for her and her sad story, it was impossible for Jewel to be longer associated with her in so close a relationship as that of mother and daughter.... [T]he social position of Mrs. Sumner demanded a prompt separation" (269, 265). Just like George, who is torn between the two images of Rena, the "fair young beauty" and a "hideous black hag" (364), Cuthbert struggles with the paradoxical nature of US race divisions, and in reference to the revelation regarding Mrs. Bowen and his former fiancée, Aurelia, he states that "I think that the knowledge of her origin would kill all desire in me.... The mere thought of the *grinning, toothless black hag* that was her foreparent would forever rise between us" (271; emphasis added). As a result of his desire to separate Mrs. Bowen and Jewel—the slave mother and her daughter (which triggers associations with the slave trade)—his repeated insistence that he would "*never wed with one of colored blood!*" (251, 238; emphasis in original; see also 269, 281), and, ultimately, his rejection of his wife, Jewel (once he finds out that she is, in fact, Mrs. Bowen's biological daughter), he dramatically fails in his role of the melodramatic hero.

Interestingly, the novel links the limitations of Cuthbert's chivalry with his imperfect charity. As Ellis Enson states in response to the young man's views on intermarriage, "[T]his is the sum total of what Puritan New England philanthropy will allow—every privilege but the vital one of deciding a question of the commonest personal liberty which is the fundamental principle of the holy family tie" (271). A similar statement comes from the narrator, who states that it was "beyond a certain point his New England philanthropy could not reach" when Cuthbert fails to empathize with Aurelia (238). The hypocrisy and flaws of white northern postabolitionist charity are conspicuously visible in one of Cuthbert's internal monologues: "He had heard the Negro question discussed in all its phases during his student life at 'Fair Harvard,' and had even contributed a paper to a local weekly in which he had warmly championed their cause; but so had he championed the cause of the dumb and helpless creatures in the animal world about him. He gave large sums to Negro colleges and on the same princpal [sic] gave liberally to the Society for the Prevention of Cruelty to Animals, and endowed a refuge for homeless cats. Horses, dogs, cats, and Negroes were classed together in his mind as of the brute creation whose sufferings it was his duty to help alleviate" (265–266).

Charity toward the underprivileged people and animals—emphatically grouped together—is his "duty," a necessary part of Cuthbert's noble manliness. His performance of his "duties" does not stem from empathy for or identification with the ones who suffer. Thus Hopkins is even more critical of white charity, reform, and the democratic potential of sentimental compassion related to them than was Lauren Berlant in her indictment of sentimentality as a mode that enables "the culturally privileged to humanize those very subjects who are also, and at the same time, reduced to cliché within the reigning regimes of entitlement or value" (Berlant, "Poor" 636). Cuthbert is appalled by the vision of a "wholesale union between whites and blacks"; "[t]hink of our refinement and intelligence linked to such *black bestiality* as we find in the slums of this or any other great city where Negroes predominate!" he posits vehemently (270). Yet, as Elise Bradford states, Cuthbert is "a victim of the plot" (155), and apart from falling into the "vile" snares of "the archconspirators" (164), he also gets lost in the "tangled web which [Hopkins has not so] unwittingly woven," to signify on Aurelia's deceptive statement (132). In the twists and turns of the melodramatic plot, Cuthbert himself, despite all his "refinement and intelligence," is juxtaposed with and likened to the "black bestiality" figured in the dark "monstrous bodies" of the snake den's inhabitants from his dream. In such commentary on the limits of philanthropy, Hopkins reveals the darker, antidemocratic, or overtly exploitative aspects of white northern middle-class reform activism. An comparable critique is even more central in African American novels directly engaged in anti-alcohol discourse. As I will demonstrate in the following chapters, black temperance narratives expose the privileged reformers as, at best, unknowingly ignorant, and as, at worst, willfully exploitative.

Overall, both George and Cuthbert aspire to chivalric manliness. Both are initially introduced as melodramatic heroes and foils to the deceptive villains and their "designs" against the mulatta heroines. As such they evoke the reader's sympathy and desire. Yet both dramatically fail to deliver due to their race prejudice and the "[i]dolatry of the Moloch of Slavery" that continues in the postbellum United States and weakens "the sacred family relation" and "the holy institution of marriage" (283–284). Once they find out about the mixed-race origins of their beloved ones, their perceptions of Rena and Jewel are superimposed with retrogressionist images of black femininity: "hideous" and "toothless hags." Just like the patriarchs, they dishonorably break promises given to their fiancées. Their failures are dramatically expressed through the tragic deaths of the young mulattas. In both cases, those dysphoric closures are cast in pastoral images: Jewel dies of Daisy Milleresque "Roman fever" and is buried "across a daisied field"; Rena dies of "brain fever," and her death is also linked to an abundance of flowers (*Hagar's Daughter* 283; *House* 449). Hence the bucolic, premodern longings—whose critique in mulatta melodrama's representations of the mother figures have been discussed in chapter 2—are also challenged in its portrayals of the failed knights and their romantic aspirations, which prove to be hypocritical and fatal as well as—more subtly—in the tragic images of mulattas' deaths configured in pastoral settings. Again, although modernity is not without its flaws, pastoral images in mulatta melodrama—closely related to the South's anti-industrial ideology and aristocratic, patrician aspirations—tend to correlate with tragedy and dysphoric endings.

Familial Villains

In Harper's and Hopkins's novels, the ethically ambivalent father and the failed white hero are contrasted with a close male relative whose villainy and plotting against the interracial family are the driving forces of both mulatta melodramas. The villain in Chesnutt's *The House behind the Cedars*, the burly mulatto Jeff Wain, is also to some extent parallel to the figures I focus on in this section. Introduced at different points as a "grinning hypocrite," a "saddle-colored scoundrel," "a liar and a scoundrel," Jeff has "obviously evil designs" against Rena (413, 421, 455–456). He deceives and "takes her away" from her mother even though he is married to another woman, whom "[h]e abused . . . most shamefully, and had to be threatened with the law" (456, 428). Yet Chesnutt is careful to problematize his "lurking brutality" and distance it from the ideology of black bestiality (431). The narrator explains that "to do him justice, [Jeff] had merely meant to declare his passion in what he had hoped might prove a not unacceptable fashion" (432). Thus Wain—together with Frank Fowler, who, as I have shown, is the true black hero—serves as a foil for George's failed heroism. His mixed-race identity and Chesnutt's insistence on the unintentional character of his assault on Rena differentiate him from the archvillains of *Iola Leroy* and *Hagar's Daughter*. Interestingly, he serves to problematize the talented, educated, and privileged mulattoes celebrated in other novels, such as George from *Clotel* or Dr. Latimer from *Iola Leroy*.

In *Iola Leroy* and *Hagar's Daughter*, the sheltered condition of mixed-race women in the private sphere does not protect them against the villains' evil designs since the threat is not posed by strangers but by greedy white relations who challenge the legitimacy of their marriage licenses and manumission papers. The use of a family member as the villain who triggers the tragic peripeteia in the novels problematizes the ideology of separate spheres and challenges the popular Victorian dichotomy between safe domesticity and the dangerous public sphere. The malevolent relatives in the texts are not, however, a simple and straightforward example of the melodramatic polarization of good and evil. Harper's and Hopkins's novels' reform logic links the characters' personal villainy to the system of slavery. Moreover, the fact that it is the post-Reconstruction black Woman's Era novels—rather than the antebellum *Clotel*—that use the figure of the villain and thus resort to a more explicit attack on the southern gentleman can be explained as a reaction to the revival of patrician ideology at the end of the nineteenth century.

Alfred Lorraine, the villain in *Iola Leroy* and the cousin of Iola's father, Eugene, actually went through a peripeteia resulting from the termination of male protection parallel to that experienced by the mulatta protagonists. Comparable to Clotel, Hagar, Marie, and their daughters, after his "easy and indulgent" father dies, Alfred has to "face an uncertain future, with scarcely a dollar to call [his] own" (63–64). His family had lived beyond their means, and Alfred, spoiled by the lavish lifestyle and surrounded by rich people who benefit from the work of slaves like the Leroys, feels entitled to their wealth. Hence his motivation does not simply stem from an inherently evil disposition but from poverty, resentment, and the ideologies of race he lives by. All these factors encourage him to exploit his cousin's death for his own ends. His position is implicitly contrasted with independent manliness: even though Alfred has an education and a trade, he chooses to rely on the fortune of the Leroys and his own wife's slave-trade money rather than follow the path of self-reliance and financial independence. His unmanly indolence is even more evident when compared with the heroism of the mulatta characters, in particular with Iola's incessant attempts to hold a job as a nurse, teacher, and shop assistant in the postbellum reality.

Eugene, whose seemingly reasonable vision turns out to be "too blurred to read the signs of the times," does not see through Alfred's plans. As pointed out earlier, for him Alfred is "the only relative ... who ever *darkens* [their] doors" (90; emphasis added). His "nervous" wife, Marie, reads this conventional metaphor in a more insightful way. For her, "with [Alfred's] coming, a shadow fell upon her home, hushing its music and *darkening* its sunshine" (89; emphasis added). These two different readings expose the precarious character of the security guaranteed by family ties in the antebellum South. After Alfred's successful takeover of Eugene's money, this problematization of family protection and the private sphere is also visible in the description of distant family members of the Leroy family, who make themselves "offensively familiar" (95). The notion of "offensive familiarity" is interestingly ambivalent. The phrase is used either to refer to the assumption of equal status by inferiors or to euphemistically suggest sexual harassment. Both readings fit the story: Marie feels superior to Alfred's wife, whose "social training [is] deficient" and "her education limited" (89), while at the same time the novel is peppered with implicit references to the rape of bondwomen under slavery. Hence, in the text, both the "familiar" and "familial" are revealed to be a source of cruelty and threat. Once the second "reversal of fortune" takes place, the narrative only marginally mentions the "offensively familiar" Alfred. The reader only learns that he "had at first attempted to refugee ... in Texas, but, being foiled in the attempt, he was compelled to enlist in the Confederate Army, and met his fate by being killed just before the surrender of Vicksburg" (192). This attempt at desertion exposes his lack of courage and hence emasculates him. His unmanly conduct is even more conspicuous when juxtaposed with Iola's brother's actions. Harry Leroy voluntarily enlists as a black Union soldier and declares that he "should like to meet Lorraine on the battle-field" (125).

Using an uncannily parallel phrasing to *Iola Leroy*, *Hagar's Daughter* portends the imminent end of the happy idyll with "a shadow falling across the doorsill shutting out the light for a moment," which announces the arrival of the evil St. Clair Enson, the brother of Jewel's father, Ellis (41). Just as Marie's forebodings turn out to be correct, so too in Hopkins's novel Aunt Henny, "born wif a veil," accurately predicts that the coming of the pair is a bad omen (42–43). Thus women's "nervousness" is presented as an occult gift or at least an astute intuition, which is parallel to the redeeming women's predictions regarding the fall of rich drunkards in temperance narratives—a trope discussed in chapter 5—in Harper's *Sowing and Reaping*. Ellis, like Eugene and the thoughtless characters in temperance stories, distances himself from this prediction, referring to it as a "mere ignorant superstition" (46), and his judgment is equally mistaken. *Hagar's Daughter* is divided into two parts—one set just before the war and the second one in 1882, and the tragic peripeteias in both parts are driven by St. Clair's actions. In the antebellum days, like Alfred, he takes over the property of Ellis and remands his wife, Hagar, and daughter, Jewel, to slavery. Additionally, he is also directly responsible for Ellis's alleged murder. In the postbellum part, he plots against Jewel (unaware that she is his niece) as he plans to take over her foster father's fortune. In order to implement his scheme, he murders a woman he has seduced and has a child with and frames Jewel's fiancé for the murder. This brief summary of his story accurately exemplifies the melodramatic excess of the novel, with the exaggerations serving to highlight the villainy of southern manhood.

Apart from the above parallels between St. Clair and Alfred Lorraine, both are similarly accustomed to self-indulgence and are suddenly cut off from financial means by their fathers. Furthermore, in St. Clair there is a streak of unchecked passion that has characterized the white fathers of interracial families. Yet whereas the narratives have subtly criticized the fathers' lack of manly self-discipline, in the case of St. Clair passion and sensuality are explicitly represented as sinister traits: "sensual, cruel to ferocity," St. Clair has "a fiery temper that kn[ows] no bounds when once aroused" (20). Even more clearly and melodramatically, he is frequently compared to the devil (20, 21, 24, 42, 51, 64). Yet the explanation of his disposition, which the reader receives from the second-sighted Aunt Henny, is intricately related to white violence against slaves. In the story, St. Clair's mother sees the devil on the night she gives birth. The appearance is conjured by Uncle Ned as a defense against the overseer's brutality (64–65). Thus the text acknowledges the possibility that the evil plottings of St. Clair are deeply related to the systemic violence of slavery. Accordingly, his villainy, just like Alfred Lorraine's, is not simply individual but closely linked to the systemic corruptions of the antebellum South.

No character in the selected novels epitomizes southern self-indulgence more than St. Clair. In this sense, he foreshadows the racially ambiguous fallen men from the black temperance discourse discussed in detail in the second part of this book. He believes that "a reckless career of gambling, wine and women [i]s the only true course of development for a typical Southern gentleman" (23), and his lifestyle is a metaphor for antebellum southern culture as a whole. If, as Mayfield claims, for the southern gentleman, "[l]ife became a series of public displays which the male literally performed through hunting, treating, conspicuous consumption, a little learning for good measure, and so forth—for the approval of his peers" (Mayfield, "'The Soul'" 481), then St. Clair perfectly exemplifies such a lifestyle, but his extreme villainy also positions it as unequivocally vain, idle, and corrupt. More importantly, however, in the context of the ideology of manliness championed by the contemporary reform discourse and its politics of self-discipline, such lack of restraint emasculates his character. The novel's intricate assaults on his masculinity are perfectly illustrated by a long description of the office of St. Clair, who assumes the name of General Benson in the latter part of the novel:

> The ceiling of the apartment was lofty, there were elegant paintings on the walls, and the furniture was luxurious. There were rich hangings at the windows, carpets and rugs on the floor, lounges were grouped about the spacious room giving it more the appearance of a *boudoir* than a public office. The style of the wardrobes ranged about the walls would lead one to infer that all conveniences for dining and longing could be easily found within its four walls.... General Benson, it was evident, though a servant of the people was using their resources freely to gratify an extravagant taste. His was the life of a popular official floating at the ease of his own *sweet* will.... General Benson sat before his splendidly covered table where cut-glass bottles of eau de cologne gleamed, vases of fragrant flowers charmed the eye, and ornamental easels of costly style held pictures of fashionable ladies. (148–149; emphasis added)

In contrast to masculine self-restraint, the luxurious extravagance that defines the room was perceived as characteristically effeminate in the contemporaneous public discourse (Dorsey 144). In such a context, even the epithet "sweet" that is supposed to highlight St. Clair's autonomy becomes charged with feminine connotations. Instead of a desk, he works at what seems to be a dressing table, covered with perfumes and flowers. He looks at pictures of "fashionable ladies" that fill the place of a dressing mirror. His office is compared to a boudoir, a woman's private chamber, and the abundance of perfume and flowers reinforces this simile. Another place where the term is used in the novel is a scene set in Hagar's room, where she rests "reclined in semi-invalid fashion on the couch" in a "dress of white cashmere, profusely touched with costly lace" (273). The juxtaposition of these two boudoirs—St. Clair's office and Hagar's repose—further challenges the villain's masculinity and work ethic, as it highlights that such spaces were associated with nineteenth-century leisure-class femininity and the notions of extravagance, indolence, and unproductiveness it triggered.

The novel implicitly posits a connection between St. Clair's extravagant lifestyle and his seduction of stenographer Elise Bradford, whom he murders after she gets pregnant and insists on a wedding. St. Clair's office poses a threat to female employees because of its privacy and limited public surveillance rather than because it is part of the public sphere. Through the figure of St. Clair, this pathological privatization of the public seems to be an inheritance from the slave system, where intimacy and business were deeply interwoven, and slave masters reproduced their property through sexual exploitation.[11] Even though the novel contests the separate-spheres ideology, it does so in the revelatory drive of melodrama, which seeks to "express it all," to make all that is secret and private public. The sheltered domestic sphere in which Hagar and Jewel are remanded to slavery is revealed to be dangerous exactly because of its privacy and isolation. When, on the other hand, the public—like St. Clair's office—becomes privatized or secret, it results in a pathological transgression. In the climactic moment of the novel, all the private secrets of St. Clair are made public in a court scene. Prophetic Aunt Henny, who has the "skeleton key" to the building, opens the Pandora's box of his crimes and reveals she had seen St. Clair kill Elise Bradford in his "private office" (254). The novel's melodramatic aesthetic of revelation makes the intimate secrets of the "private office" public, and its poetic justice punishes villainous St. Clair with an accidental death.

Furthermore, if Hopkins's representation of Washington's officials is read as yet another reference to *Clotel*, St. Clair's boudoir functions in parallel to Jefferson's presidency and the White House in Brown's novel: all represent the glaring discrepancy between democratic institutions and the legacy of slavery. Hopkins further highlights the similarities between St. Clair's individual plottings and the collective political endeavors of the South when she mentions "conspiracy ... by fraud or violence" planned by the Confederate forces after the election of Lincoln (6). The setting in which "leading Southern politicians" gather—the magnificent hotel hall "used for dancing" with "the glittering mass of glass, plate and flowers"—seems to have shaped St. Clair's aesthetic sensibility (13). In these introductory chapters, politics is, in general, positioned on par with gambling as imprudent and unpredictable. When luck deserts St. Clair "at cards and dice," he invests his hopes for "fame and fortune in the service of the new government" (22). Such a narrative evaluation of politics as irrational, precarious, and tragic in consequences is another element that resonates in *Clotel*, where Horatio's change of heart and the disintegration of the subsequent interracial family result directly from his newly discovered political ambitions.

Slaves to the Bottle & Lowly Passions

St. Clair's self-indulgence and affinity for gambling and alcohol are reinforced through other images of male weaknesses, both in *Hagar's Daugh-*

ter and in other African American mulatta melodramas. The narratives explicitly criticize the lifestyles of southern gentlemen as unmanly and contrast them with the northern ideology of manliness based on self-discipline, work ethic, and a hegemonic "marketplace manhood" rooted in economic productivity. Significantly, the immoderation that characterizes white masculinity in mulatta melodrama powerfully resonates in the black temperance narratives: whereas the former corpus exposes and chastises white men's complicity with the system of bondage, with its sexual exploitation of the black female body and slave family separations, the latter body of writing targets the dangers of male privilege in general.

As Elaine Parsons has demonstrated in *Manhood Lost*, the effectiveness of the fallen man trope in nineteenth-century reform discourse is inherently connected with the anxieties about masculinity it triggers: the influence of alcohol becomes inextricable from the loss of masculine mastery. "The drunkard... was not a true man because he was unable to exert his will over his body and interests" (55). Since masculine identity was at the center of the apprehensions stirred by the temperance movement and was in "crisis," or at least in the process of being remade at the time, the repeated representations of slave owners' alcoholic indulgence in the novels are a powerful tool to confront the patrician paradigm of masculinity. What further adds to the force of these images is the residual presence of the central metaphor of temperance discourse: "slave to the bottle" (Parsons 19; Dorsey 122–124). The novels, by presenting drunken white men, implicitly invest them with the stigma of enslavement. Furthermore, the residual echoes of the apologetic rhetoric of "wage slavery"—which is used to present "chattel slavery" as a more humane institution—suggest that in the postbellum days, all men could become enslaved "wage laborers." Undercut by such sentiments, in the late nineteenth century male identity in the South was drenched with insecurity. Whereas in the antebellum era it was safely anchored in the opposition between slavery and freedom, after the Emancipation Proclamation this symbolic difference was abolished, even though the structural conditions of interracial relations sometimes did not change very dramatically. This anxiety was symbolically resolved in the revival of patrician ideology and, in turn, was sharply challenged in the African American postbellum texts. The mulatta novels' images of drunkenness are an important element that links them to black uses of temperance discourse, as discussed in the next part of this book.

Additionally, just as in the case of black novels that recast temperance narratives, the subplots of white man's decline due to gambling and alcohol, especially prominent in Harper's and Hopkins's novels, exemplify structural similarities with the contemporary naturalist fiction published in the 1890s and thus express analogous insecurities regarding the social and economic instability of the era, as discussed by June Howard (95–103), who argues that such instabilities in the South were exacerbated with the specter of "wage slavery" and the mythical threat of black supremacy. The plots of decline in the two post-Reconstruction novels also evoke dominant bourgeois anxieties of proletarianization and represent it as a direct result of failed white masculinity. This naturalist undercurrent of white downfall serves as a foil for the self-determination and newly gained freedom of black characters, which is especially visible in *Iola Leroy*. The recurrent images of white male decline and failure also serve to counter the retrogressionist mythology that specifically postulated indolence, intemperance, and shiftlessness as defining features of blackness. As Tate argues, racist references to blacks as "coons" and "sambos," which presented black men as "lazy, ugly, intemperate, slothful, lascivious, and violent, indeed bestial," were omnipresent in the late nineteenth-century United States (9–10). Black postbellum representations of white irresponsibility, laziness, and recklessness uncannily mirror the retrogressionist image of the "sambo," whereas the way that they depict the unrestrained passions and self-indulgence of southern gentlemen mirrors the black "coon." Thus African American mulatta melodramas enter into a dialogue with the retrogressionist mythology concerning blackness and suggest that it projects white anxieties onto the black Other. The novels' representations of white southern masculine recklessness, indulgence, and intemperance meaningfully complement their constructions of patriarchs, suitors, and villains.

In *Clotel*, Brown offers many long, digressive scenes—which seem scarcely related to the main narrative—to depicting and critiquing the recklessness and irrationality of the southern lifestyle and its most popular masculine entertainments. For example, through the words of a northern minister, introduced in one such tangential episode, the novel condemns intemperance and bloody animal fights, both associated with the South. Furthermore, although the metaphor of "slave to the bottle" is not directly used in the dialogue, it is implicitly evoked. The minister expresses outrage at his servant's unrestrained appetite for alcohol, which is manifested in the latter's willingness to drink whiskey and black shoe polish. As Robert Levine argues, this suggests that "to drink intemperately is to transform oneself into a 'black' slave to the bottle" (94). In contrast, the opponent of the minister in the stagecoach, a model southerner, vigorously speaks out against temperance laws and states that he wouldn't "bet a red cent on these teetotlars" (163). The minister most likely expresses Brown's own abstinence approach to alcohol. Apart from inebriety, in the dialogue, the South is associated with sensational animal fights, which took place on Sundays in New Orleans. The minister cites a bloody eleven-paragraph-long newspaper account of the victory of an Attakapas bull over a grizzly bear named General Jackson from California, which are not mentioned again in the text. The animals represent southern entertainment and at the same time symbolically point to the frontier territories, which suggests an affinity between the South and the "Wild West."

In a similar, largely irrelevant digression, in a chapter tellingly entitled "Going South," Brown's narrative almost completely ignores its main characters and devotes its attention to the technical details of slave trade transactions, to a steamboat race, and to gambling. The latter two references seem to have no other function in the narrative apart from exposing the absurdity of southern entertainments. "The *wildest* excitement prevail[s] throughout amongst both passengers and crew," when the race of two ships begins (54; emphasis added). This bravado results in a huge explosion and fills the vessel with "shrieks, groans, and cries" (55). "The saloons and cabins soon had the appearance of a hospital," and nineteen people are "killed and scalded." Since the scene refers neither to the mulatta protagonists nor to the practices of slavery, its sole function is to demonstrate that slavery is the cruelest of the many irrational, fatal, and barbarous customs that formed southern culture. The temerity of the race is matched with the recklessness of a gambling scene that follows. As the narrative points out, it "was now twelve o'clock at night, and instead of the passengers being asleep the majority were gambling in the saloons" (55). Hence, instead of subscribing to the work ethic of daytime productivity and nighttime rest, the "majority" of passengers engage in nighttime leisure, which precludes any daytime labor. As a result, "many men, and even ladies, are completely ruined." Brown swiftly moves from the ruination of white passengers to the resultant changes in the ownership of slaves, who are lost in gambling debts. "He [the slave] goes to bed at night the property of the man with whom he has lived for years, and gets up in the morning the slave of some one whom he has never seen before!" (56). Concluding the fragment, the narrator again points to the representativeness of such scenes: "To behold five or six tables in a steamboat's cabin, with half-a-dozen men playing at cards, and money, pistols, bowie-knives, all in confusion on the tables, is what may be seen at almost any time on the Mississippi river." Thus southern entertainments in the novel are similar to frontier rodeos and saloons rather than European sophistication and the refined traditions that the southern aristocracy supposedly aspired to.

The association between gambling and the South rather than the West is also interestingly inserted into *Hagar's Daughter*. Senator Bowen, Hagar's second husband and Jewel's foster father, loses a considerable amount of his fortune in a gambling "palace" organized by St. Clair. Bowen's predilection for gambling does not surprise the reader as he is introduced as a good-hearted but slightly uncouth entrepreneur from California. Yet the narrative explicitly confounds this expectation and links his weakness with the South rather than with the saloon in the West. "Gaming was Senator's Bowen only vice, a legacy from the old days when as mate he played every night for weeks as the cotton steamer made her trips up and down the river highways in the ante-bellum days" (132). This reference to gambling on the steamer is yet another way in which Hopkins alludes to Brown. Moreover, she also recasts the scene from *Clotel* of losing slaves in gambling debts and thus repeats Brown's argument about the cruelty of southern recklessness. Following the conventions of temperance rhetoric, *Hagar's Daughter* represents the saloon as seductive, attractive, and glamorous (cf. Parsons 115). The "glittering" bar, in which the reader gets acquainted with St. Clair, is filled with the "clink and gleam of gold" and decorated with "gilded mirrors" that reflect "the rays of a large chandelier depending from the center of the ceiling" (24–25). When St. Clair loses his loyal servant in a game of cards, the dazzling character of the place highlights his shock. "The lights from the chandelier shot out sparkles from piles of golden coin, the table heaved, the faces were indistinct" (27). St. Clair's earlier-analyzed office furnishings seem to be inspired by this glamour. In the second part of the novel, apart from his work for the government, St. Clair runs a gambling "palace" together with his opportunistic, ex-slave trader associate. In St. Clair's palace, the allure of glamorous décor is reinforced by the presence of a mulatta temptress passing as white: "the Madison house was a gambling palace where men were fleeced of money for the sake of the smiles of the beautiful Aurelia" (253). Thus the gamblers are represented as seduced by the femininely decorative interiors as well as the presence of an actual seductress. Additionally, in both places, alcohol is a significant factor that draws "inveterate gamblers" (25, 252). In dramatic contrast to hegemonic temperance narratives and naturalist classics, the forces of seduction are not correlated with modernity and its urbanization and metropolitan migration but are positioned as defining of the "olden days": the antebellum southern culture and its aristocratic aspirations to the premodern feudal order.

Though the issue of temperance was less central in the activism and texts of Hopkins than in those of Harper and Brown or even Chesnutt, her literary career symbolically opened with the 1874 essay "The Evils of Intemperance and Their Remedies," for which she received an award in a contest organized by Brown. In *Hagar's Daughter*, alcoholic intemperance is predominantly used as a metaphor and is linked with other types of unchecked passion and lack of discipline. The South is "drunk with rage" or "drunk with power and dazzled with prosperity" (3, 4). As the Confederacy is founded, "mad passions" leave a mark on American history (6); "the most intemperate sentiments" are "voiced by the zealots in the great cause," "vociferous cheers" shake the assembly, "the crowd [goes] mad" and tears "the decorations from the walls" (15). "Pandemonium reign[s]," while the "wild and "brute," "vast crowd" goes "wild with enthusiasm" (18). Intemperance of all kinds, passion, and wildness are positioned in the novel as key features of the lifestyle of southern gentlemen. The text presents such a lifestyle as lacking in manly self-restraint and independence, and at the same time barbarous and savage.

Chesnutt's youthful involvement in the temperance movement is scarcely researched, yet Richard Brodhead notes that under "his management, the Fayetteville Colored Normal School had two student organizations, a literary society and a temperance society based on the principle of total abstinence," and that Chesnutt's journal makes "clear that he also tried to teach the control of other fleshly appetites, to impart a norm of sexual continence not familiar to his charges" (14). In his journal entry of January 9, 1875, he states, "I spent the whole Christmas Holidays in preparing for an entertainment at the 'Templar's Hall[.]' On Thursday after Christmas we played 'The first Glass' a temperance Drama" (54; original capitalization). This is followed by the full cast and synopsis of the play, an 1868 text authored by Nellie H. Bradky, which is a typical temperance comedy that euphorically ends with two marriages between teetotalers (55–56). Though *The House behind the Cedars* does not employ the dramatic dark-temperance images used by Harper or Hopkins, the fact that only the failed hero George and the villain Wain are portrayed as drinking (wine and eggnog, respectively) correlates alcohol use with moral imperfection. Additionally, the novel employs two images of intoxicated women—an image rare but not altogether absent from temperance rhetoric and a trope centrally significant for naturalist classics such as Crane's *Maggie*. Chesnutt juxtaposes Rena, fed with whiskey when what she needs is medicine, with the sallow, sand-hill woman, who is cordially tipsy out of her own will. The comparison is encouraged as the two images are temporarily simultaneous, and additionally, as I have shown, George's final failure as a hero is due to his following the "false scent" and finding the female lower-class inebriate instead of his "Queen of Love and Beauty." The woman's tipsiness serves to highlight her difference from Rena and her departure from the Victorian ideals of passionless womanhood.

Since Harper was a key African American temperance activist and a member of the WCTU (Woman's Christian Temperance Union), *Iola Leroy*'s representations of white slave owner's failures are more deeply interlinked with inebriety than their equivalents in the other two texts and resonate with her temperance-oriented oeuvre, which includes a number of poems, a short story, and the novel *Sowing and Reaping* (analyzed in the second part of this book). *Iola Leroy* is interpolated with images of white men drinking themselves to bankruptcy and loss of health. Iola's last owner and oppressor, Frank Anderson, gets "reckless and dr[inks] himself to death" (153). Comparably, for her uncle's former owner, "drink [is] ruination" (188), and "he dr[inks] up ebery thing he c[an] lay his han's on" (158). Yet another former slave owner takes "to drink, an' all his frens is gone, an' he's in de pore-house" (174). The images of white poverty and the fall of white men into ruin are explicitly contrasted with the rise of black people, visible in "evidences of thrift and industry" among the newly emancipated black households (153). The metaphor "slave to drink," profusely used in *Sowing and Reaping* (100, 103, 110, 121, 134, 165, 172), reverberates through these repeated images of intemperance and consequently marks the white gentlemen with the stigma of slavery. In *Iola Leroy*, slavery and alcohol are also juxtaposed when white men selling alcohol to black people are compared to slave catchers: "mean white men ... settin' up dere grog-shops. ... Deys de bery kine ob men dat used ter keep dorgs to ketch de runaways" (159). Moreover, the text also links the two problems in a speech by Iola's husband, who speaks against "slavery and the liquor traffic" and claims that the "liquor traffic still sends its floods of ruin and shame to the habitations of men" (250). Finally, Harper uses the same metaphor—a snake, whose significance in temperance discourse has already been discussed—to represent the dangers of both: "wine at last will bite like a serpent and sting like an adder"; and "Slavery is a serpent which we nourished in its weakness, and now it is stinging us in its strength" (185, 130). Thus, as the text intricately constructs the parallel between slavery and intemperance while at the same time repeatedly representing white gentlemen as addicted to alcohol, it marks them with the specter of enslavement, which symbolically emasculates the men according to the southern dichotomy of masters and slaves. The bankruptcies that accompany their drinking gain additional significance in the context of postbellum fears of "wage slavery" and the late nineteenth-century proletarianization, which further undercuts their masculine autonomy and mastery.

In sum, one of the most trenchant refrains in the mulatta melodramas' critique of slavery and segregation is directed at southern manhood. Their repeated portrayals of southern gentlemen as failed patriarchs question their masculinity within the patrician paradigm of benevolent protection, the hegemonic model of manhood in the South. Male characters in the novels do not meet the central requirement of this ideology: the defense of their subordinates. In the four texts, no white man is presented as a reliable protector of his dependents. The fathers break the promises given to their loved ones, and thus they violate the sacred word of honor, deemed to be a unique feature of the southern gentleman. The white lovers fail as melodramatic heroes by rejecting the women they love and breaking such oaths as engagements or, in the case of Cuthbert, even wedding vows. As the white aristocrat Frank Oakley, from Paul Laurence Dunbar's *The Sport of the Gods*, bitterly comments in one of the epigraphs to this chapter, southern honor, instead of producing gentlemanly and truly chivalric men, actually turns them into liars and thieves. Additionally, the mythical safety of the domestic realm is contested in the novels, as the villains are close relatives, and thus the danger for the mulatta protagonists does not come from the outside but precisely from within the family circle. As a result, the male protectors fail to provide a safe private sphere for their daughters and wives, who in turn become slave chattels and are repeatedly sold on auction blocks. Thus the white men repeatedly fall short of the standards of southern masculinity.

At the same time, the texts question the very ideology of genteel patriarchy. They expose the contradiction inherent in the model of the benevolent master. Even the actions of the most lenient white slaveholders in the novels show the cruelty of chattel slavery and thus demonstrate that it is impossible to reconcile benevolence with mastery over human property. Additionally, the African American melodramas continually demonstrate that the foundation of southern paternalism, the idea of absolute private property, is actually far from safe and secure. Even in the cases in which the men believe they have provided for their families, their legal guarantees are rendered void and the wills are overturned. Not only is private property taken from the rightful heirs, but the heirs themselves become private property. Thus Brown, Harper, Chesnutt, and Hopkins repeatedly discredit the basis of southern masculinity as outlined by Kimmel, which is "property ownership and a benevolent patriarchal authority at home" (16). Furthermore, in their portrayals of the failed white lovers, Chesnutt and Hopkins expose the hypocrisy and fatal consequences of the patrician ideology of chivalry, which applies to white people only and leads to the deaths of two mulatta girls.

As an alternative to the patrician model, the texts champion the ideology of self-restraint and compassionate manliness promoted by the contemporary reform discourse. Paradoxically, the juxtaposition of the two gender ideologies makes the southern gentleman simultaneously effeminate and barbaric. When measured against the norm of manly self-discipline, southern slaveholders in the novels seem idle, irresponsible, indulgent, and intemperate. Their self-indulgence and fondness for luxury trigger associations with "parlor ornaments" and upper-class women (63), which feminizes southern gentlemen. In the novels' challenge to southern masculinity and their advocacy of disciplined manliness, the theme of temperance emerges as a central issue. The predominantly northern rhetoric of abstinence regularly presented drunkards as unmanly, but when positioned in the southern context, the power of images of intemperance to question the characters' manhood is additionally strengthened by the more immediate relevance of the "slave to the bottle" metaphor. The abundant images of white male inebriety in the African American mulatta melodramas present the white men as enslaved by their appetites and thus emasculated in the southern dichotomy of masters and slaves. Additionally, their alcoholic decline triggers fears of proletarianization and wage slavery, which loomed large in the South during the Nadir.

The excessive alcohol use is represented as an extension of the more general southern intemperance and inclination for recklessness and gambling. These, in turn—in part through associations with the "Wild West"—are represented as uncivilized, uncouth, and even barbarous, and thus black authors scornfully mock the aristocratic pretensions of southern patricians and cavaliers. Inasmuch as the white male characters assume the savage characteristics stereotypically associated with black men at the time, the novels both challenge the southern manhood ethic and question the retrogressionist images of blackness. Thus the critique of white masculine failures in mulatta melodramas meaningfully resonates with those African American novels which feature racially ambiguous characters that recast the tropes of temperance discourse (as is shown in the next part of this book). Intertextually, the intemperate white patriarchs, lovers, and villains serve to whiten the images of drunkenness in Harper's *Sowing and Reaping*, Johnson's *Clarence and Corinne*, and Dunbar's *The Uncalled*, and thus help distance the drunkards in black temperance narratives from the Nadir's retrogressionist images of black bestiality. Furthermore, the majority of men so scathingly criticized in mulatta melodrama are patricians, aristocrats, politicians, or professionals and thus represent the very elite of US society, which lends the novels a subtle but distinguishable anti-elitist tone. Such sentiment is even more explicitly present in the black temperance novels, which either melodramatically attack the intemperate elites or pay careful attention to the material context and naturalistically expose the deterministic force of the underprivileged environment—namely, the world of rented tenements and economic exploitation invisible to the middle-class observer.

PART 2

BLACK TROPES OF TEMPERANCE

CHAPTER 4

The Genre Mergers of the Nadir

ANTIDRINK LITERATURE, SENTIMENTALISM, AND NATURALISM IN BLACK TEMPERANCE NARRATIVES

> There is a fearful curse upon us, ... a canker eating into the very heart of society, and sapping the foundations of our dearest and best institutions.
>
> —JANE E. STEBBINS,
> *Fifty Years History of the Temperance Cause*

"This gigantic evil, this cruel monster," depicted in such graphic terms by a postbellum American writer, "is Intemperance," a central theme of mid- and late nineteenth-century American literature (Stebbins 18). As Elaine Parsons persuasively argues, the temperance narrative was one of the most popular stories of the era. Rewritten, sung, drawn, retold, and performed across the country since the 1830s until the end of the Progressive Era, it accompanied antidrink activism, "arguably the largest social movement of the nineteenth-century United States" (Parsons 3–4). Although in the postbellum days the overwhelming majority of its activists did not advocate moderation but total abstinence, their discourse retained the notion of "temperance," rather than introducing "abstention" or "teetotalism," mostly due to its larger connotative field and, as a result, greater rhetorical potential. Accordingly, the significance and influence of the antidrink discourse vastly transcended its immediate objective. As Holly Fletcher states, throughout the nineteenth century, "temperance became a way to explore [diverse] social issues in a safe environment" (123). The antidrink rhetoric was formed of diverse and at times conflicting narratives that were related in a complex way to the ideologies of race, ethnicity, class, and gender. Such heteroglot discourse enabled activists and writers to use the temperance cause in different ways, which ranged from radically democratic and progressive to reactionary and conservative. Anti-alcohol activists championed radical egalitarianism as well as social control of the lower classes and ethnic minorities; some supported woman's suffrage, while some celebrated traditional domestic womanhood. Such contradictions paradoxically contributed to the movement's impact, and they partially accounted for its widespread appeal.

As my analysis of masculinity in mulatta melodrama has demonstrated, intemperance also emerged as a central motif in African American literature of this period, and black temperance narratives form a corpus that both overlaps with and complements mulatta melodrama. The presence of temperance tropes in African American literature dates back to the days of the abolitionist movement and could be easily explained as a residual trace of the close rhetorical and historical ties between different nineteenth-century reform movements. The frequency with which the theme recurs during the Nadir suggests, however, that like the mulatta figure, it gained some additional usefulness for African American activists and Arican American literature at the turn of the twentieth century. This might seem surprising since, at the time, "chronic drunkenness was so rare among blacks that they were thought to be physiologically immune from alcoholism" (Herd, "Ambiguity" 158).[1] One of the factors that helps explain this paradox is the postbellum retrogressionist mythology that represented black men as unable to control their urges and appetites (Tate 9–10). More specifically, their inability to restrain their lust for white women was both mirrored and fueled by their alcohol consumption. This predominantly southern ideology was also embraced and perpetuated by the conservative flank of the temperance movement (Fletcher 69, 118), which argued that the freedmen could be easily bribed with liquor or, more radically, warned that white women were threatened by "the drunken debauches of half-crazed [black] men" (Christmon 328; see also Herd, "Prohibition" 77), which made black appropriations of the hegemonic antidrink discourse wrought with pitfalls. Even though the retrogressionist mythology of black bestiality and corruption did not become dominant until the 1880s (Herd, "Prohibition" 77–83), its emergent traces were discernible already in the years immediately following the

Civil War, when as Eric Foner states, for example, some politicos claimed the black community could be easily corrupted with "a jug of whiskey" (292).

As a result, African American postbellum writers—representatives, historically, of one of the most abstinent demographics in the United States—necessarily had to address the contemporary exaggerated savage and bestial images of their community, which were frequently complemented with drunkenness and which stood in direct contrast to representations of white intemperance, which typically evoked empathy for "the most promising young men" trapped by the demon in their drink (Arthur 132, 137, 236; cf. Parsons 11). In strategically rewriting temperance discourse, black postbellum writers used its powerful appeal and heteroglot structure not only to challenge the retrogressionist mythology but also to represent the condition of freedmen under the emerging Jim Crow regime. The parallel between intemperance and the post-Reconstruction era is visible in the common metaphor used to depict them. In 1882 the *National Temperance Advocate* compared intemperance to "a second slavery" (qtd. in Fletcher 11), and the Jim Crow regime was famously referred to as "a second slavery" in Du Bois's *The Souls of Black Folk* (7), published immediately after the Nadir. The metaphor of enslavement, one of the most powerful tropes of nineteenth-century reform discourse, mobilized the energy of the antebellum abolitionist movement, whose activism successfully ended with the Emancipation Proclamation. Moreover, as I mentioned in the previous chapter, both intemperance and slavery were metaphorically depicted as biblically satanic snakes, serpents, and adders, which is illustrated by Jessie Shepherd's 1887 image "The Worm of the Still" from *Harper's Weekly* (fig. 2). These reptile images further cement the relationship between the two ideas and thus make the use of temperance discourse to talk about the Nadir even more relevant. Echoing the previously quoted passage from Pauline Elizabeth Hopkins, "the slave-power" is represented as a serpent, who "was scorched, not killed." Harper, the most renowned black temperance activist, repeatedly used the biblical motto "[a]t the last it [wine] biteth like a serpent, and stingeth like an adder" (Proverbs 23:32). This powerful image, together with its religious connotations, exerted an intensive affective force. Additionally, the notion of "slavery" in black temperance narratives became, due to its abolitionist echoes, less abstract and more literal than the hegemonic antidrink rhetoric, which further added to its effectiveness.

Another way in which black writers bent the hegemonic temperance discourse to their needs was in their scrupulous attention to class divisions. In contrast to many white antidrink narratives, black depictions of "slavery to the bottle" emphasized the structural limitations of the economic context and the economic factors behind the liquor trade. Whereas before the Civil War, Harper called for a boycott of slave-made products (cf. Stancliff 7), in the postbellum era she used analogous argumentation and encouraged a comparable practice of "commodity consumption as a liminal site of intersubjective connection and a field of ethical choice" to challenge the liquor traffic and make the antidrink reform movement more effective (Stancliff 7). Yet all the novels discussed here in part 2 complement such Marxist insights regarding economic and social determinism with a belief in the efficacy of self-determined teetotalers' efforts and the social reform of drunkards. Using the notion of alcohol as the common human foe, black activists and writers argued for an interracial antidrink platform and, by extension, for an integrated vision of US society. Pointing out that shared vulnerability was an effective strategy, which encouraged the building of a free, cross-class black community and a more democratic and inclusive nation.

Ultimately, in light of the expectations of racial authenticity in African American studies, the most striking feature of Harper's, A. E. Johnson's, and Dunbar's novels is their omission of clear markers of racial differences. I argue that this meaningful and strategic evasion, despite its downplaying of the race question, was deeply involved in progressive race politics. The conflicting significances of racial indeterminacy in the novels can—at least partially—be explained using Gabrielle Foreman's notion of simultextuality, an interpretive mode that covers the multivalent, simultaneously available readings of black fiction (*Activist* 6). On one hand, the lack of racial markers in stories about intemperance distances the narratives from the retrogressionist mythology of black bestiality that emerged in the 1880s. On the other hand, the racially unmarked images of bourgeois success, home-ownership, and fulfillment of domestic ideals, which are frequently juxtaposed with family disintegration in rented spaces, well illustrate the black domestic allegories of political desire as outlined by Claudia Tate in her study of the black female text. Yet the central and (due to the significance of masculinity in temperance discourse) inescapable presence of the male protagonists—*Sowing and Reaping*'s Paul Clifford, A. E. Johnson's eponymous Clarence, and *The Uncalled*'s Fred—illustrates that while the novels cannot be reduced to "female texts" as defined by Tate, at the same time they all do "implicitly construct[] an external, fictive world in which marriage as the sign of private prosperity is also the sign of civil justice," and thus they present "fictions of connubial happiness to the community of their first readers" as well as "histories of racial prosperity within a matrix of sanctioned Victorian social, political, and economic viewpoints" (Tate 8–9).

As was signaled in the introduction, the early black novel was driven by the dialectic of ethical temperance and aesthetic excess. These seemingly paradoxical elements are even more conspicuous in black temperance discourse than in mulatta melodrama, and it is a characteristic that was borrowed from the hegemonic antidrink literature. Although temperance novels promote self-discipline, their poetics in general and representations of alcohol use, in particular, are spectacularly excessive in character. As David S. Reynolds and Debra J. Rosenthal argue, since the 1830s the canon of reform literature was dominated by "the dark-temperance mode" (23; Reynolds 68–69). Detailed depictions of lurid scenes of violence, insanity, and crime resulting from alcohol use contributed to the popularity of the genre (Reynolds and Rosenthal 25–28). Apart from the predilection for brutality, the aesthetic excess of reform fictions was additionally visible in their melodramatic plot construction. As the three novels examined in part 2 illustrate, when adapting the conventions of reform literature to their ends, black writers retained the tension between an excessive aesthetic and temperance.

Another dynamic that drives the structures of the black temperance narratives is the intersection of sentimentalism and naturalism. Its roots are not specifically related to the African American tradition but go back to the early—and dramatically understudied—presence of European naturalism in the United States, which was strictly related to the theme of temperance and the aesthetic of melodrama. The following brief overview of the merger of these two aesthetics—frequently perceived as polar opposites—elucidates their presence and significance in the black novels of the Nadir. Naturalism's entry into the United States predates the moments traditionally recognized as the introduction of naturalism to North America: Frank Norris's 1896 essay glorifying Émile Zola as a romantic writer as well as the release of the first (pirated) translations of the French author in the early 1880s (Chase 185–204; Pizer, *Realism* 41, 110). The presence of Zola in US culture can be traced back to the year 1879, when several companies staged theater adaptations of his novel *L'Assommoir*. This study of a family's decline and alcoholism was published in weekly installments in *La République des Lettres* in 1876–77 and released as a book in 1877. Only two years after its publication in France, at least three different directors adapted it for the US stage, and at the same time, a British company was successfully touring the United States with Charles Reade's adaptation of the novel under the title *Drink* (Frick 169–170).[2] Although all these productions highlighted the melodramatic elements of Zola's text and significantly altered the narrative to make it more compatible with sentimental compassion and reform optimism, the works were received as "an example of Zola's sordid realism, rather than a resurrection of mid-century temperance melodrama" (Cummins 161). Reade managed to combine "the then-popular melodramatic mode with Zola's original naturalistic mode," which is considered to be central to the success of his production (Frick 174–175). Thus the introduction of Zola into the United States illustrates the significance of temperance discourse and its sentimental strategies for the emergence of American naturalism. This intersection, as I suggest above, is equally fundamental for *Sowing and Reaping* (published in the same years as *L'Assommoir*—1876–77—and also in installments), *Clarence and Corinne*, and *The Uncalled*. Just like the theater adaptations of Zola, these novels showcase the crucial interconnectedness of naturalism, sentimentalism, and melodrama at the turn of the twentieth century.

The above-outlined trajectory of naturalism's emergence in the United States is absent from the dominant histories of American literature, and naturalism and sentimentalism are conventionally perceived as two distinct, almost oppositional traditions, frequently strongly gendered as masculine and feminine, respectively (Campbell 1–13).[3] Yet the most insightful studies of naturalism do point out and attempt to account for the continuing presence of sentimentalism in the canonical works of Frank Norris, Theodore Dreiser, and Jack London. As Donald Pizer argues, the US naturalist "often describes his characters as though they are conditioned and controlled by environment, heredity, instinct, or chance. But he also suggests a compensating humanistic value in his characters or their fates which affirms the significance of the individual and of his life" (*Realism* 11). The belief in the worth of the individual and humanistic values is closely related to sentimental pedagogy.[4]

Whereas Pizer's arguments need elaboration to become relevant for the sentimental/naturalist dialectic that informs so many late nineteenth-century novels, Amy Kaplan addresses the issue head-on and devotes her study's final chapter to "The Sentimental Revolt of *Sister Carrie*."[5] She argues that "the critical opposition associating sentimentalism with consumption and desire, and realism [meaning here the aesthetic that includes, rather than is opposed to, naturalism] with work and deprivation" is "a way of imagining and managing the contradictions of a burgeoning consumer culture" (143). A more recent and equally astute study of the post-Reconstruction era, Fleissner's *Women, Compulsion, Modernity*, devotes one of its chapters to the issues of "Sentimentality and 'Drift.'" Fleissner claims that it is "nostalgic men like Carrie's lover Hurstwood [that] become the preeminent sites of a sentimental worldview" (33), and Carrie's figure—a working woman *adrift*, filled with elusive, never-to-be-satisfied desires (24)—acts "against sentimental insistences made to women like her in the 1890s that the conventional marriage plot could ensure female fulfillment" (33).[6] Whereas Kaplan's and Fleissner's perceptive analyses interpret the canonical works of the era in the context of dramatic socioeconomic changes, unprecedented class conflicts, and shifts in gender ideologies (9), I will complement their studies with attention to race relations in the Nadir, an issue altogether absent from Kaplan and only marginally present in Fleissner.[7]

Apart from forming the merger that characterizes many canonical US fin-de-siècle texts, which is most visible though not limited to the works of Dreiser, Norris, and Wharton (Fleissner 160–200), sentimentalism and naturalism share several features that are especially relevant for a study of black works signifying on white reform discourse in general and on temperance literature in particular. Thematically, both aesthetics are primarily interested in the underprivileged: sentimentalism draws its affective power from the construction of an innocent and humane victim that evokes the reader's sympathy, and the naturalist canon, closely related to social reforms of the Progressive Era (Howard 74–75), painstakingly investigates "how the other half lives," to use the title of Jacob Riis's publication. More precisely, as Kaplan argues, naturalism "actively construct[s] the coherent social world [it] represent[s]" as a way of confronting, managing, and reimagining the "fragmented and competing social realities" produced by "intense and often violent class conflicts" (9). The sentimental tradition eulogizes the domestic sphere, whose basis—sometimes invisible and unconscious yet necessary—was homeownership, and it sympathizes with the literarily and symbolically homeless demographic. In a parallel way, US fin-de-siècle naturalists were deeply "preoccupied with the problem of inhabiting and representing rented spaces.... Rented spaces constitute a world filled with things neither known nor valued through the well-worn contract, but cluttered instead with mass-produced furnishings and the unknown lives of strangers" (Kaplan 12). In response to sentimentalism's and naturalism's frequently obsessive or instrumental, yet always intense, interest in the oppressed and the other, African American fiction does not turn away from the reforming gaze but returns it, signifying on their conventions.

In order to evoke affective reactions in the reader—either those of sentimental empathy or of a naturalist protest against social injustice—both aesthetics stress the significance of external influences. Structurally, their sensational plotlines, abounding in coincidences, are in opposition to the expectations for verisimilitude and plausibility set by literary realism. Sentimental uses of the melodramatic mode are perfectly illustrated by mulatta melodrama, where euphoric coincidences bring about poetic justice, while dysphoric recognitions or missed connections hyperbolically highlight the utter absurdity and oppressive sides of the Jim Crow racial divides. Analogously, as intrusive naturalist narrators explicitly declare and as many literary critics argue, the improbable and chance events are a defining feature of naturalist narratives (Fleissner 165–166),[8] and in the US canon, they are even more visible than in European literature. Naturalism's foregrounding of chance and coincidence is primarily a sign of its engagement with a particular historical moment of the emergent modernity, inescapably linked to an awareness that "we are but ciphers in either a cosmic storm or a chemical process" (Pizer, *Realism* 40). It strongly parallels the cultural significance of the melodramatic mode, whose emergence is explained by Brooks as a reaction to the rise of modernity and the secular state (12–15). The use of coincidence and chance, as well as the attention to external factors in black temperance narratives, subtly undercuts the ideology of the American Dream, whose assumptions regarding the efficacy of hard work explained away the oppression of minorities by their inborn indolence and slovenliness. Yet, as I have mentioned, in the US canon of naturalism this engagement with indifferent external forces does not come in the form of an uncritical embrace of such nihilist and proto-existentialist vision but is undergirded with the belief in the importance of community-building as well as in the efficacy of human struggle against pessimism.

From the perspective of this study, an even more important parallel between sentimentalism and naturalism is the significance of temperance, or rather intemperance, in both aesthetics, which is aptly illustrated by the earlier-mentioned sentimental and melodramatic adaptations of Zola's naturalist work. As Parsons states, temperance advocates "made their argument largely through the melodramatic language of sentimental fiction" (172; cf. Fletcher 33). Baym also admits that it does "become intertwined with woman's fiction ... when it centers on the feminine victims of the drunkard," although she argues that "the temperance novel is a genre in itself" (267). Hence antidrink discourse forms a significant part of the US nineteenth-century culture of sentiment. Depictions of the use of alcohol and intemperance are equally central for the naturalist canon. As will be demonstrated, black novels, especially in their recastings of the hegemonic tropes of temperance, strongly resonate with such seminal works of US classical naturalism as Stephen Crane's *Maggie: A Girl of the Streets* (1893) and *George's Mother* (1896); Frank Norris's *McTeague* (1899); Theodore Dreiser's *Sister Carrie* (1900) as well as "Nigger Jeff" (1901); and, most importantly, Jack London's *John Barleycorn: Alcoholic Memoirs* (1913).

The primary sources examined in "Black Tropes of Temperance" exemplify these general structural similarities between sentimentalism and naturalism as well as their shared concerns, such as representations of social reform and intemperance. Yet they go beyond just exhibiting parallels between canonical naturalism and sentimentalism. Through the practice of black-on-white signifying, they recast them in meaningful ways. In all three novels examined, the protagonists, from the underprivileged class and drunkard's homes, are orphaned, but none is burdened with the traditional naturalist plot of decline (Howard 142). The characters manage to transcend both their biological heredity of alcoholic parents and, in the case of Dunbar's and A. E. Johnson's texts, the inhibiting middle-class conditioning of their adoptive milieu. Having rejected the paradigm of biological determinism and social Darwinism, with their deeply racist, eugenic underpinnings, the novels embrace social determinism and argue for the possibility of social change and redemption. Their focus on the underprivileged and the weak, as well as their foregrounding of a common vulnerability to demonstrate the shared humanity of different social groups, results in the advocacy of "lived ethics of connection, a structure of identification within an intersubjective social network" (Stancliff 8).[9] Just as mulatta melodrama implodes the Jim Crow racial divide through its melodramatic revelations that evoke epistemological uncertainty regarding kin relationships in US postbellum society (and thus show that we are all "of one blood," to borrow a title from Hopkins's novel), black temperance narratives expose the inescapable interconnectivity, which is figured in the omnipresent flows of liquor traffic and its all-pervading influence among all social strata and all races.

CHAPTER 5

Aesthetic Excess, Ethical Discipline, & Racial Indeterminacy

FRANCES ELLEN WATKINS
HARPER'S *SOWING AND REAPING*

> Night after night he tore himself away from John Anderson's
> saloon, and struggled with the monster that had enslaved him.
>
> —FRANCES ELLEN WATKINS HARPER, *Sowing and Reaping*

Whereas mulatta melodrama's representations of masculinity emphasize southern patricians' lack of control and unchecked indulgence, and thus portray the drunkard as white, male, and upper class, black temperance narratives endow him with racial ambiguity. The racially indeterminate drunkards in A. E. Johnson's and Paul Laurence Dunbar's novels that I discuss in the following chapters come from the economically underprivileged strata and thus, to that extent, diverge from the white aristocrats discussed in chapter 3. Yet Frances Ellen Watkins Harper's didactic drama *Sowing and Reaping*, which primarily stigmatizes the drinking of expensive wines in upper-class social circles, very distinctly echoes the undisciplined characters from mulatta melodrama and juxtaposes them with a new generation of reformers.

Serialized in 1876–77 in the *Christian Recorder*, the journal of the African Methodist Episcopal Church, *Sowing and Reaping* largely follows hegemonic temperance aesthetics. Its form is characterized by traces of dark-temperance rhetoric, narrative coincidence, and the melodramatic oppositions characteristic of antidrink discourse. Although Harper's critics tend to disregard the significance of the novel's sensational elements (Rosenthal 158; Fulton 212), in this work I show how gothic imagery and aesthetic excess meaningfully inform its reform message and also, indirectly, its race politics. Moreover, although Harper uses hegemonic temperance discourse in a more direct manner than Johnson or Dunbar, she subtly but strategically rewrites it, primarily through omission of the antidrink rhetorical tropes that could associate intemperance with blackness. Harper's political awareness is also visible in her emphasis on the significance of the socioeconomic context and in her criticism of the mechanics of power, including patronage politics and reform activism.

"Stranger Things": Beyond the Commonsense Logic

Sowing and Reaping represents its less-than-probable and paradoxical narrative trajectory as more logical than the dominant, apparently reasonable, and commonsense paradigms of laissez-faire capitalism and biological heredity. Harper openly comments on the use of implausibility in the novel through the words of the main character: events remind him "of the stories [he has] read in fairy books" (119). Paul Clifford has one hour to raise five hundred dollars and prevent his business from going bankrupt when he is visited by his debtor's son, who pays back his father's old debt. Yet even though Paul is amazed by the opportune timing of the payment, he has actually predicted this event. Twelve years earlier, in refusing to foreclose a mortgage on the property of a man in financial difficulty, he envisages that it could be one of his "best investments" as "[s]tranger things than that have happened" (97). Thus Paul Clifford, the model temperance man in the text, undermines the cold rationality of financial profit and loss with the ethics of "lending a helping hand." The novel melodramatically juxtaposes him with another businessman, John Anderson, who believes in "common sense" and in "every man looking out for himself." John's rationale is represented as typical for "worldly men" and the masculine public realm (98). This is in stark contrast to Paul's alternative approach to investment, which stems from his mother's domestic influence. Another motherly intervention into the unstable economy of the postbellum United States brings about a last-minute financial rescue of Paul's shop, which is explained by "the blessed influence of the [debtor's son's] mother" (119). For both men, maternal suasion has been a formative influence. They represent the model of compassionate manhood promoted by women's reform movements, the antithesis of the southern patricians' self-indulgent excesses discussed in chapter 3. The logic that they embrace, far from irrational, is represented as grounded in the laws of nature. Paraphrasing a biblical quotation, the narrator explains that Paul's mother "sowed the seed which she hoped would blossom in time" (99), and accordingly her son "sowed the seeds of kindness and they were yielding him a harvest of satisfaction" (122). Hence, even though the last-minute rescue may seem to be an implausible "fairy tale" twist, the novel ultimately represents it as a logical and natural outcome of Paul's past decisions.

Apart from the laissez-faire rationale, *Sowing and Reaping* indirectly challenges another commonsense logic dominant at the time. According to Parsons, "[M]any reformers believed that an individual could inherit an alcoholic tendency so strong that drinking one drop would bring to life an uncrushable inner demon" (33). At first, it might seem that Harper's text supports this belief since it contains a number of references to hereditary determinism. The threats that "the appetite for strong drink" can be transmitted to the drunkard's children "as a fatal legacy" (99) or that the child "received as an inheritance a temperament which will be easily excited by stimulants" recur in the novel (101). Yet even though such fears are voiced by the narrator and the characters, they are not realized. Both model protagonists—Paul Clifford and Belle Gordon—are the offspring of drunkard fathers, and neither shows any inclination toward intemperance. To the contrary, not only are they antidrink activists, but both demonstrate moral self-discipline in other ways. Paul is lured several times with the opportunity to make an unethical profit, which he rejects despite financial difficulties. Belle is also tempted by an advantageous marriage offer from a "handsome, agreeable, and wealthy" Charles Romaine (113), and despite her affectionate feelings for the man, not to mention his social and economic position, she exercises great self-restraint and decides not to marry him after he refuses to abstain from alcohol. She shows much better judgment than her peers or even her mother, who, as I mentioned in chapter 2, recalls Rena's money-struck parent, Molly Walden, from *The House behind the Cedars*. Belle's mother, despite her age and experience, is represented as foolish and shortsighted, which highlights the future-oriented character of the novel and its hopeful investment in the new generation. Belle's social milieu cannot understand her rejection of "an excellent offer" and the decision to "sacrifice a splendid opportunity" (99–100). They perceive her as a "*monomaniac* on the temperance question," going "*crazy* on the subject" as well as "*nervous* and giving way to *idle fancies*" and "*squeamish* notions" (101, 111, 157, 100; emphasis added). By unfolding a plot of decline for Charles and confirming Belle's predictions, the narrative not only criticizes her elite milieu in general and her mother in particular, it also challenges the controlling image of the irrational and mentally unbalanced woman in a manner similar to Harper's *Iola Leroy*. Just as the last-minute rescue is represented as true to the laws of nature, here the novel demonstrates the rationality of feminine nervousness.

Belle Gordon's and Paul Clifford's ability to transcend the biological heritage of intemperance through self-discipline is contrasted with the story of Belle's jilted fiancé, Charles Romaine. Carla Peterson claims that his drinking is a result of "a poor genetic makeup" (48), yet even if he is constitutionally susceptible to alcohol use, it is not an inherited trait. A conspicuous foil to Paul, Charles is the son of a man who is completely immune to the effects of alcohol: his father always has "wine at the table" and never appears to be "under the influence of liquor" (157). Yet despite such a family history, as Belle predicts, Charles is ultimately buried in a drunkard's grave. Another drunkard in the novel, Joe Gough, also does not come from a drunkard's home but is well educated and "belongs to a good family" (140). Thus the fates of the main characters disprove the hereditary character of intemperance. Such downplaying of biological determinism repudiates social Darwinist thought, which posited that both lower classes' and black people's inferior position reflected the natural evolutionary hierarchy (L. Baker 27).[1] The doctrine was closely related to laissez-faire logic since it argued that any social reform was against the laws of evolution. As the most influential American social Darwinist, William G. Sumner, wrote in his 1883 study, a "drunkard in the gutter is just where he ought to be, according to the fitness and tendency of things" (114), and—strongly echoing John Anderson's words—"[t]o mind one's own business is . . . a sociological principle of the first importance" (105–106). Thus Harper's narrative logic undermines both the notion of laissez-faire individualism and social Darwinism, with their implicit race and class politics.

Such a narrative challenge to the logic of heredity in the text is complemented with its embrace of social determinism, which evidences its affinity with the protonaturalist and naturalist works discussed in the following chapters. Harper's novel is not unique in its foreshadowing of the naturalist logic of social determinism: many reform activists believed that "environmental influence could be irresistible" (Parsons 33). In *Sowing and Reaping*, on the one hand, society's impact is manifested by the force of moral suasion that overpowers the heritage of intemperance. For example, Paul Clifford, the son of a drunkard, becomes a temperate man thanks to the moral guidance of his "dear sainted mother" (106), and drunkard Joe Gough is reformed thanks to his wife and Belle Gordon. On the other hand, a number of characters become inebriates as a result of the detrimental influence of their environments. Young men are corrupted by the typical temperance literature villains: immoral women, thoughtless fathers or uncles, and greedy saloonkeepers (Parsons 113).

Among this cast of traditional antagonists, the novel's father figures are most frequently blamed for making their children "slaves to appetite" (165), and such a critique of the older generation further evidences the text's future-oriented character and additionally echoes the sins of the failed fathers in mulatta melodrama. Bad paternal influence is presented in an exaggerated way that draws on the gothic images of demons and possession. For example, a single glass of wine—offered to a boy by his uncle—"awaken[s] within him a dreadful craving," and "as if a spell was upon him," liquor becomes his "master" (134). Analogously, Charles Romaine is "enslaved" by a "monster" (172), which stands for alcohol and the saloon, but also metonymically for his father: "it was from his hands, and at his table [he] received [his] first glass of wine" (146). "The curse that John Anderson had sent to other homes had come back darkened with the shadow of death to brood over his own habitation" (170–171): the son of the saloon owner dies in an attack of delirium tremens as a result of his father's participation in liquor trafficking. Whereas temperance literature typically emphasized the emasculation that accompanied inebriation, the scenario in which a younger man is lured to drink by a father figure offers a double critique of masculine inadequacies. It both depicts the loss of the drunkard's manhood and the deficiencies of paternal protection.[2]

Sowing and Reaping's father figures, as I signaled above, strongly resonate with the patrician patriarchs of mulatta melodrama, who fail to protect their mixed-race children. In both cases, father figures are responsible for the enslavement—literal or metaphorical—of their offspring, and their claim to civilized manhood is questioned. Moreover, *Sowing and Reaping* echoes another central conflict of the typical mulatta plot, which is the disintegration of interracial families. Once Charles Romaine's father realizes his son is a "wreck" on a "downward course" (144–145), he decides to "cast him off" and forces him to sign "the articles of dissolution" from their law office (144, 146). The event is thrice referred to as "separation" (147), which parallels the numerous "cruel separations" of mixed-race families in *Iola Leroy* and the slave-owning patriarchs who "cast off" their offspring and "send them to the auction block" (148, 54).[3] It also reminds one of the chapter title "Separation" in the ur-mulatta melodrama, William Wells Brown's *Clotel*, in which Horatio Green discards and hence enslaves Clotel and their daughter, Mary. Such dramatic separations of mixed-race families have an intense affective force and evoke sentimental sympathy, but, more radically, the mixed-race body of the mulatto offspring evidences the impossibility of ultimate racial separation and hence undermines the Jim Crow regime of racial segregation. Harper's rhetoric suggests that, in the case of temperance, any plans of separation from intemperate relatives and the liquor traffic are likewise either hypocritical or illusory due to the inescapable interdependence of the community depicted in the novel. Furthermore, in both types of narratives, the threat to family integrity is not external but embodied by the failed patriarch, who in *Sowing and Reaping* is additionally cast with the specter of supernatural monstrosity through the demonic images of dark-temperance rhetoric.

"Gorgeous Palaces of Sin":
Liquor Traffic, Social Reform, & Consumer Desire

More often than not, the fatal impact of the environment in the novel is positioned in a respectable milieu, and *Sowing and Reaping* explicitly challenges the associations between binge drinking and the lower class and targets the privileged class with its critique. Most of the drunkards are not "in the gutter" (Sumner 114), and the most popular drink is not beer or cheap corn whiskey but wine. Wine, in general, is mentioned as many as thirty-eight times in the novel and champagne an additional three times, which is in stark contrast to whiskey and rum, which each appear twice, while beer remains altogether unmentioned. Such a choice of drink might seem surprising as the historical and economic significance of wine in the nineteenth-century United States was minuscule in comparison to distilled spirits or beer (Rorabaugh 106, 238).[4] Apart from the community of Italian Americans, it was a popular beverage only among the upper classes, who served it during formal entertainments, as the high cost of imported European wine helped them display their high social status (Murdock 55–63).[5] As John Koren reports, wine was almost absent from African American drinking patterns of the Nadir. In their generally low alcohol consumption, there was "scarcely any wine, very little beer, and not much cider ... whiskey [was] the standard drink" (163).[6] The lower classes' lack of familiarity with wine, and in particular with champagne, is ironically signaled in Norris's naturalist classic, *McTeague* (1899), in which the protagonist, having been served champagne at his wedding, declares that it is "the best beer [he] ever drank" (168).

Although it definitely surpasses the historical accounts of US wine consumption, wine's presence in the temperance discourse is not dominant. As Madelon Powers points out, the leading position belongs to rum (which is also quite surprising, given that its popularity slumped with the introduction of tariffs after the Revolutionary War [80–85]).[7] Characteristically, antidrink narratives that focus on the threat of wine call for self-discipline among the upper classes rather than for the social control of the lower class. For example, Jane E. Stebbins, in her history of the temperance reform published only two years before *Sowing and Reaping*, condemns "the favorites of wealth and the devotees of fashion" who serve wine at their social gatherings (73–74). The racial connotations of such alcohol use are predominantly white. In the corpus of Harper's texts, there is a close textual parallel that might serve to further whiten the novel's wine-drinking class. The main upper-class drunkard, Charles Romaine, is warned by Belle Gordon that he is "drifting where he ought to steer" and "floating down the stream" (101–102). Analogously, Iola Leroy's father, a rich white planter, "learned to drift where he should have steered, to float with the current instead of nobly breasting the tide" (*Iola Leroy* 69). As I mentioned earlier, the strong similarity between the two passages links the two characters, and the whiteness of Eugene Leroy is cast on the racially unmarked Charles. This analogy is further reinforced by the earlier-mentioned parallel between *Sowing and Reaping*'s critique of paternal corruption and *Iola Leroy*'s representation of white slave owners.

Thus *Sowing and Reaping*, by its foregrounding of wines, forges a strong connection between inebriety and upper-class conspicuous consumption, which evokes racial associations with whiteness. Apart from the narrative's closures, in which two upper-class men are buried in drunkard graves, the indictment of upper-class intemperance is directly pronounced by the novel's model characters. In a conversation with her friend Jeanette Roland, Belle Gordon questions the distinction between vulgar drinking in saloons and decent drinking at social gatherings of their "set" and argues that alcohol consumption at such events is more of a threat to young men than the "horrid" bar rooms (101). Respectable members of the set legitimize intemperance with their social position: it is "most dangerous" when "sin... is environed by success," which lends it "a fearful fascination" (111). Harper's character, echoing contemporaneous temperance arguments (cf. Stebbins 73–74), aptly elucidates the work of hegemony as defined by Antonio Gramsci: the spontaneous consent to act against one's interests "caused by the prestige (and consequent confidence) which the dominant group enjoys because of its position and function in the world of production" (190). Such proto-Marxist insights are not limited to Belle. Paul Clifford—a paragon of compassionate manhood—makes a comparable argument regarding class and alcohol in his conversation with John Anderson. Despite his difficult financial situation, Paul refuses John's offer of partnership in a "first class saloon," "well lighted and splendidly furnished," and overall too pricey for "rough, low, boisterous men" (105). He contends that such places are "just as great a curse to the community as the low groggeries" and thus, just like Belle, undermines class boundaries in the patterns of alcohol use. The narrative's closures, in which Jeanette Roland becomes the wife of a drunkard and John Anderson witnesses his son's death in a fit of delirium tremens, mock their assumptions that class privilege will protect them from the brutal results of intemperance.

Although some critics fail to see it (A. Williams 47, 52), in her depictions of the community's interconnectedness Harper also introduces the voice of working-class characters. Their presence is related in a complex way to the novel's advocacy of the power of the environment and its championing of reform work. Belle Gordon, just like the New Negro women in mulatta melodrama, is "an earnest ally" of every reform that aims to "lessen human misery." "A real minister of mercy," she enters the lower-class neighborhoods: "There was no hut or den where human beings congregated... too vile and repulsive to enter" (123). Strongly echoing the representation of Iola, she is portrayed as an angelic bringer of joy and light to the "darkened homes" and "depths of sin and degradation" (123, 155). Yet the novel complicates this saintly image of the racially ambiguous middle-class reformer among the "poor and needy" by introducing the perspective of the underprivileged (156). Belle is juxtaposed with another charity worker—Mother Graham, whose name alludes to the antebellum temperance and health reformer, Sylvester Graham. The effects of Graham's activism were praised in reform discourse: as Bruce Dorsey puts it, magazines such as "*Genius of*

Temperance raved over the consequences of Graham's labors" (118).[8] Furthermore, the title "Mother" resonates with Mother Stewart and Mother Thompson, the two leaders of the 1873 temperance crusade—the momentous historical event that Harper refers to in *Sowing and Reaping* (167) as well as in "The Woman's Christian Temperance Union" (281). According to Carol Mattingly, the title honored Stewart's and Thompson's "special capacity and power" (42). Histotextually, this dignity is transferred onto Harper's less prominent but highly noble character. Mother Graham's "poverty of her dress" unequivocally indicates her lower-class status. In contrast to Belle, who is both metaphorically and socially located above the "depths of sin" (123), Mother Graham makes a point of not looking down on the people she helps (126). Moreover, whereas Belle's reform activity primarily consists in bringing abstract aid such as sunlight, brightness, counsel, and sympathy (123), her lower-class foil first feeds the people she helps: "I never like to preach religion to hungry people" (126).[9] Thus the text subtly suggests that there are limits to Belle's empathy and understanding, and despite her function as a model temperance protagonist, she is not a melodramatic embodiment of pure virtue. As Peterson convincingly argues, Harper's "model [of uplift] was no longer that in which authority figures (often female) exercise discipline—whether through coercion or through love—over their charges" (43). Mother Graham accurately illustrates an alternative model of horizontal self-help that does not assume social control over the less privileged. Moreover, the novel's presentation of reform that goes beyond the practice of moral suasion is also manifest in its—at the time radical—embrace of woman's suffrage. One of the female characters uses economic arguments to show that without the right to vote, women's interests are not truly protected.

Mother Graham's perspective is not the only way in which the novel gives the floor to underprivileged women. Throughout the text, Harper exhibits a keen awareness of the way in which gender and class oppression coincide, and, as Michael Stancliff correctly points out, she meticulously "put[s] the woman's fate in an economic context" (103). The significance of socioeconomic conditions is most conspicuously depicted in *Sowing and Reaping* when one of the women assisted by Belle Gordon speaks up about the exploitation of workers. After the protagonist suggests that her protégée could get employment with an "excellent" and "religious" Mrs. Roberts (129), Mary Gough responds that her experience is quite the contrary: Mrs. Roberts is "a very hard person to deal with" and wants "much work for so little money" (130). Although she spends large sums on dressmaking, she saves when "dealing with poor people" who do not have the power "to resist her demands" (130–131). The greed of Mrs. Roberts, next to the intemperance of Joe Gough, is one of the narrative reasons why Mary Gough faints from "overwork and want of proper food" and cannot afford to move to "a respectable neighborhood" (130). Mary's story dialogically rewrites Belle's statement that "the times are very hard; and the rich feel it as well as the poor" as a naïve and thoughtless fantasy. Thus, despite her embrace of the bourgeois ideal of self-discipline and her use of hegemonic temperance rhetoric, Harper criticizes upper-class condescension and exploitation of the lower class. The greed of Mrs. Roberts is linked to the greed of saloonkeepers, who incidentally also think that they "are paying [their] servants too high wages" (167). Thus the owner class, with its insatiable appetite for wealth, is explicitly judged as immoral and exploitative, taking profit from "the loss of others" (106).

Mrs. Roberts's greed is narratively positioned as akin to Joe Gough's inebriety, since they both not only lead to Mary's overwork and illness but are also metaphorically analogous. The parallel between intemperance and extravagance is used throughout the novel to criticize the excessive materialism of the upper class, and the link evidences the diverse meanings of temperance that were mobilized in antidrink discourse, which went far beyond abstention from alcohol. Additionally, the novel's critique of conspicuous consumption echoes mulatta melodrama's representations of southern aristocratic culture with its indulgence and love of excess, which has already been discussed as central to the critique of patrician masculinity. *Sowing and Reaping* employs the well-established association of the saloon with luxurious display: in the "gorgeous palace of sin" (165), "sparkling champaign [sic] and ruby-tinted wine [a]re served in beautiful and costly glasses," and men can rest on "rich divans and easy chairs" (107). The tempting luxury is also embodied by prostitutes, who parallel the representation of Aurelia Madison from *Hagar's Daughter*. "Debased" women with "costly jewels and magnificent robes" lure men into drinking (107). Such lavishness corrupts the patrons, but it stimulates the liquor traffic moguls. Just as liquor "fires the brain" of a drunkard (137), "visions of wealth dazzle [the] brain" and "unsettle [the] mind" of John Anderson (165). Neither the saloonkeeper nor the drunkard is capable of restraint.

The immoral excesses of John's conspicuous consumption are additionally emphasized by gothic images. His residence is "a marvel of decoration"

(171), "a home of wealth, luxury and display" (165), but it is overcast with "[t]he darkness of the tomb... not gilded with the glory of resurrection" (171), and all his "money... is the price of blood" (118). In a parallel way, the house of a whiskey dealer is "a brilliant array of wealth and fashion," but as the narrator imagines it, blood oozes "from every marble ornament or beautiful piece of frescoe" as they are acquired at "the price of blood" (109). The liquor traffic, driven by the excessive appetite of dealers and inebriates alike, is represented as a system that saps the blood of drunkards and their families and inevitably leads to an untimely death. Such a perception of alcohol as a depressant (rather than stimulant), causing lethargy, exhaustion, and, ultimately, death was, although not dominant, residually present in the contemporary temperance discourse. For example, Stebbins argues that liquor "has taken vitality from the blood, and filled it with poison and seeds of disease and death" (61). Additionally, the novel's blood-related images can further explain Harper's choice of wine as the central drink in the text despite its relatively low popularity. Not only do its connotations with upper-class conspicuous consumption emphasize the excessive display of liquor dealers, but its visual similarity to the human body fluid reinforces the analogy between the flows of blood and alcohol.

In addition, such appetite for blood and imported European wines resonates with the early and mid-nineteenth-century images of vampires. In Byron's *The Giaour*, the eponymous character is cursed with the vampire's fate: as a "livid living co[r]pse," he will "suck the blood of all [his] race" (71). Harper's narrator claims that, like the living corpses of vampires, the patrons and prostitutes in the saloon are "dead while they live[]" and their "souls [a]re encased in living tombs" (107). The liquor industry turns people into vampires, who in turn suck the life out of their predominantly female family members like the cursed Giaour, who shall "drain the stream of life" from his "daughter, sister, and wife" (Byron 71). Although critics tend to disregard the use of dark temperance in *Sowing and Reaping*, the scene of Joe Gough cutting his wife's hair is cited as one of the exceptions to Harper's relative moderation (Rosenthal 158; Fulton 212). "[T]he wreck of what was once [her] husband" with "wild and bloodshot" eyes and "pale and *haggard* face" approaches Mary's bedside with "a pair of shears" to cut her "wealth of *tresses*" (131–132; emphasis added). The scene bears an uncanny resemblance to Byron's vampire passage, in which the "demon" with "gnashing tooth and *haggard* lip" attacks his daughter and tears "[t]he *tresses* of her yellow hair" (71; emphasis added). In the free-market circulation of goods, Mary Gough's body is literally commodified: her hair is exchanged for money, which in turn is spent on alcohol. The novel also suggests that insatiable consumer desire is analogous to the drunkard's appetite. Such a portrayal echoes Karl Marx's repeated allusions to the vampire, which "perfectly embodies the way in which human life nourishes the machine of capitalist production" (Punter and Byron 269).

In Harper's gothic representation of the liquor traffic, ultimately it is the saloonkeeper and whiskey seller that feed on the bodies of the intemperate men and their dependents. In the text, the vampiric tropes of capitalist exploitation resonate with images of drunkards and their failed fathers: they all embody the monstrosity of exaggerated patriarchal oppression. Furthermore, the vampire narrative typically evokes the figure of a "white male who penetrates both society and the bodies of his victims" (Brox 391), and African American writers traditionally have used "the gothic to haunt back, reworking the gothic's conventions to intervene in discourses that would demonize them" (Goddu 138). Hence it is possible to read the novel's vampiric images of capitalist circulation in general and of the liquor traffic in particular as marked with the shadow of monstrous white masculinity.

While *Sowing and Reaping* exposes the gothic horrors of the liquor traffic and extravagance, it also suggests that there is a reasonable and positive pattern of consumption, and the model protagonist, Belle Gordon, is twice represented as a purchaser. At the beginning of the novel, she asks for Jeanette Roland's assistance with shopping as she believes in her friend's "excellent taste" and in the "the utility of beauty" (110). Later, she "replenishe[s] her basket with some of the good things of life": "refreshing tea" and "bread and milk" for the Gough family (125). Analogously, Paul Clifford pays for Joe Gough's barbers and a new suit so that "appearances" do not work against the reformed drunkard, and he is happy to see his "return of self-respect" (151). In this scene, Harper appropriates a specific temperance discourse that goes back to the Washingtonian movement dominant in the 1840s. In contrast to other, mostly middle-class antebellum antidrink reformers who emphasized self-mastery and policed the lower-class bodies, the Washingtonians, rooted in the working-class milieu, were much more democratic and open to women's active involvement (Fletcher 31–37). They combined the narrative of temperate self-control with the doctrine of communal self-help, which specifically included a change of the drunkard's clothes. As an 1843 history of the movement states, a "half-clad reformed inebriate" "could receive such early tokens of sympathy as would enable him, by the time he was clothed and in his right mind, to appear out in the condition of a respectable candidate for any place of industry his previous trade or profession had qualified him to fill" (L. Johnson 9). Thus Harper, through Paul Clifford's model character, appropriates the Washingtonians' temperance narrative and ideology, which, though rooted in the antebellum working-class culture, suited the needs of the postbellum African American community. Its democratic rhetoric strongly echoes the reform activism represented by Mother Graham. Communal self-help, central to the Washingtonian thought, is also illustrated in the novel when temperance men hire abstinent drunkards: the reform club works to the economic advantage of its members. *Sowing and Reaping* emphasizes that the materiality of self-help needs to complement the spiritual uplift: as Mother Graham puts it, reformers should not "preach religion to hungry people" (126).

Thus, rather than melodramatically reject material concerns, Harper positions ethical consumer choices and fair business conduct at the center of her didactic rhetoric (cf. Stancliff 83–84). The novel's poetic justice rewards the honest grocery owner Paul Clifford and shows how the anticonsumer action of the 1873 temperance crusades "has made quite a hole in [John Anderson's] business," and its impact could even "affect the revenue of the [entire] state" (167). Just as Harper's antebellum works embraced the free produce tactic—i.e., consumers' choice of articles, mainly cotton clothing, not marked with the "blood and tears" of slave labor ("On Free Produce" 45)— her temperance reform transcends moral suasion. The text's antidrink rhetoric both enters the market realm and advocates political action.[10] The novel is peppered with the discourse of economics, which primarily functions in two ways. On the literal level, *Sowing and Reaping* points to the significance of the economic context: the "general depression in every department of trade and business" influences "men of business," who "have grown exceedingly timid about investing" (104). It also represents the limitations of the laissez-faire "business is business" motto and champions the kind of entrepreneurship that receives the blessing of moral women and God (96, 95, 105). On the other hand, Harper's work appropriates the jargon of the marketplace to metaphorically portray its characters' spiritual condition. John's soul is "poverty stricken" and gnawed by "unappeased hunger," and as a result, he will "go into the eternities a pauper and a bankrupt" (97). In contrast, Belle is "affluent in tenderness, sympathy, and love" (124), and Paul's "life has been a grand success" due to "the enrichment of his moral and spiritual nature" (175). Thus, whereas the novel unequivocally condemns laissez-faire market logic, it does not naïvely reject social reality and material concerns. *Sowing and Reaping* offers models for using the market tools of strategic consumption and business integrity and also bends the materialist rhetoric to suit its sociopolitical purposes.

Racial Excess:
Intemperance in Black & White

Characteristically, although the novel is firmly grounded in the hegemonic antidrink discourse, much more so than A. E. Johnson's and Dunbar's texts (discussed in the following chapters), the drunkards in *Sowing and Reaping* are not presented as marked with one of the most recurrent traits of inebriate bodies in temperance fiction, that is, sensuality and redness (Parsons 140). The former frequently recurs in Stebbins's history of temperance, where she repeatedly portrays the drunkard's face as "distorted with passion" and marked with "sensuality and brutishness" (Stebbins 58, 61; see also 20, 50, 95). In a similar vein, in the most popular nineteenth-century temperance text, which Harper quite likely alludes to in the names of her characters (Peterson 48), Timothy Shay Arthur's *Ten Nights in a Bar-Room and What I Saw There* (1854), drunkards' faces are "marred by sensual indulgence" and "gross, sensual expression[s]" almost every time they are introduced (Arthur 10, 43; see also 113, 157, 205). Similarly, both Stebbins's and Arthur's works profusely illustrate the discourse's tendency to portray the "alcoholic's skin as red or 'flushed'" (Fletcher 26), as they mention the reddened complexions of inebriates time and time again (Stebbins 37, 74, 60, 87, 108, 325, 347; Arthur 16, 21, 108).

In contrast, Harper's victims of liquor are repeatedly portrayed as lifeless and pale (124, 138, 164), which further emphasizes the blood-draining powers of alcohol and its depressing rather than stimulating effects. By eschewing the link between sensual passion and inebriety, Harper also avoids triggering the emergent retrogressionist images of "liquor-crazed" and "sexually depraved" blackness (Herd, "Prohibition" 77). Her choice not to depict the reddened faces of drunkards can also be related to ideologies of race and ethnicity. The drunkard's loss of "whiteness in physical appearance" expressed the hegemonic fears of racialization and emasculation (Fletcher 26). Fletcher points to the similarities between the inebriate's red-colored faces and Native American complexion; she also discusses examples of brown and dirty faces of drunkards that directly connoted blackness (26). As other scholars argue, redness at the time was most commonly associated with lower-class Irishness (Banerjee 107–110), and in turn, Irishness was frequently paired with blackness (Stancliff 109–114). Hence, by emphasizing the pallor of inebriates and their lifelessness, Harper avoids these diverse ethnic and racial connotations and further strengthens the association between intemperance and privilege, including the racial privilege of whiteness.

Her avoidance of racialization, however, goes beyond the omission of redness and sensuality. Like the other narratives discussed in this part of *The Nadir and the Zenith*, the novel is altogether devoid of unambiguous bodily signifiers of race. The only character whose hair is described, Joe Gough, has a "wealth of raven hair," and the only eyes whose color is specified belong to an intemperate boy and are "brown" (138, 133). Such a consistent lack of unequivocal racial markers needs to be seen as carefully designed and thus intentionally loaded with meaning. Its significance, however, has been read in contradictory ways. Rosenthal argues that since the novel was published in an African American magazine, its readers "did not find the deracialized discourse curious, but instead assumed Harper's characters to be black" (Rosenthal 155). This, she adds, had the effect of "the normalizing of blackness," which was an empowering alternative to the images of "black-as-victim-of-racism-and-discrimination" (156). A scene from a recently recovered chapter of *Sowing and Reaping*, in which Mr. Follard, the head of an upper-class household, is mistaken for a servant when he opens the door, might be used to further support Rosenthal's argument that the novel's characters were read as black. In the postbellum era, the servant identity was deeply racialized across the United States (Branch and Wooten 179), and in some southern towns, there were no white servants at all (Fleming 2), which suggests that if Mr. Follard was confused with a servant he was an African American. In direct contrast, the racial connotations in my analysis of Harper's choice of wine in the novel, the parallels between Charles Romaine and Iola Leroy's white father, as well as the vampiric images indicate whiteness rather than blackness. These contradictory readings can be reconciled with DoVeanna Fulton's thesis that racial indeterminacy in the novel needs to be perceived as a strategic act, which "allows Harper to proffer a radical integrationist vision of America" (Fulton 211; see also Peterson 45). This claim could be further supported by the fact that *Sowing and Reaping* takes place in the city of A.P., which is also the setting of *Trial and Triumph* (1888–89), another magazine novel authored by Harper. In the later novel, A.P. is inhabited by a multiethnic population, and the black protagonist, Annette Harcourt, attends an integrated school (182). Although the novel is far from depicting a blissful interracial harmony, it does portray a racially diverse community. Developing Fulton's line of reasoning, I see *Sowing and Reaping* as a work that participates in racial simultextuality, a practice characteristic for black women's nineteenth-century fiction, whose complex layers enabled multivalent contested readings (Foreman, *Activist* 6–8).

In Harper's overall oeuvre, such racial simultextuality is not limited to *Sowing and Reaping*. As Fulton and Foster point out, her temperance writings, in contrast to the texts primarily concerned with abolition and racial discrimination, are generally devoid of clear racial markers. Whereas they exemplify this claim based on Harper's short story "Two Offers" and her antebellum poetry (Fulton 210; Foster xxxii), even closer parallels can be found between *Sowing and Reaping* and the second edition of Harper's *Sketches of Southern Life* (1886). The speaker in the latter volume's first section is Aunt Chloe, whose folk, rural, unsophisticated persona insightfully judges Reconstruction politics (Stancliff 75; Foster 137). This race-oriented part is complemented with a series of temperance poems devoid of racial markers. The juxtaposition of the postbellum era and intemperance in a single volume echoes their representations as "a second slavery" in the contemporaneous reform discourse, as pointed out in the previous chapter. The racially ambiguous poems strongly resonate with images from *Sowing and Reaping*. The drunkard's bride from "Signing the Pledge"—with "orange blossoms in her hair" (255)—is a close recasting of Jeanette Roland with "her wreath of orange blossoms" at the altar (148). Analogously, consider the merchant from the fourth stanza of "Something and Nothing":

> As over his ledger he bent his head;
> I'm busy to-day with *tare* and *tret*,
> And I have no time to fume and fret.
> (252; emphasis added)

The lines clearly echo the novel's assessment of John Anderson, who changes "his heart into a ledger on which he will write *tare* and *tret*, loss and gain, exchange and barter, and he will succeed, as worldly men count success" (98; emphasis added). The latter poem criticizes the individualist doctrine of self-interest and self-sufficiency as an "idle sleep," and in its six stanzas, each of which is devoted to a different socioeconomic milieu, it shows that intemperance is an issue impacting all members of US society.

By avoiding references to unambiguous bodily markers of race, Harper represents a future US republic that, as she imagines in another text, "shall be so color-blind, as to know no man by the color of his skin or the curl of his hair" ("We Are All"). Paradoxically, this strategy of omission produces a simultextual excess of meanings when it is positioned in the deeply racialized postbellum context. Instead of a univocal story of a sympathetic white drunkard's fall (as outlined in Parson's analysis), the inebriates in *Sowing and Reaping* have the potential to be either white or black, which destabilizes the racialized connotations of drinking in the late nineteenth century. The novel thus enables readings that could be empowering for the black audience of the *Christian Recorder*, ranging from a portrayal of the prosperous black upper classes that, despite their intemperance, do not become "sensual hyenas" (qtd. in Herd, "Prohibition" 84); to a depiction of a multiracial community—a reading that could be reinforced with the conviction, common in the Nadir times, that "the saloon promoted race-mixing and social equality" (89); to an emphasis on the white upper-class context of intemperance and its bloodthirsty exploitation of the (possibly black) proletariat.

Racial indeterminacy in the novel is underscored by its representation of alcohol, the impact of which, as I have argued, cuts across class lines and illustrates social interdependency. This boundary-defying character of drink is further reinforced in the metaphors of the apocalyptic deluge that resonate in Zola's depictions of the distillery in *L'Assommoir* (whose last installment was published simultaneously with Harper's, in 1877). In old Colombe's cheap tavern for the Parisian proletariat, the still goes on "sweating out its alcohol like a slow-flowing but relentless spring, which would eventually flood the bar-room, spill over to the outer boulevards, and inundate the vast pit that was Paris" (42): the mechanistic force of the distillery spreads its influence from the slums to the entire city. In the upper-class setting of *Sowing and Reaping*, the alcohol's flow is more organic than mechanistic, and it starts from the top, not the bottom, but its inevitable escalation is largely analogous: "the wine flow[s] out like a purple flood" during Jeanette Roland and Charles Romaine's wedding (148), and John Anderson's saloon sends "a flood of demoralizing influence" (106). Also, the earlier-mentioned gothic images that link alcohol traffic to blood circulation produce a comparable effect.

The fluidity of images of alcohol in the novel parallels the uncertain flow of blood in mulatta melodrama. In Harper's overall oeuvre, the genre, apart from *Iola Leroy*, is exemplified by her early serialized novel *Minnie's Sacri-*

fice (1869). Both mulatta protagonists, Iola and Minnie, are brought up to believe they are white, which undermines the notion of pure white identity and questions Jim Crow segregation. Similarly, in *Sowing and Reaping*, no class and no race is immune from the all-pervading influence of the liquor traffic. As she puts it in her address "The Woman's Christian Temperance Union and the Colored Woman," alcohol is "an enemy to all races" (281). In the postbellum era, as Fletcher demonstrates, the Woman's Christian Temperance Union used "the common foe of alcohol" to reunite the North and the South, frequently alluding to images of drunk freedmen, destroyed by freedom (117–121). Harper, in contrast, recasts "the common foe" as a platform for interracial unity and communal self-help, highlighting the all-human vulnerability to foster community-building and relation-building processes. The uncertain flows of alcohol and the all-pervading liquor traffic cannot be stopped without interclass and interracial collaboration. Significantly, Harper's avoidance of racial bodily markers does not result in an abstract and disembodied representation of the community; to the contrary, instead of racial differences, she emphasizes the human bodily universality and the corporal vulnerability central to it, which was a powerfully political intervention during the Nadir era.

Overall, although it has not attracted as much critical attention as the more explicitly political *Iola Leroy*, which is firmly set in the black community, *Sowing and Reaping* is also a forcefully critical work, which evidences Harper's commitment to "a pragmatic poetics" (Foster 135), or as her protagonist puts it, her belief in "the utility of beauty" (110). It uses aesthetic excess and dark-temperance imagery to challenge the doctrines of autonomous self-sufficiency, laissez-faire economy, and social Darwinism, with the class and race politics embedded in them. The novel places emphasis on the disciplining of the upper class rather than on social control of the lower class, which produces a more democratic uplift rhetoric. Its main critique is targeted at the male figures of authority rather than at women or less privileged men. Even though Harper strongly draws on the predominantly white temperance discourse and its powerful affective and political appeal, she also strategically selects its elements to form a narrative that offers a counterhegemonic reading. Her avoidance of sensual images and of mentions of alcohol's discoloring effects distances the narrative from the contemporaneous notions of racialized inebriety and uncontrollable sexual appetite. As I have demonstrated, the racially ambiguous cast of characters in *Sowing and Reaping* provides a simultextual excess of meanings and reinforces the text's critique of self-sufficient individualism and of the viability of race or class divisions. The novel exemplifies the correlation between racial indeterminacy and the theme of temperance, which is characteristic not only of Harper's antidrink works in general but also of other postbellum African American novels on alcohol use, such as Amelia E. Johnson's *Clarence and Corinne* (1890) and Paul Laurence Dunbar's *The Uncalled* (1901), which will be discussed in the following chapters.

CHAPTER 6

Tropes of Temperance, Specters of Naturalism
AMELIA E. JOHNSON'S
CLARENCE AND CORINNE

> How could she live, battered and beaten, and starved as she was, and by our father too; the one who could have made us all comfortable and happy. But instead of that he's made us miserable—no, it wasn't him either; it was that dreadful, dreadful stuff, whisky. Yes, drink ruined our father, and now it's killed our mother; and nobody cares for us because we're the children of a drunkard.
>
> —AMELIA E. JOHNSON, *Clarence and Corinne*

Amelia E. Johnson's *Clarence and Corinne* (1890), a relatively little-known and understudied novel of the black Woman's Era, is an evangelical conversion narrative published by the American Baptist Publication Society. Since it features racially indeterminate characters and hence does not meet the expectations of authenticity set for African American literature, and additionally since its author, unlike Frances Ellen Watkins Harper and Paul Laurence Dunbar—whose temperance narratives it is juxtaposed with—did not become popular for other works that would satisfy such expectations, *Clarence and Corinne* has not attracted much scholarly attention. Though at the time of its release it was read by a largely white audience, it was also promoted by black magazines as a significant novel by a black female author, thus its reception in the African American community largely paralleled that of *Sowing and Reaping*.

Like the mulatta melodramas discussed in part 1 of this book, the novel begins with the disintegration of a family, climaxes with a moment of anagnorisis, and ends with an extended family reunion. As several critics have argued, *Clarence and Corinne* parallels the tradition of white woman's fiction, as defined by Nina Baym, and the sentimental tradition as discussed by Jane Tompkins (Spillers xxvii; Tate 5–6; duCille 4, 17). It also uses reform discourse aimed at the expansion of the private sphere (Tate 14; Foreman, *Activist* 3–4), which further highlights its similarity to mulatta melodrama. Following the gender critique embedded in the hegemonic tradition, Johnson's text challenges unchecked patriarchal authority and women's financial dependence on men, rather than simply "reiterate the conservative female gender prescriptions of white culture," as critics highlighting its conventional gender representations have argued (Tate 98–99).[1] In my analysis, I show how Johnson's appropriation and revision of hegemonic ideologies and fiction formats may be read as meaningful and usable for the African American community at the turn of the twentieth century. Just like Harper's *Sowing and Reaping*, her text voices a trenchant if implicit critique, not only of gender politics, but also of the Nadir's free labor ideology, the capitalist marketplace, and patronage politics. I posit that the text's narrative parallels with mulatta melodrama make it possible to read these challenges as specifically targeted against white privilege.

In the following analysis, I specifically focus on *Clarence and Corinne*'s appropriation of temperance rhetoric and its gender politics. The tropes of temperance, in which reformers voiced their anxieties related to volition, compulsion, and contentment, enabled black writers of the Nadir such as Johnson to express the tension between structural determinism and symbolic self-determination, which was central for the newly freed community, whose post-Emancipation optimism clashed with the social realities of Jim Crow segregation, disfranchisement, sharecropping, and lynching violence. More specifically, Gabrielle Foreman convincingly shows that it is possible to read Johnson's temperance rhetoric—in particular, the images of white intemperance—as a response to the contemporary retrogressionist discourse of black bestiality, and more specifically to the southern temperance discourse, in which activists such as Rebecca Latimer Felton warned against "liquor and lust-filled Black threats to the nation" (*Activist* 166). Building on Foreman's insights, I argue that Johnson's challenging of the racial and gender politics of white masculine authority and her critique of the limitations of hegemonic femininity do not stem from her appropriation of woman's fiction and the rhetoric of the temperance movement alone, but are significantly informed by the emergent naturalist aesthetic, whose employment in the novel has not been explored by literary critics.

The Emergent African American Naturalist Aesthetic

Johnson's use of the drunkard motif in the novel resonates with naturalist narratives of decline and human bestiality, whose emergence coincided with the black Woman's Era. As June Howard has convincingly argued, the naturalist brute and the plot of decline both express and manage the fin-de-siècle anxieties of proletarianization. The naturalist brute draws on the former myths of savages and wild men, yet the figure is "imagined as living not outside the bounds of human society, not in the wilderness ... but within the very walls of the civilized city" (Howard 80). Those specters of atavism were primarily projected on the persona of the immigrant worker, who in the bourgeois imagination "easily succumbed to alcohol, sex, crime, and violence" (Melvyn Dubofsky qtd. in Howard 80). Thus, according to Howard, naturalism internalizes representations of brutality and positions it on the US territory, in US cities, and within US bodies. Consequently, the brute becomes more immediately threatening than the distanced exotic otherness. On the other hand, naturalist discourse manages the anxieties of proletarianization: it ethnicizes the working class and contrasts it with the passive observer, a position that the text frequently encourages the reader to identify with (Howard 70–103), and which largely parallels the function of the sentimental compassionate reformer. Although Howard's study has been quite rightly criticized for its overt emphasis on pessimism and decline, which many works in the US naturalist tradition actually transcend, the contrast between the brute and the observer and the power dynamics that she theorizes are definitely at the center of US naturalist classics. This opposition, in turn, is analogous to the tension between determinism and reformism, which is at the heart of *Clarence and Corinne*.

Even though Johnson's novel was published before the classical phase of American naturalism, Howard traces the origins of naturalist discourse in the United States back to 1877, the year of the first national strike (75), which, incidentally, is also the year that, according to Rayford Logan, marked the beginning of the black Nadir era. Such a reading adds additional support to M. Giulia Fabi's claim that *Clarence and Corinne*'s preoccupation with "the impact of the environment on the individual" and the representation of "urban outcasts ostracized by their poverty" can be referred to as "proto-naturalist" ("White Lies" 14). When approached in this way, the book foreshadows the canonical works of American naturalism released several years later. Additionally, Johnson's novel aptly illustrates the thesis, outlined in chapter 4, that the emergence of American naturalism was decidedly marked by a dialogue with temperance discourse and its twin techniques of sentimental compassion and melodramatic excess. This intersection, most vividly illustrated by the introduction of *L'Assommoir* to the United States via the temperance stage, is equally fundamental for Johnson's narrative. *Clarence and Corinne*, just like the theater adaptations of Zola, showcases the crucial interconnectedness of naturalism, sentimentalism, and melodrama in the postbellum United States.

Clarence and Corrine begins with images that prefigure the introductory chapters of Crane's *Maggie: A Girl of the Streets* (1893), frequently listed as the earliest work in the American naturalist canon and most likely the bleakest among its representatives (Holton 37). In both cases, young children, a brother and a sister, are positioned at the threshold of the unfriendly and unsafe private sphere of the drunkard's home. Crane's novel opens with the protagonists, Maggie and Jimmie, in a Bowery street (135–138). The significance of this image is highlighted in the depiction of their tenement, in which "a dozen gruesome doorways gave up loads of babies to the street and the gutter. . . . In the street infants played or fought with other infants or sat stupidly in the way of vehicles" (139). The building is represented as a woman in labor, whose grotesque body, riddled with a "dozen gruesome doorways" and "an hundred windows," merges with the external world. Although the house rented by the Burton family in Johnson's novel is a cottage, not a tenement,[2] the boundaries of its private sphere are equally volatile. "The rough door hangs on a single hinge" and is half-open; the palings are broken and the gate is never closed (5–6). The threatening character of the cottage (and its environs) is also conspicuously visible in the first illustration in the novel, which precedes the text. It shows that apart from the broken door, many other elements of the house, such as shutters and drainpipes, are in need of repair. As Clarence, the eponymous brother, stands on the threshold, about to enter the house, he seems to hesitate, which suggests his sense of insecurity. Moreover, even though at other times he acknowledges the rules of etiquette (10), in the picture he is not opening the door for his sister, Corinne, to enter ahead of him. She is standing one step behind him, which—especially when read in the context of contemporaneous standards of politeness—further indicates that the space they are about to enter is far from being secure.[3] The interior of the house is described as being even more dismal than when viewed from the outside. The narrator conscientiously lists a dirty, uncarpeted, broken floor, dusty and broken windows, and rough and rickety items of furniture (6), which foreshadow "the broken furniture, grimey walls, and general disorder and dirt" in *Maggie* (154). Both Johnson's and Crane's novels problematize the ideology of separate spheres and its easy equation of the safe idyll with domesticity, and danger with the public realm, in ways that echo mulatta melodrama's challenge to the ideology of the pastoral private realm. More specifically, both *Clarence and Corinne* and mulatta narratives focus on the dependents left without parental protection: mulatta melodrama's mixed-race daughters are abandoned by their fathers, just as Clarence and Corrine are left by Mr. Burton.

Even though the Burtons' home is far from the domestic ideal, Mrs. Burton can be read as a hyperbolic image of domestic femininity. Parallel to the "perverse patriarchs" in gothic fiction analyzed by Kari Winter, she "fill[s] [her] role so exactly that [her] behavior calls attention to the injustice embedded in patriarchal ideology" (22). Radically relegated to the private realm, as Hortense Spillers (not entirely correctly) pointed out, Mrs. Burton "never leaves her chair" (xxxi), where she is found dead in the second chapter by her daughter.[4] Almost all she does before her death is sit in the rocking chair, apathetic and listless. The continuous monotony of rocking is reinforced by Mrs. Burton's never-ending darning: she "draw[s] the needle and thread slowly back and forth" (8). Even though the narrative does use the sentimental metaphor of the "last sleep," it devotes more space to a depiction of naturalist details of her dead body: Mrs. Burton's "wide-open" "dull eyes" stare from her "stony face." Her son, Clarence, moves toward her "motionless figure" and lifts "one of the nerveless hands" (17–19). Limited to the nonprogressive rocking indoors and the motionlessness of death, the drunkard's wife in Johnson's text emblematizes interiority, passivity, submission, and nonproductivity. Her exaggerated performance of Victorian hegemonic femininity, strongly echoing the mulatta mothers discussed in chapter 2, highlights its tragic limitations and drives the novel's future-directed orientation.

The relationship of Mrs. Burton's representation to the discourses of nineteenth-century femininity can be further illuminated using an intertextual analysis since her chair resonates with two influential literary representations of women rocking. On one hand, it forms a dramatic contrast with the celebration of maternity expressed in a squeaking rocking chair in *Uncle Tom's Cabin*. "For twenty years or more, nothing but loving words, and gentle moralities, and motherly loving kindness" have come from the chair of an elderly Quaker mother, Rachel Halliday (Stowe 138). As Tompkins claims, Rachel Halliday "rules the world from her rocking chair," which is the center of a utopian matriarchal order rooted in motherhood (142).[5] Her domestic confinement is represented as a source of power in the form of moral suasion rather than an instrument of her oppression or symbol of domestic entrapment. Although Mrs. Burton is also represented as a mother in a rocking chair, her figure stands in polar opposition to the boundless maternal nurturance, care, and moral influence of Rachel Halliday. Her rocking chair is silent, not squeaky, but "her voice [rings] out sharp and harsh" (8). In light of this reversal, Mrs. Burton's representation can be read as a critical rewriting of Stowe's utopian, loving matriarchy. Rather than comfort, "cure head-aches and heart-aches," her inaction and endless rocking seem to be an expression of a death drive. As Freud famously argued, the instincts "impelling towards death" are of a "regressive ... character corresponding to a repetition-compulsion," and "their aim [is] the reinstatement of lifelessness" (54). Mrs. Burton's apathetic repetitive movement aptly illustrates that, and furthermore it presages her imminent actual death.

Rather than follow Stowe's sentimentalist politics, Johnson's image prefigures naturalist imagery. The rocking chair, as numerous scholars have argued, at the turn of the twentieth century becomes a fundamental image of static, illusory motion.[6] Since its most famous rendering is the dreaming and longing of Theodore Dreiser's Carrie Meeber, the rocking chair image is frequently read as closely linked to femininity. As Jennifer Fleissner argues, it exemplifies the key naturalist plot centered on "the modern young woman," which is characterized by "ongoing, nonlinear, repetitive motion ... that has the distinctive effect of seeming also like a stuckness in place" (9). Despite the conspicuous difference in their conditions, both Mrs. Burton and Carrie embody a lack of contentment. In Carrie's case, such continual lack of satisfaction motivates and leads to her social advancement from a poor second-generation German immigrant to a famous New York actress. For Mrs. Burton, the final outcome is dramatically different. In light of the scant information that Johnson's narrative offers the reader about Clarence and Corinne's mother—according to which she "[was] a giddy, thoughtless girl" and married James Burton against the advice of friendly people (43)—we may assume that she neatly falls into the category of the "speculative," "discontented" wife of a drunkard, who chooses "a 'flashy' and 'fast' young man for a husband" in hopes of quick social advancement (Parsons 88–90). In contrast to Carrie's daring moves, Mrs. Burton's speculations are stigmatized and punished by the poetic justice of Johnson's novel.

Dreiser's novel, however, also features another character who frequently sits in a rocking chair and who represents a plot of decline analogous to Mrs. Burton's. After Carrie leaves him when he is not able to maintain the lifestyle she has gotten used to, her lover, George Hurstwood, "[sinks] down in his chair" with "bereaved affection and self-pity." The text, just as Johnson's novel, emphasizes his inertia: "[a]t midnight he [is] still rocking, staring at the floor" (Dreiser 436–437). The trajectory of Mrs. Burton resembles George's declining plight more closely than Carrie's rise to fame. More specifically, the last words of Hurstwood before he commits suicide by gassing himself with methane and the very last lines in the original version of the text—"[w]hat's the use?" (498)—strongly resonate with some of Mrs. Burton's scarce utterances. She repeats that "[t]here's no use talking, and there's no use trying to be decent," and asks rhetorically, "[w]hat's the good of wishing for what can't be?" (7–8). Moreover, both characters' deaths are characterized by inactivity rather than drama. Both die in the darkness of their rented rooms. Hurstwood stretches for "rest" in the bed he does not own (498), and Mrs. Burton passes away in her chair and is first assumed to be asleep by Corinne (17). These parallels encourage the reader to perceive the figure of Mrs. Burton through the prism of Hurstwood's suicide as an expression of the death instinct, a conjunction of repetition and regression. Instead of providing maternal care for her children and making the rocking chair an extension of her womb like Rachel Halliday did, she desires to return herself to "an earlier condition" of the womb (Freud 54). Her rocking toward death simultaneously foreshadows Carrie's continuous lack of contentment and Hurstwood's final resignation.[7]

What further highlights Johnson's departure from the Quaker settlement of Rachel Halliday, which represents the Jeffersonian ideal of the self-sufficient homestead (Fisher 114), and what underlines the similarity between Mrs. Burton and both Carrie and Hurstwood, is the positioning of their chairs in a rented, rather than privately owned, space. As

Amy Kaplan argues, representations of rented spaces are central to late nineteenth-century realism and naturalism since they epitomize "the threatening repository of the unreal" (12), which stems from the coexistence of "seemingly mutually exclusive realities" in the wake of late nineteenth-century urban-industrial transformations (8–11). Rented spaces trigger bourgeois anxieties since they constitute the threatening realm of "the other half."[8] Seen through the prism of such connotations evoked by rented spaces at the time, the positioning of Mrs. Burton's chair in a rented cottage further highlights the specter of the menace and anxiety of proletarianization in the text. In the novel, the continuity and changelessness of the rocking motion do not provide maternal comfort in a time of dramatic social changes and the black Nadir but are represented as a fatal paralysis, which prefigures the circular images of rise and fall, listed as a signature mark of US naturalism by Donald Pizer (*Realism* 35–36, 189).

The seemingly paralyzed Mrs. Burton, however, is not a sentimentalized victim and does not evoke the reader's compassion in the text. As the intrusive narrator critically comments, "[Mrs. Burton] had lost all energy and ambition, doing hardly anything save to sit and brood bitterly" (42–43). This judgment is repeated more explicitly in the words of Miss Rachel Penrose, the owner of the cottage, and it is further reinforced on the narrative level through the story of the children left unprotected. As Foreman states, "Mrs. Burton is situated as a poor victim and passive victimizer at best. At worst she is a bad mother complicit in her children's ruin" (*Activist* 161). Her failure as a parent and her marginal presence in the text strongly echo the representation of Belle's thoughtless mother in Harper's *Sowing and Reaping*.

The narrator's lack of sympathy for Mrs. Burton becomes even more visible when her home is contrasted with the ideal household of Helen and Mary Gray, two orphaned sisters who eventually take over the responsibility for Clarence and Corinne. Their "picturesque white cottage" with a blooming garden is kept "neat, cool, cozy," even though the younger sister, Mary, who is the main housekeeper, is a "frail and sickly" invalid (29). She is introduced, like Mrs. Burton, "sitting" in a chair, but she is placed "by the open window" and productively engaged in sewing (30). Likewise, her older sister, Helen, sits in a rocking chair after a day's work as a teacher. "Strangely"—as the text points out—the invalid, "[i]nstead of giving way under the strain of nursing the sick child every day, . . . seemed to gain strength" (83). In contrast to Mrs. Burton's self-absorption and her ultimate confinement to the home, the sisters are actively and generously engaged in the life of their community, and as Fabi argues, their household represents "a viable non-capitalistic relational economy" ("White Lies" 18). Significantly, the model household of the two sisters foreshadows the novel's happy ending, which is also based on the relationships between two pairs of siblings. Thus the novel, although conservative in its representations of femininity, emphasizes the significance of women's work and demonstrates the dangers of female passivity, dependence, and the loss of "ambition."

The Raceless Drunk

On the narrative level, *Clarence and Corinne* incorporates the drunkard narrative as defined by Elaine Frantz Parsons. In this formulaic plotline, a father's drinking problem typically leads to the disintegration of the family (Parsons 11). In Johnson's novel, as a result of the father's intemperance, the mother dies and the children are left homeless and are separated. In his deathbed confession, reported in a newspaper, the father admits that "he had deserted [his children] at the death of their mother, because he did not wish to be burdened with them" (177). Whereas Mrs. Burton represents a hyperbolic embodiment of domestic femininity, her husband represents a hyperbolic failure of male authority. As Parsons demonstrates, the effectiveness of the drunkard narrative was inherently connected with the anxieties about masculinity that it triggered: the influence of alcohol became inextricable from the loss of masculine mastery, and such a correlation was recognized both by temperance activists and their opponents. "The drunkard . . . was not a true man because he was unable to exert his will over his body and interests" (55).[9] Drunkard narratives evidence time and again that any man can become addicted to alcohol. To quote from T. S. Arthur's *Ten Nights in a Bar-Room:* "In a tavern . . . an angel could scarcely remain without corruption" (208). Accordingly, in *Clarence and Corinne*, it is also emphasized that it is "that dreadful stuff, whisky" which leads to the tragedy at the beginning of the novel rather than any innate weakness of Mr. Burton (19).

Nevertheless, as historians have argued, the significance of the slave to the bottle metaphor and other tropes of temperance express anxieties that are not limited to alcohol abuse (Epstein 100–103). In antidrink discourse, men's addiction is exposed as one of the systemic weak links positioned at the juncture of the patriarchal culture and capitalism rather than treated as an individual and isolated phenomenon. Furthermore, although temperance literature highlights the problem of the "bottle," it needs to be seen in the wider context of the nineteenth-century reform rhetoric of self-discipline, which metonymically links alcohol with other stimulants of appetite—from meat to a modern urban lifestyle—and inebriety with other weaknesses, forces, and desires—from sensual passion to pecuniary greed (Epstein 125–127; Dorsey 116–120; Parsons 78–81). When read as an element of such an extended disciplinary discourse, Johnson's representations of intemperance automatically evoke a whole family of ideas, many of which rhetorically target two interconnected loci of power: masculinity with its passions, and capitalism with its speculative marketplace. Their interconnectedness also explains why the text assigns the roles of villains to figures as different as the intemperate Mr. Burton and accumulating Miss Penrose. As will be argued in the last part of this chapter, these can be additionally linked with the racial privilege of whiteness in the novel, which strongly resonates with the failed patrician patriarchy in the mulatta melodrama discussed in the first part of *The Nadir and the Zenith*.

In temperance narratives, masculine authority is further challenged by the fact that the fallen drunkard's complement is a "redeeming woman," who through her temperance work can gain access to the public sphere and control over the lower-class neighborhoods (Parsons 51–52). Accordingly, in *Clarence and Corinne*, the neighboring women immediately take charge of the Burtons' house and children. As in many texts representing "woman's fiction," the novel juxtaposes good and bad guardians (Baym 37). Miss Penrose, the antagonist in the novel, is a middle-class, financially secure woman, whereas the good guardians—the earlier-mentioned Gray sisters—are extremely poor. Such a juxtaposition can be read as an expression of anxiety over the bourgeoisie's control of lower-class neighborhoods guaranteed by the former's economic privilege. In a way that parallels Harper's juxtaposition of Mother Graham and Belle's blindness to economic exploitation, Johnson's novel exposes the limits of compassion of privileged reform activists by representing a respectable woman with a complete lack of empathy for her disadvantaged protégée, whose condition clearly alludes to slavery. After Mrs. Burton's death, Miss Penrose takes Corinne to her house and trains her as a domestic. The girl is "overworked and underfed," while the guardian "pays her no wages" and forbids her to leave the house. Even though the novel represents a reformist strand of literature, Johnson is clearly aware that reformist protection might easily turn to slavery-like economic exploitation. As Sánchez-Eppler argues, unlike the freed black population, female northern charity workers and teachers "remained largely blind to the ease with which their humanitarian concern could produce patterns of authority and subordination, dominance and dependence not wholly dissimilar from those associated with the ministrations of the plantation mistress" (*Touching* 7).

What further intensifies the antagonist's exploitative attitude is the fact that she owns the house in which the children live, and the rent is not commensurate with the dilapidated conditions of the cottage. The Burtons "paid but little, but more than the place was worth" since it "was only fit to be torn down" (44). After the mother's death and father's abandonment, the children are told "it would be no longer their home," even though the cottage is closed up rather than rented to someone else (40). Such positioning of the capitalist landlord and reformer in one and the same person foreshadows the depiction of the Dalton family in *Native Son*, Richard Wright's classic of twentieth-century black naturalism published exactly fifty years after Johnson's novel.

Apart from its parallels with the sentimental drunkard narrative, the depiction of Mr. Burton also resonates with the discourse of the brute, as outlined by Howard. "Drink-maddened," he "knock[s] and beat[s]" his wife, who as a result has a swollen eye and other signs of "ill-usage" (8, 15, 7). After he falls asleep, he becomes a dehumanized object, a "figure" in the "form of a man" (15–16). In the narrative, he is just as immobilized as his wife. In the evening, the children find him lying upon the bed unconscious. In the morning, he is in the same position: "on the bed, across which he had thrown himself, hat, boots, and all" (17). He does not utter a single comprehensible sentence, which is in contrast both to the well-developed grammatical statements that come from his children and to the general eloquence of the drunkard in temperance literature, in which he frequently later becomes the chief speaker against alcohol (Parsons 23–24). After the children ask him about the reasons for their mother's death, Mr. Burton mutters a brief "I dunno" and leaves the room, not to be mentioned until the end of the novel (18). This ideally fits Howard's characterization of the naturalist brute as "necessarily inarticulate," "the animal who does not use language and is named but never names" (81). Mr. Burton's representation thus evokes analogous hegemonic anxieties to those triggered by the other brutes: the threats of proletarianization and masculine insecurities that vexed the US imagination at the turn of the twentieth century. These fears, however, are not mediated by any of the othering devices that characterize naturalism. Mr. Burton is not ethnically marked; he is not an inhabitant of the slums. He is a nondescript all-American male like the characters in the drunkard narrative.

Another element that emphasizes the novel's affinity with naturalist images of drinking and signals a departure from the drunkard narrative is its lack of compassion for the husband, which is central for the hegemonic temperance story (Parsons 21). In antidrink literature, the white and middle-class identity of the protagonist encouraged the target reader's identification with the inebriate. Additionally, the reader's sympathy was evoked by the narrative's focus on the moment of the fall of the "finest young man in our neighborhood," to quote again from *Ten Nights in a Bar-Room* (11). In contrast, as Foreman has pointed out, "Johnson offers no backstory to affirm Mr. Burton's essential goodness" (*Activist* 168). Moreover, whereas the typical drunkard narrative focuses on the causes, *Clarence and Corinne* presents only the results. Since, as Philip Fisher claims, "[t]o give the narration a past is to recognize and implicitly adopt the point of view of the oppressor," the shift from causes to results sharpens Johnson's critique of masculine authority (116). Mr. Burton is represented only at the beginning of the narrative, and he is only barely conscious, hence the narrative presents a much less sympathetic and more critical image of the patriarch than the typical drunkard's story.

In temperance discourse, the seductiveness of alcohol was frequently gendered as feminine and positioned in the multiethnic metropolis, where a naïve young man arrived from a pastoral village (Parsons 110; Dorsey 91–92). This rhetoric capitalized on the long-standing, nostalgia-drenched dichotomy between the innocent country and corrupt city and conflated it with residual representations of the temptress (Parsons 86, 100–125). Mr. Burton, however, is not tempted to take his proverbial first sip in a town saloon by a scheming foreigner or a prostitute. Even though, as Fabi points out, the family's deterioration follows its urban migration ("White Lies" 14), Mr. Burton is already "given to hard drinking" before his marriage (43). Thus Johnson's novel complicates the standard rural-urban dichotomy with its nostalgic undertones. The origins of patriarchal intemperance are located in the country, and it is only transferred to the city by the forces of urbanization. Such a configuration firmly locates the text in the antinostalgic and future-oriented politics that characterize the African American novel of the Nadir.

Johnson's work, therefore, draws on the drunkard narrative, which is primarily visible in Mr. Burton's lack of ethnic markedness and in the narrative logic, in which his intemperance leads to family disintegration. Additionally, her novel incorporates the emergent naturalist discourse of the brute, which is evidenced by Mr. Burton's violence, inarticulacy, and immobility as well as the narrative's lack of compassion for his fate. Due to such a combination, Johnson's text evokes the contemporary anxieties of proletarianization without projecting them onto ethnic minorities, problematizes middle-class reform activism, and rejects urbanization and European immigration as the primary origins of intemperance. Also, the gender criticism of the novel draws much of its significance from such recasting of women's reform and temperance rhetoric and its blending with the emergent naturalist aesthetic. Johnson uses the image of the fallen drunkard to challenge the patriarchal order and presents exaggerated hegemonic femininity to highlight its absurd limitations.

Racial Ambiguity & Mulatta Melodrama

Since the gender and class politics of the black Woman Era's fiction are necessarily entangled with race politics, an analysis of Johnson's tropes of temperance also requires scrutiny of this intersection in the novel. As different readings of postbellum black fiction demonstrate, the use of racial indeterminacy by a black author may paradoxically serve as a factor that highlights the raced character of whiteness and strips it of its invisibility. Although Hortense Spillers argues that race is not a key intratextual factor in Johnson's text and that the novel does not respond to any of the "putative urgencies of coeval black life in the United States" (xvii), many later critics see racial neutrality as an efficient political weapon for the black woman author at the turn of the twentieth century (Christian xxvii; Tate 12; duCille 62). As Fabi argues, it allows Johnson to deal with issues of urban poverty and discrimination, and at the same time, it does not perpetuate specific racial stereotypes of black vice and squalor ("White Lies" 14). She points out that the racial indeterminacy in the novel is radical and subverts the automatic assumption about the whiteness of the portrayed community: "if nothing indicates the characters' blackness, nothing indicates their whiteness either" ("Taming the Amazon?" 239). She also emphasizes the potentiality of the indeterminate characters' blackness. Specifically, Johnson's focus on the protagonists' dark eyes encourages black readers to identify with them (Fabi,

"White Lies" 10). Tate accordingly includes *Clarence and Corinne*'s female characters as examples of what she labels as specifically a "black heroine's text" of self-determination and fulfillment (4). Foreman, although positing that racial indeterminacy is an example of "simultextuality," claims that the narrative gains more political power and gives more narrative pleasure for black readers when its milieu is read as specifically white (*Activist* 162). She argues that Johnson's depiction of a potentially white dysfunctional family challenges contemporary southern temperance rhetoric, which racialized drink and positioned "the drunk black man" as a threat to the white household, and especially to the mythical purity of white womanhood (164–168). As my analysis has shown, it should be added that Johnson is able to engage in a dialogue with the black brute rhetoric more effectively because her narrative combines the sentimental drunkard's story with naturalist imagery of the brute. If the father, positioned as a menace rather than a victim or an object of reformers' sympathy in the novel, is read as white, he constitutes a more pinpointed response to the black brute rhetoric than a typical protagonist of the drunkard narrative.

The failure of the white father, which leads to family disintegration, also resonates with the separation of slave families, whose central significance for mulatta melodrama was discussed in part 1 of this book. In several novels, when patriarchal control is terminated, the mulatta, in a melodramatic recognition scene, learns that she is black and not white, enslaved and not free, and in some cases, such an anagnorisis is followed by a resultant peripeteia in which the narrative moves from an Anglo-American to African American setting in order to showcase the protagonists' self-determined identity and self-reliance. Mr. Burton's failure to protect his family analogously forces his daughter into slavery-like servitude. This narrative parallel may further complicate the claims about racial indeterminacy in the novel. If Johnson's text is read in conjunction with the changes in racial identities of characters in such postbellum novels as Pauline Elizabeth Hopkins's *Hagar's Daughter*, Frances Ellen Watkins Harper's *Minnie's Sacrifice* and *Iola Leroy*, or Julia C. Collins's *The Curse of Caste; or, The Slave Bride*, the race of the original milieu can be read as connotative of whiteness, while the final destination of the characters' narrative trajectories is connotative of blackness. Such an experimental intertextual reading would diachronically reconcile divergent synchronic readings of racial indeterminacy in Johnson's novel. The text would then potentially criticize white patriarchy and the limitations of hegemonic feminine domesticity at the beginning, and its closure would envision a happy, extended, horizontal black community, made up of brothers and sisters. *Clarence and Corinne*'s employment of the aesthetic and affective structures characteristic of mulatta melodrama, which was a well-established and influential genre by the 1890s, added to the potential impact of Johnson's temperance novel.

Before the community is built, however, the eponymous brother and sister need to face many oppressive experiences. Corinne's life after her mother's death and her father's abandonment of the family brings clear associations with slavery. As I have mentioned earlier, she is heavily exploited by the stern Miss Penrose, who does not pay her and forbids her to leave the house. The child is constantly hungry, and there is not "a moment of the day which she [can] call her own" (47). Furthermore, Corinne's guardian, although a member of a church herself, does not allow the girl to attend the services, which showcases not only her religious hypocrisy but also her inability to see in Corinne a fellow human being, possibly due to the race difference. Characteristically, Miss Penrose is the only character in the novel whose eyes are described as gray (rather than dark or unspecified), and thus she might be positioned as white in contrast to black-eyed Corinne (50, 9; see also Fabi, "White Lies" 10). Hence Johnson's novel evokes the specters of slavery and uses them primarily to comment on the conditions of contemporary domestic service and child labor. If we read the race of the children as black, the text more specifically comments on "a second slavery" of the Nadir and the failure of the free labor ideology (Foner 562–563).

These associations with slavery are less visible in Clarence's subplot, as the text more parallels mulatta melodrama's focus on female characters. His figure bears more resemblance to the protagonist of Paul Laurence Dunbar's debut novel, which is discussed in the following chapter. Yet Clarence's declaration of his desire to "run away" in a conversation with his sister does recall black males' dilemmas in slave narratives (9).[10] Both exemplify the conflict between a wish for escape and devotion to female relatives, whose escape is less plausible. Most of the images of Clarence's oppression highlight his powerlessness, stemming from his class and age, but the novel also points to the tragic influence of the omnipresent eugenic logic that sees his heredity as his destiny. Clarence claims that "people don't even want to give" anything to do to "old drunken Burton's boy" because of his parentage (19–20). Later, after he experiences the competition and corruption of the capitalist marketplace and finds himself homeless and penniless, he is afraid that a naturalist plot of decline necessarily awaits him: "I was born to be down-trodden—crushed!" (116). In Clarence's subplot, intemperance and capitalism are juxtaposed as the two obstacles to the boy's self-determined success, which reflects the positioning of his father and Miss Penrose as villains in the novel as well as the coupling of inebriates and insatiable capitalists in *Sowing and Reaping*. Ultimately, just as Reade in his adaptation of Zola lets the female protagonist live and ends the play in a triumph of reform optimism, Johnson's protagonists overcome the limitations of heredity, and the novel ends with the founding of an extended household of Clarence and Corinne and their spouses, who also happen to be siblings. The brotherly and sisterly bonds guarantee greater gender equality than the traditional heterosexual romance. Additionally, the quartet of brothers and sisters represents the favorite professions of woman's reform literature: a teacher and a doctor.

In contrast to the postbellum black male text, which as Tate argues dramatizes "the frustrated moral claim of black patriarchal desire" (67), black women-centered novels, notably including mulatta melodrama (as demonstrated in the first part of the book), repeatedly present white patriarchal failure. This is also exemplified by Johnson's novel if we read the opening milieu as connotative of whiteness. Her rhetorical strategy to draw on temperance discourse and recast it so that it foreshadows the emergent naturalist aesthetic enables her to challenge white masculine authority and expose its lack of mastery. Johnson's assaults on masculinity play into a wide range of interrelated turn-of-the-twentieth-century anxieties of the dominant classes: proletarianization; the sense of crisis of hegemonic masculinity, especially visible among defeated Confederates; and southern fears of black supremacy. Johnson rewrites temperance scripts to voice anxiety about the reformers' patronage politics and the abusive aspect of economic privilege. What she presents as a foundation of the happy ending in the corrective vision of her novel is, in fact, a horizontal cohesive community of brothers and sisters, which emerges as a response to the vertical power structures of capitalism and the limitations of upper-class patronage. As such, it differs from Dunbar's *The Uncalled*, whose narrative trajectory is linear and individualist rather than circular and relational, despite the many striking similarities between the two novels, which are discussed in the following chapter.

CHAPTER 7

Enslavement to Philanthropy, Freedom from Heredity
PAUL LAURENCE DUNBAR'S
THE UNCALLED

> A genuine attachment had sprung up between the
> lonely old woman and the friendless boy.
> —AMELIA E. JOHNSON, *Clarence and Corinne*

> The man stood smiling down into the child's face: the boy,
> smiling back, tightened his grasp on the big hand. They were
> friends from that moment, Eliphalet Hodges and Fred.
> —PAUL LAURENCE DUNBAR, *The Uncalled*

Like the two novels discussed in the previous chapters, Paul Laurence Dunbar's *The Uncalled* (1898) is largely absent from the canonical debates about American or African American fin-de-siècle literature. At the time of its release by Dodd Mead, a publisher who had released Dunbar's volume of poems *Lyrics of Lowly Life* two years earlier, Dunbar's text was read by a mostly white audience even though he was reviewed as a black writer, a "man of pure African blood," to quote from W. D. Howells's introduction to *Lyrics of Lowly Life*. Although, after Howells's characterization, all of Dunbar's texts were read as belonging to the African American tradition, in the twentieth century the race significance of the novel was considered as negligible by most critics. The racial indeterminacy of its characters and its blending of naturalism and sentimentalism violated the regime of racial authenticity and placed it outside both US and African American canons.[1] This absence comes as a surprise when one considers that in dramatic contrast to the almost unknown *Clarence and Corinne* and the only recently rediscovered *Sowing and Reaping*, *The Uncalled* is one of four novels authored by the most famous black writer of postbellum belles lettres who, although frequently misread, has never disappeared from American literature anthologies.

In this chapter, I attempt to partially fill in this gap in the critical discourse. I will use Dunbar's debut novel to show how it simultaneously draws on sentimentalism and naturalism, and as such it aptly illustrates the overlapping spaces between the two aesthetics that are the focal point of *The Nadir and the Zenith*. Furthermore, I demonstrate that there are many parallels between *The Uncalled*, on one hand, and, on the other, *Sowing and Reaping* and *Clarence and Corinne*, the two racially ambiguous black novels that recast the tropes of temperance analyzed in the two preceding chapters. This resonance suggests that Dunbar, in his first novel, enters into a dialogue with the black Woman's Era, represented by both Frances Ellen Watkins Harper and Amelia E. Johnson, which evidences the dominant position of this still-understudied body of African American writing during the Nadir. It is impossible to provide a comprehensive reading of *The Uncalled* without a recognition of Dunbar's signifying on the black Woman's Era.

As I have suggested earlier and demonstrated in the analysis of *Clarence and Corinne*, although naturalism and sentimentalism are conventionally perceived as two distinct, almost oppositional, traditions, they share significant features. Thematically, both are primarily interested in the underprivileged, and they highlight the significance of external influences. Structurally, their sensational plotlines, abounding in coincidences, have been defined against the expectations for verisimilitude and plausibility set by literary realism. *The Uncalled* exemplifies these general similarities between sentimentalism and naturalism as well as their more specific shared concerns, such as social reform and intemperance. The dynamic tension between naturalism and sentimentalism in the novel strongly echoes A. E. Johnson's evangelical narrative, yet whereas her work represents protonaturalism while being firmly grounded in sentimental rhetoric, in contrast, Dunbar's debut is a naturalist text with strong residual traces of sentimentalism (cf. Jarrett, "Second-Generation Realist" 290). In both novels, the protagonists come from the underprivileged class and are orphaned at the beginning of the narrative, but none of them is burdened with the naturalist plot of decline (Howard 142).

Like *Clarence and Corinne*, Dunbar's work opens with a depiction of a lower-class neighborhood. Characteristically for naturalism, it is interpolated with philosophical enunciations about natural instincts that are suppressed by culture. Yet it avoids typical naturalist pessimism, since the main character, Fred Brent, manages to transcend both his biological heredity of alcoholic parents and the inhibiting middle-class conditioning of his adoptive milieu. Like mulatta melodrama and A. E. Johnson's racially ambiguous novel, *The Uncalled* begins with a family disintegration and ends with a family reunion. Whereas in mulatta melodrama and in *Clarence and Corinne* it assumes the form of a circular trajectory that closes with a homecoming, in *The Uncalled*, the father-son reunion, although it follows the return of both men to their hometown, does not end the novel. Fred linearly moves on: he goes back to his city life and gets married to a namesake of Dunbar's wife, Alice. Thus, although many critics have attempted to frame Dunbar as a city-phobic and disturbingly nostalgic writer (Morgan 233), the linear trajectory oriented toward the future, toward modernity, but also toward the urban context optimistically closes with an announcement of marriage, thus disproving such claims and firmly grounding *The Uncalled* in the antinostalgic and antipastoral body of black Nadir novels.[2] The different but similarly euphoric endings of A. E. Johnson's and Dunbar's novels largely stem from their residual sentimental optimism regarding social change, which is guaranteed by a genteel identification and empathy with the oppressed as well as with narrative coincidences that reunite broken families.

As will be shown, overall Dunbar—following in A. E. Johnson's footsteps—merges, recasts, and bends naturalist determinism, sentimental compassion, and melodramatic coincidence to tailor the tropes of temperance to his own authorial purposes. Just like Harper and A. E. Johnson, Dunbar's text undercuts the image of the benevolent agent of uplift. He uses the metaphors of slavery to depict the power of the newly adopted environment of a respectable middle-class home, which strongly echoes A. E. Johnson's depictions of Rachel Penrose. Moreover, akin to Harper's and Johnson's meticulous attention to the socioeconomic context, Dunbar, in his appropriation of naturalism, privileges social rather than biological determinism. Thus his debut novel supports a belief in the decisive impact of the environment, which logically correlates with a conviction about the effectiveness of reform work and the possibility of social transformation. On the other hand, by representing Fred's charitable guardian as an enslaver, *The Uncalled* complicates the sentimental discourse of empathy and uplift and problematizes the opposition between the benevolent agency of the reformer and the helplessness of the brutalized victim in a way parallel to Harper's and A. E. Johnson's temperance texts. When the blends of naturalism, sentimentalism, and melodrama in the three novels are read in the context of the racial politics of the Nadir, the three authors analyzed in this part of the book successfully balance their hope for change of the Jim Crow regime with consideration of the structural conditions that powerfully shaped the lives of the oppressed black minority. The tropes of temperance that they all employ in their writing are instrumental for the effectiveness of their rhetoric.

Freedom from the Bottle

As this book argues, one of the most significant points of intersection between naturalism and sentimental reform fiction is their preoccupation with alcohol use and intemperance. In naturalism, alcohol highlights human powerlessness, whereas in sentimentalism it serves to construct images of victimhood and thus to increase its affective force. *The Uncalled*'s embeddedness in both aesthetics is also closely related to its recasting of the canonical temperance narrative of a fallen drunkard who abuses or deserts his family. The novel presents the story of Fred Brent, a boy deserted by his intemperate father and orphaned by his maltreated and intemperate mother, an account that uncannily echoes the plot of A. E. Johnson's narrative.

The similarity between Dunbar's debut and *Clarence and Corinne* (as well as *Sowing and Reaping*) is further highlighted by the author's decision to avoid unequivocal racial markers. This choice was reinforced by Dunbar's cooperation with a mainstream publisher, Dodd Mead, which marketed the book to a mostly white audience. On the other hand, at the time of his novelistic debut, he was already the most popular black poet in the United States, and the critical reviews of the novel contrasted it with his dialect poetry (which, as mentioned earlier, was praised for its racial authenticity by Howells). As Dunbar's race was a key factor in the readers' responses to the novel, the racial identity of *The Uncalled*'s characters was not as transparent as in the case of a text by a white author. As a result, contemporaneous readers could entertain the possibility that the novel's protagonists were black, and Dunbar, in turn, might have used the racial indefiniteness of the protagonists and their intemperate parents as a strategy that distances the narrative from the contemporary retrogressionist images of black drinking, analogously to Harper and A. E. Johnson.

The retrogressionist mythology was instrumental in the escalation of anti-black terrorism—including white-on-black lynching and rape—after the Civil War. At the turn of the twentieth century, this oppressive ideology had not withered. In fact, owing to the growing fears of proletarianization, frequently cast in ethnic and racial terms, and the rise of the naturalist brute in American literature, it reinforced its appeal (see Howard 80). As Sherri Broder argues, although "temperance advocates used the term [brute] to refer to all men who abused their families by their addiction to alcohol, by the late nineteenth century the brute had become a short-hand for immigrant and African American men" (100). Such fin-de-siècle controlling images of black intemperance can be illustrated with a short but representative quote from Thomas W. Dixon's *The Leopard's Spots* (1902), a classic of retrogressionist literature, which depicts an African American soldier disrupting a wedding ceremony to kidnap the white bride: "The burly figure of a big negro trooper from a company stationed in the town stood before them. His face was in a broad grin, and his eyes bloodshot with whiskey. He brought his musket down on the floor with a bang" (125). This grotesque characterization of the figure is deeply related to his prior alcohol use: the large mouth dominates his face in an uncontrolled smile, and his red eyes lend it a threatening edge.

A less explicit but largely similar image can be found in a contemporaneous naturalist classic, namely, Theodore Dreiser's "Nigger Jeff" (1901) (see Pizer, "Theodore Dreiser" 337). Unlike Dixon, Dreiser, even though he had not been a loud champion of racial equality and integration, was definitely not an explicit advocate of retrogressionism. In his articles, he argued that "there is room for a black republic or a black empire" and that many African Americans evince "intellectual power" (*Political Writings* 33). Yet the text's eponymous character is referred to as a "groveling, foaming *brute*" (44; emphasis added), and throughout the story, he is depicted as a dehumanized, animalistic, and grotesque beast. Lynched for accosting a white girl, he explains that he "didn't go to do it. [He] didn't mean to dis time. [He] was just drunk" (43–44), which positions alcohol at the center of the narrative. Pizer, discussing the text in a formalist way, disregards the factor of race and argues that Jeff simply represents sexual desire, "a dominant, uncontrollable force in almost all of Dreiser's principal male characters" ("Theodore Dreiser" 336). Yet although "sexual desire may not lead to the destruction of such a figure as Frank Cowperwood," Jeff is tortured and killed because his act is perceived as living proof of a retrogressionist mythology, not as a result of a universal human or male desire. Both Dixon's black soldier and Dreiser's Jeff embody and serve to further racialize uncontrolled desires: drinking both evinces their lack of restraint and additionally increases their indulgences. Thus Dunbar's debut novel, written at the turn of the twentieth century, dissociates itself from such dominant retrogressionist images of blackness through the elimination of racial markers, just like Harper and A. E. Johnson.

By choosing racially ambiguous characters, Dunbar avoids the retrogressionist connotations in their depictions of alcohol use, but he also departs from the hegemonic, racially unmarked temperance rhetoric. As has been mentioned, in the traditional drunkard narrative as defined by Elaine Parsons, the enslaved drunkard is "a particularly promising young man" who falls because of "external influences": he is tempted by older men or by palatial urban saloons (11). Thus, in direct contrast to the drunken brute of retrogressionism, he is cast as a victim, not an aggressor, and evokes the reader's sympathy, not fear or outrage. One of the central metaphors of this discourse was "slave to the bottle," which identified intemperance with slavery and evoked in abolitionist discourse an effect akin to sympathy for the enslaved. Even though its use goes back to antebellum days, as Parsons observes, it "continued well after emancipation, even to the end of the century" (28). In the late 1800s, the sentimental metaphor of enslavement to one's appetites began to resonate with the emergence of naturalist determinism. Determinist skepticism regarding human volition was largely analogous to the sentiments expressed in temperance rhetoric. Hence, although devoid of the emotional excess that characterizes sentimentalism, the naturalist denial of free will largely overlaps with the rhetoric of enslavement and victimhood in reform fiction.

In contrast to the hegemonic drunkard narrative, Dunbar does not use the metaphor of slavery to depict intemperance. Furthermore, just like A. E. Johnson (but unlike Harper), he avoids sentimental empathy for the inebriate. Fred's drunkard father is not represented as "a promising young man," and an explanation of the causes of his intemperance is absent from the novel. Such an absence of the character's background history precludes both the reader's sympathy and identification with Tom Brent. He is explicitly introduced in a dialogue as "a brute" who used to give his wife "sich beatin's... when he was in liquor you never heerd tell of," so she has divorced him (6). Brent reappears as a reformed temperance activist, to die just before the narrative's ending. Despite his marginal presence in the novel, he performs a significant narrative function. Throughout the text, due to the dominance of social Darwinism and eugenics, his haunting image determines society's attitudes toward and expectations for his son, just as in the case of A. E. Johnson's Clarence. Since, again just like Clarence, Fred struggles to separate from his heritage and emerges triumphant, Dunbar's narrative undermines the theory of hereditary determinism and the idea that "blood will tell" (*The Uncalled* 69). As Gene Jarrett rightly argues, the ending of *The Uncalled* "resists portraying Fred, and even his father, as insurmountably degenerate" (293). The novel's ambivalent closure—in contrast to the final destruction by alcohol or complete redemption that characterize hegemonic drunkard narratives—does not offer easy sympathy for the inebriate and does not position him as a victim. At the same time, like the black Woman's Era writers, *The Uncalled* expresses a belief in change and transformation.

Dunbar's *The Uncalled*, apart from revising the drunkard narrative in its plot, also offers an implicit metatextual commentary on temperance discourse and sentimentalism. Its young protagonist, Fred, exposes the paradox of sympathy for inebriates and, more specifically, the celebration and renown of reformed drunkards such as John Gough, who, as I indicated, is histotextually alluded to in Harper's novel. When thinking about his father's conversion, Fred cannot forget about his unreformed past, that is, "Tom Brent, temperance advocate, sometime drunkard and wife-beater" (223). Fred is outraged that "his father, after having led the life he had, should make capital out of relating it" (228). As a former minister, Fred refers to biblical rhetoric in his divagations, but rather than embrace it he challenges its logic, which constitutes a decided departure from Harper's and A. E. Johnson's use of the Bible and signals the dominance of naturalist philosophy over evangelical sentimentality in the novel: "[T]hey tell us that there is more joy over the one lamb that is found than over the ninety and nine that went not astray; it puts rather a high premium on straying" (230). The narrative enables Fred to vent his anger at his father, which is much more elaborately depicted than their understated reconciliation preceding the imminent death of old Tom Brent. His father's homecoming is important for Fred because he is able to tell him that he has ruined his life and "left [him] a heritage of shame and evil" (237). In contrast to anger, forgiveness does not come easily: "Could he forgive him? Could he forget all that he had suffered and would yet suffer on this man's account?" Only the moral suasion of his adoptive father, Eliphalet, enables Fred to say, "I forgive you, father." Thus *The Uncalled* enters into a dialogue with the sentimental sympathy for the drunkard in temperance rhetoric, both by revising the plot of the temperance tale and by an explicit rhetorical attack against it in Fred's internal monologue, focused more on anger than forgiveness.

There is one more way in which Dunbar rewrites the drunkard story, for which "the maleness of the subject" was traditionally central (Parsons 21). Even though the inebriate father is the dominant image haunting Fred in Dunbar's novel, the text also presents his mother as intemperate. Strongly resembling the mother of Stephen Crane's Maggie, rarely sober "Margaret had never been a particularly neat housewife," and her house is dilapidated and "miserably dirty" (6). The image of female drinking is also repeated toward the end when, during a temperance meeting, the audience listens to "experiences from women whose husbands had been drunkards and from husbands whose wives had been similarly afflicted" (218). Thus the text problematizes the easy identification of intemperance with masculinity, which was wholeheartedly embraced by the black Woman's Era writers. This peculiar gender equality parallels the lack of racial markers in Dunbar's novel. When read in the context of determinist philosophy and eugenic discourse, *The Uncalled*'s downplaying of race or gender markers deemphasizes the significance of internal, biological, and hereditary factors. Moreover, as men can also be victims of their wives' intemperance, the text further challenges the correlation between black masculinity, the stereotypical drunken brute, and its white female victims.

The novel undermines the notion of hereditary intemperance and the determinist force of "demon drink" in yet another way. Just like *Clarence and Corinne* and *Sowing and Reaping*, it does not depict any moment when a drunkard's child is drawn to drinking, although Fred, like Clarence, migrates to the city and is exposed to its mythical temptations. Such behavior stands in stark contrast both to the sentimental drunkard narrative and to the naturalist classics dealing with the notion of alcohol use. The central significance of the saloons that determine the fates of characters is already signaled in titles such as Arthur's *Ten Nights in a Bar-Room* and Zola's *L'Assommoir*—whose meaning, in the slang of the French working class, denotes a cheap tavern, and it directly refers to the bar frequented by its characters, whose still floods the room to unavoidably "inundate the vast pit that was Paris" (Zola 42; cf. Baguley 73). Analogously, the saloon exerts a powerful influence over young men in Crane's *Maggie* and *George's Mother* or Jack London's *John Barleycorn*, whose protagonists enter saloons at the first invitation. London's autobiographical persona states that "here was John Barleycorn, prevalent and accessible everywhere in the community": "I found saloons, on highway and byway, up narrow alleys and on busy thoroughfares, bright-lighted and cheerful, warm in winter, and in summer dark and cool" (953). More figuratively, in *Maggie*, "the open mouth of a saloon call[s] seductively to passengers to enter" (30): a female anthropomorphization of a barroom lures its male victims in the dark corners of the city. *George's Mother* applies a parallel technique to introduce the bar that drives the novella's plot of decline: they "made toward a little glass-fronted saloon that sat blinking jovially at the crowds. It engulfed them with a gleeful motion of its too widely-smiling lips."

In stark contrast to these naturalist classics, in *The Uncalled* the protagonist easily avoids the seductive calling of saloons and accessible alcohol. After his arrival in Cincinnati, Fred is "surprised and sickened" when he sees children fetching beer for their parents or "a mother holding a glass of beer to her little one's lips" (203). Moreover, the narrative stops him from entering a beer garden, which his roommate wants to patronize to introduce Fred to city life. Thus the novel balances attention to the meaningful impact of the social context with the protagonist's self-determination and volition. The use of the intemperate parents helps Dunbar underline the possibility to transcend biological heritage, but he also portrays the difficult struggle against the eugenic logic that was all-pervasive during the Nadir in a way that echoes *Sowing and Reaping* as well as *Clarence and Corinne*. Whereas the metaphor of slavery was used to talk about intemperance in the hegemonic reform discourse, Dunbar, Harper, and Johnson use intemperance to talk about the powerful impact of social expectations rooted in eugenic thinking and the possibility of self-determined action and advancement. In *The Uncalled*, images of slavery are reserved for a different theme.

Slaves to Charity

In Parson's analysis, "slaves to the bottle" are complemented by the "redeeming women" who reform them. Dunbar's novel uses metaphors of and allusions to slavery, yet these do not concern intemperance per se but rather the female figure who "charitably" takes over control of the drunkard's broken home in a way that strongly resonates with A. E. Johnson's depiction of Rachel Penrose. In *The Uncalled*, Fred is adopted by the strict and unmarried Hester Prime and forced by her to enter the ministry. The stifling religiosity and discipline of his guardian are represented as parallels to slavery and bondage. At some point he rebels and decides to leave his new family. Fred announces then that he is "going to spend the first few days just in getting used to being free," to which Miss Hester bitterly responds that he "think[s] that [he has] been a slave" (194). Even though he politely objects, his later thoughts on the powerful impact of religious education actually reinforce the simile of enslavement: "He had hated the severe discipline of his youth, and had finally rebelled against it and renounced its results as far as they went materially. This he had thought to mean his *emancipation*" (209; emphasis added). Thinking about Hester Prime's training, Fred uses vivid metaphors of physical bondage, such as "a chain that galled his flesh" (57), "iron bands" (209), or a "yoke whose burden he hated [but which] he was placing about his own neck" (210). Even away from her, he feels "bound, irrevocably bound" (170). "He had run away from the sound of 'right' and 'duty,' but had not escaped their power" (210). Hence the rigid religiosity and controlling influence of Hester Prime are presented as analogous to slavery and antithetical to freedom and growth. These images strongly echo the representation of Corinne's guardian, Rachel Penrose, who treats the girl protagonist as a slave. Corinne is "overworked and underfed," her custodian "pays her no wages," and the girl is confined to the space of the household. Thus, in both texts, genteel agents of uplift are represented figuratively as slave owners.

Additionally, there are many more detailed parallels between the two guardians. Both are referred to as "stern," and their judgmental perspective on the lower class is highlighted. Just as A. E. Johnson's Rachel Penrose cannot understand how lower-class people "could be so *shiftless*" (22–23; emphasis added), Hester Prime's voice is "a trumpet of scathing invective against the *shiftlessness*" of the "denizens of the poorer quarter" (34; emphasis added). She concludes that Fred's mother "ought n't never to 'a left her husband" and "the child is better off without her example" (7–8; emphasis added). In the emergent eugenic rhetoric, shiftlessness, next to crime and disease, was a code word for racial and class difference. As Robin D. G. Kelley contends, the notion of shiftlessness was central to what he calls the "Cult of True Sambohood," an ideology that soothed white anxieties about black presence on the labor market (21–22). Accordingly, the use of the term by the two white female guardians possibly invests their protégées in particular, and the lower class in the novels in general, with a racial difference.³

The whiteness and privileged position of the guardians are further emphasized in the representations of their *white gaze*. Whereas in *Clarence and Corinne* the "[k]een grey eyes of the seamstress" are depicted as looking sharply at people (50), in *The Uncalled*, Hester Prime has a "cold grey eye" that phallically "impales" her lower-class neighbor with "an annihilating glance" (27). As I have pointed out in my analysis of A. E. Johnson's text, the guardian's judgmental "grey" eyes are contrasted with the—racially ambiguous but potentially raced as black—dark eyes of the children. In Dunbar's debut novel, Hester Prime's stern gray glance is juxtaposed with Fred's "brown eyes," which "sparkl[e] with amusement" (26). Additionally, the protagonist's name is quite likely an allusion to Frederick Douglass, who employed Dunbar as his secretary in 1893 and died three years before *The Uncalled* was published. In an elegiac poem written after Douglass's death, Dunbar praises "his power" and "kindness" and states that:

> he was no soft-tongued apologist;
> He spoke straightforward, fearlessly uncowed.
> *(Lyrics 8)*

Significantly, using the ambiguous first-person plural pronoun—standing for humanity, the black community, or when used as a royal "we" instead of the first-person singular to refer to Dunbar himself—the speaker emphasizes the close intimacy between him/them and Douglass:

> we have touched his hand,
> And felt the magic of his presence nigh.
> *(Lyrics 9)*

Hence, if the scant bodily markers of the gray and brown eyes and the histotextual allusion to the most renowned black leader of all time are taken into account, Fred's guardian's gaze, apart from class superiority, may also be imbued with racial condescension.

Like Rachel Penrose's house, Fred's adoptive household is very respectable and pristine, which follows the domestic ideal in the sentimental tradition (Tompkins 143, 178). The devotion to cleanliness also parallels the critical gaze of the narrator-observer in naturalist fiction, which painstakingly records the lower-class lack of hygiene and marks it with an ethnic difference (Banerjee 122–123). Dunbar, like A. E. Johnson, problematizes the identification of a clean household with moral purity and thus challenges the ideology of genteel respectability, while at the same time highlighting the dominance of such thinking. The devotion to the cleanliness of the middle-class guardians is manifested in *The Uncalled* already at the beginning of the story, when Hester Prime takes over the cleaning of the dilapidated and dirty household of the deceased Mary Brent. Her own home is accordingly immaculate, and it accurately mimics the patronizing attitude of the owner. Miss Prime's windows look at the "mean street" like "a pair of accusing eyes" (32). The "prim cottage" is "painted a dull lead colour," and—in a dramatic contrast to the heterotopic gardens from mulatta melodrama discussed in chapter 2—the flowers are "planted with such exactness and straightness" that they look "cramped and artificial and stiff as a party of angular ladies dressed in bombazine." Unlike A. E. Johnson's novel, Dunbar's text explicitly expresses the lower-class perspective on Hester Prime's "maidenly neatness" (12). Mrs. Warren, one of Fred's mother's friends, expresses her sympathy for the boy: he "won't dare to breathe from this hour on" (31). Even though Mrs. Warren does not evoke much sympathy in the narrative—after the funeral, she robs the orphaned Fred of his mother's belongings—her judgment regarding the guardian's approach to upbringing is largely correct and challenges the idea of noble charity. Overall, the images of the compulsively clean household highlight the condescension of naturalist observers and dispute the goodwill of sentimental angels of charity.

Hester Prime, like the almost villainous Rachel Penrose in the more melodramatic reality of *Clarence and Corinne*, shows a dramatic lack of understanding and empathy for her lower-class protégée, and, as has been demonstrated, she restricts his life in a manner metaphorically compared to slavery. Her patronizing attitude and privileged economic position connotatively comment on middle-class reform activities. According to Broder, in the 1890s, in response to labor unrest, conservative reform activists expressed a "desire to exert more control over the immigrant and African American working class" (18). Dunbar's *The Uncalled*, as well as A. E. Johnson's 1890 text, might constitute responses to such increased policing. Significantly, both novels imagine the reform workers as females that are raced as white. This can be read as a critical commentary on the evangelical missionary zeal of privileged white women and their crusades in lower-class neighborhoods, which provided them with an opportunity not only to introduce social change but also to exercise control over the disadvantaged and improve their own position in US society's power structures.

Additionally, the ease with which Dunbar's and A. E. Johnson's guardians take charge of the orphans' homes and the orphans themselves can be linked to their unmarried status. That such a correlation forms a pattern is evidenced by the fact that Belle from Harper's novel is also single when she takes over the Gough household. The link between the automatic, effortless manner with which the reform women take over the control of other people's homes and children and "spinsterhood" is subtly suggested in *The Uncalled*: "Miss Hester move[s] about the room, placing one thing here, another there, but ever doing or changing something, all with *maidenly neatness*" (12; emphasis added). As Anna Lepine argues, without a full "home and hearth" of her own, "the spinster unsettled established notions of domestic space by seeming to be 'at home' anywhere" (v). Partly as a result of such an expansive presence, at the turn of the twentieth century "the single woman was a threatening figure, suggesting women's independence from men" (Holmes 68). In their critiques of the increased policing of the "other half," Harper, A. E. Johnson, and Dunbar activate these anxieties, marking them with anti-elitist class and possibly race resentments.

Blood Does Not Tell: Emancipation from Heredity

Dunbar's dialogue with temperance discourse and naturalist philosophy is most conspicuous in his novel's preoccupation with the notion of heredity. As has been mentioned, in contrast to both hegemonic temperance fiction and naturalist classics, *The Uncalled* does not show any moments when Fred is drawn to drinking, despite the proximity of mythical urban temptations. In Dunbar's debut novel, the protagonist struggles thus not as much with his biological heredity as with the eugenic thinking of society. Fred, since childhood, is confronted with the idea that "blood's bound to tell, an' with sich blood as he's got in him [no one knows] what he'll come to" (23). People object to his entrance into the ministry because it is "ag'in' nature" that "Old Tom, drunken Tom, swearin' an' ravin' Tom Brent's boy [should become] a preacher!" (114). A manipulative animalistic metaphor is used to support this eugenic logic: a "panther's cub ain't a-goin' to be a lamb." As a minister of his small congregation, Fred constantly feels that he is "fighting old Tom

Brent" (179). The struggle with the image of his father accompanies the climactic twist when Fred resigns from his position as the church's minister. After the elders oppose his decision not to stigmatize a young pregnant girl, he decides to leave and explains that he is "drunken Tom Brent's son" and "would rather be the most roistering drunkard that ever reeled down these streets than call [himself] a Christian and carouse over the dead characters of [his] fellows" (187–188). Fred uses the image of his father to highlight the hypocrisy of the congregation and subsequently migrates to the city to leave behind his "past of sorrow and degradation" (222). Dunbar's explicit challenge to Christian hypocrisy might seem at first to be a decided departure from the evangelical and deeply sentimental works of the black Woman's Era writers. Yet both Harper and A. E. Johnson—although in more subtle ways—also criticize the hypocrisy of religious zeal exhibited by two villainous and economically privileged characters: the "excellent" and "religious" Mrs. Roberts, who exploits the wife of a drunkard, Mary Gough, in Harper's novel (*Sowing* 129); and "pharisaical" Rachel Penrose, who makes "a great show of piety" but simultaneously takes advantage of Corinne and does not even try to convert her in A. E. Johnson's narrative (57). These images also resonate with abolitionist reform discourse and its reliance on "anti-Christian irony," which pinpoints the slave owners' many "abuse[s] of Christian theology" (Heermance 86).

The struggle against eugenic logic does not end with Fred's move to Cincinnati. Instead of being able to free himself from his father's shadow, the protagonist is forced to face him in his new hometown. Through a melodramatic coincidence, the city, instead of providing anonymity, reunites the son with his father. Now a newly reformed drunkard, Tom Brent has become a temperance advocate. Fred feels that he "comes and lays a hand upon" him and that he is "more the son of Tom Brent to-night than ever before" (222). After the encounter, Fred's "eyes [are] bloodshot, his face [is] pale, his step [is] nervous and weak" (224), and his landlady assumes that he is intoxicated. Thus at this moment, his father's former intemperance is mirrored in what the novel tellingly refers to as Fred's "beastly condition"—the contact with his father has symbolically touched the son with a temporary inebriety. As has been mentioned, the Oedipal confrontation, after much inner struggle on Fred's part, ultimately ends in reconciliation. Characteristically, Fred does not take up his father's position, but on the contrary, his father takes the room and bed of the son. Dunbar thus rewrites the scene of a drunkard's reformation in his child's bed, which, according to Karen Sánchez-

Eppler, is a staple image in temperance fiction ("Temperance" 1). In contrast to the scenes analyzed in her article, Fred is empowered by the reunion with his father, which enables him to separate himself from the haunting images of hereditary intemperance. The reconciliation ends Fred's Oedipal crisis: he is able to enter into a relationship with a woman and get married.

The Converted & the Uncalled

Despite the many parallels between Harper's, A. E. Johnson's, and Dunbar's texts, there is an important difference; namely, their representation of the conversion experience. As if issuing a challenge to the evangelical rhetoric of the black Woman's Era and its narratives—including *Sowing and Reaping*, serialized in the *Christian Recorder*, and *Clarence and Corinne*, subtitled *God's Way* and originally published by the American Baptist Publication Society—Dunbar tellingly entitles his debut novel *The Uncalled*. Such an anti-evangelical gesture can be read as a reaction to the specific black women's tradition, but it also fits the all-American context of what Ann Douglas famously dubbed "the feminization of American culture," a process in which the "Victorian lady and minister" changed the literary scene (8). In the course of the nineteenth century, the religious sphere was domesticated and, as a result, became part of the women's realm. Just as in the temperance narrative analyzed by Parsons, in sentimental conversion narratives, a woman was positioned as a redeemer. As Jane Tompkins states, in sentimental rhetoric women served as mediators between the unconverted and God (219). Women's religious mission was strongly related to the rise of the ideology of suasion—the specifically feminine power of moral influence (Dorsey 116). This special ability to affect the behavior of children, males, and females who did not meet the expectations of Victorian "true womanhood" enabled women to transcend the limits of the domestic sphere since, as Tompkins argues in her generous reading of the sentimental tradition, "religious conversion" was positioned as "the necessary precondition for sweeping social change" (132), and the "process of redemption" could "change the entire world" (131). Conversion was supposed to lead to social transformation, as it helped to build a community alike in interests and feelings, and the woman's power of influence was instrumental in its emergence.

Dunbar's novel recasts the hegemonic scenario of women's religious mission as analyzed by Douglas and Tompkins and signifies on the scenes of conversion and reformation in *Sowing and Reaping* and *Clarence and*

Corinne. In contrast to the religious and moral epiphanies of Joe Gough, Clarence, and Corinne, the protagonist of Dunbar's text does not have a minister's calling. To the contrary, the awakening and emancipation he experiences in the novel result from his resolution to leave the ministry (170, 209), which is the first autonomous decision he makes. The ostentatiously religious women in the novel—again as in Harper's and A. E. Johnson's texts—are not successful "mediators between God and the unredeemed" (Tompkins 219). Hester Prime, as has been demonstrated, is depicted as an agent of enslavement. She is paired with the minister's daughter, who is unfavorably judged by the narrator as a "fool" and a "shallow woman," who with complacency "skims the surface of tragedy and thinks that she has sounded the depths" (121). The true redeemer in the first part of the novel is "Brother Hodges," Fred's adoptive father, Eliphalet. This "kindly-faced man" is introduced during a service he conducts. His supplication is "very tender and childlike." He leaves "all to God, as a child lays its burden at its father's feet, and many eyes were moist as the people rose from their knees" (17). Hodges's prayer strongly recalls the biblical verse frequently repeated by female characters in A. E. Johnson's novel: "[c]asting all your cares upon him; for he careth for you" (65, 73, 109). When Fred leaves Dexter, "[p]oor Eliphalet ... br[eaks] down and we[eps] like a child" (197). The incident takes "sunshine ... out of the old man's life." Not only is Eliphalet a more successful mediator between "God and the unredeemed," but he is also represented as a better parent than his wife. Thus Dunbar gender-bends the traditional domestic narrative. Whereas in woman's fiction or in black Woman's Era novels the protagonist is typically a female orphan and the redeeming figure is also a woman, in Dunbar's novelistic debut, both the orphan and the compassionate mentor are male. Such a refiguration clearly challenges the sentimental tradition's celebrations of mothering and of the feminine power of religious suasion that were strategically appropriated by the black Woman's Era writers and activists.

On the other hand, like *Clarence and Corinne*, *The Uncalled* also problematizes the moral corruption related to the city in the sentimental tradition. In contrast to Hester Prime's predictions that in "a strange city full of wickedness an' sin," Fred might fall victim to "temptation sich as is layin' in wait fur young men" (195), migration to the city helps him renounce stifling religiosity, grow, develop, and find fulfillment. Significantly, his stern guardian is juxtaposed with an urban woman, whose influence is represented in a much less restrictive way. Fred meets "a young lady ... who is very much interested in church work, and somehow she has got [him] interested too, and [he goes] to her church every Sunday" (245). Alice's influence is positioned as parallel to that of Fred's adoptive father, Hodges: "'I been a-prayin' fur you,' [Hodges] said. 'So has Alice,' replied the young man, 'though I don't see why she needs to pray. She's a prayer in herself'" (254). Thus Dunbar, like A. E. Johnson and even Harper (who blames intemperance on men's rather than women's influence), challenges the stereotypical ideas of urban temptations and seductive women. Even though during his first days in Cincinnati the protagonist admits that the "city indeed was full of temptations to the young" (206), the euphoric closure of the novel, which ends in Fred's settling down in the metropolis and in his marriage to Alice, disproves the uniform identification of the city with sinfulness and depravity. Fred's story represents the positive side of urban immigration, which was common for millions of turn-of-the-twentieth-century Americans. When Fred's narrative is read more specifically as a commentary on the situation of the African American community, it represents the Great Migration of black people to the northern cities as a possible way to emancipate themselves from the Jim Crow regime. As will be argued in chapter 8, such a euphoric ending in Dunbar's debut novel needs to be considered in any reading of his most influential work of fiction and his only novel firmly set in the black urban community, *The Sport of the Gods*, which is frequently misinterpreted as a city-phobic text (Morgan 233).

As has been demonstrated, Dunbar's novel decidedly belongs to the tradition of US naturalism, which, as its most insightful critics have demonstrated, incorporates residual traces of sentimentalism and melodrama. In its blending of these aesthetics and its engagement with contemporary reform discourse and determinist philosophy, *The Uncalled* signifies on the black Woman's Era rhetoric, which is exemplified in its many uncanny parallels with A. E. Johnson's evangelical narrative and significant similarities to Harper's temperance text. All three novels examined in this part of the book revise the drunkard narrative and sentimental conversion narrative, and they focus attention on balancing meaningful impacts of the social context and external influences, on one hand, and the characters' self-determination and volition on the other. The racial indeterminacy of the characters in the novels enables the authors to avoid the immediate associations with the black lower-class population and retrogressionist ideology. Furthermore, if the racial indeterminacy is read as white, then the texts evoke images of white male brutality and white female drunkenness, thus even further challenging the ideology of retrogressionism.

Alternatively, it is possible to read the protagonists in all three texts as black, which offers a narrative of the self-determined uplift of the black community. In the case of Harper, it is quite conservatively set within the boundaries of a single town and is figured as a union of the two model protagonists: noble reformer Belle Gordon and paragon of compassionate manhood Paul Clifford. A. E. Johnson's novel strongly draws on the circular trajectory characteristic for mulatta melodrama and its family reunions, and it ends with a homecoming and a euphoric formation of two symmetrical nuclear families; such an excessive doubling might symbolically call into being the newly free black community. Finally, the linear plot of Dunbar's debut novel ends with the promise of an independent nuclear family in the city. His later text, *The Sport of the Gods*, is formed by more complex and conflicting plotlines, and, as the following chapter will demonstrate, it recasts many elements that are centrally important for the works analyzed in both parts of this book, such as a future-oriented narrative arc, a linear trajectory of urbanization, or a drunkard's decline.

CHAPTER 8

※ ※ ※

Metropolitan Possibilities & Compulsions
THE MULATTA AND THE DANDY IN PAUL LAURENCE DUNBAR'S *THE SPORT OF THE GODS*

> The city has its cunning wiles, no less than the infinitely smaller and more human tempter.... Half the undoing of the unsophisticated and natural mind is accomplished by forces wholly superhuman.
>
> —THEODORE DREISER, *Sister Carrie*

> To the provincial coming to New York for the first time, ignorant and unknown, the city presents a notable mingling of the qualities of cheeriness and gloom.... The subtle, insidious wine of New York will begin to intoxicate him.
>
> —PAUL LAURENCE DUNBAR, *The Sport of the Gods*

> I began to feel the dread power of the city; the crowds, the lights, the excitement, the gaiety, and all its subtler stimulating influences began to take effect upon me. My blood ran quicker and I felt that I was just beginning to live. To some natures this stimulant of life in a great city becomes a thing as binding and necessary as opium is to one addicted to the habit.
>
> —JAMES WELDON JOHNSON, *The Autobiography of an Ex-Colored Man*

"Reading Dunbar is not a harmonious experience," as Gavin Jones fittingly argues (203). This is due in part to the breadth of the multigeneric overall oeuvre, produced against the odds of his short, fourteen-year professional career, which in all comprises fourteen volumes of dialect poetry and standard English poetry, 103 short stories, numerous journalistic essays, musical lyrics, dramas, and four novels. Furthermore, each of his novels represents a different genre: from a racially ambiguous bildungsroman (analyzed in the previous chapter); to a historical novel; to a romantic western; to a melodramatic naturalist work set in the black Tenderloin (which is the focus of this chapter). But the nonharmonious nature of his work primarily stems from the conflicting discourses that his works echo, juxtapose, and dialogize. Among these contradictory strands that Dunbar engages in through his heteroglot writings, scholars point to the plantation tradition and minstrel show ideologies of blackness, which many of his critics read as an embrace of dominant white racism (G. Jones 187). The collective speaker in Dunbar's most frequently quoted poem declares that:

> We wear the mask that grins and lies . . .
> With torn and bleeding hearts we smile,
> And *mouth with myriad subtleties.*
>   (*Lyrics* 167; emphasis added)

Yet relatively few readers have fully appreciated the soundlessly or indistinctly mouthed "myriad subtleties" in his writings.[1] This is conspicuously visible in the traditional readings of his dialect poetry, short stories set in the South, and popular lyrics taken at their "face-grinning" value. It can also be traced in the studies of his most frequently discussed work of fiction, *The Sport of the Gods* (1902), the popularity of which is largely determined by the fact that, unlike his other novels, it is firmly set in the black community and as such meets the requirements of racial authenticity set for African American fiction. Most critics accept it as a "decidedly naturalist work of fiction" (Murphy 150); impose the simplistic clichés regarding naturalist decline on the text's many voices, perspectives, and subplots; and as a result fail to see the irony, polyvocality, and Dunbar's other signifying practices.[2] Based on my reading of his only "black" novel and selected "black" drama pieces he produced at the same time, I attempt to do better justice to their heteroglossia and black-on-white as well as black-on-black signifying practices, and to show how this not only extensive but also complex corpus synthesizes the central ideological, rhetorical, and aesthetic tropes of African American fiction of the Nadir. Dunbar, in *The Sport of the Gods* and two ragtime dramas from the same period—*Uncle Eph's Christmas* (1899) and *Jes Lak White Fo'ks* (1900)—recasts the two central tropes analyzed in *The Nadir and the Zenith*: the *mulatta* and the *drunkard*. He does so in conflicting ways that highlight, celebrate, and criticize the interracial, cross-class, intersectional cultural processes shaping the African American community in the era of the Nadir, including its interracial violence and allegedly fixed racial divisions. His last novel's melodramatic poetics are just as ambivalent as the mulatta melodramas analyzed in the first part of this book, and, analogously, they preclude any ultimate euphoric reconciliation. Dunbar's signifying on mulatta melodrama is visible both in the mulatta figure's central presence and in the significance of musical vaudeville in his 1899–1902 works. In entering into a dialogue with the racially ambiguous works analyzed in the second part of the book—most notably with his own first novel and Amelia E. Johnson's *Clarence and Corinne*, *The Sport of the Gods* recasts the tropes of temperance in a way that does not employ sentimental empathy. Dunbar's departure from sentimentalism in his work is best exemplified by its unapologetic depiction of the black drunken dandy and the intemperate protagonist's plunge into the urban whirlpool of bohemian New York City.

In contrast to *Clarence and Corinne*, which emerges as a protonaturalist text dominated by the sentimental paradigm, and even more decidedly the naturalist *The Uncalled*, which is nevertheless devoid of any traits of decline or philosophical pessimism, the immersion of *The Sport of the Gods* in the naturalist tradition is unquestionable. The novel presents a story of urban migration, and it ends with a closure akin to *Sister Carrie*, Dreiser's classic published only two years earlier. Both endings are melodramatic and deeply ambiguous, a fact many critics fail to see. Yet it is precisely such ambivalence and melodramatic elements—rather than an unequivocal pessimist determinism—that firmly position *The Sport of the Gods* in the specifically US tradition of naturalism (Pizer, *Realism* 9–37). In Dunbar's novel, a whole black southern family—rather than a single girl as in Dreiser—migrates to the northern metropolis, and such a multicharacter narrative echoes the familial relationality that underlies the chaotic, unruly poetics of mulatta melodrama. Much like in the complex diegetics of *Clotel*, in *The Sport of the Gods* the reader follows the family disintegration and partial reunion of the Hamiltons. Additionally, there are three white family members who serve as the black family's foils. Moreover, the novel's plots are also driven by several minor but well-sketched characters, such as the cynical black bar patron Sadness Williams, the light-skinned singing actress Hattie Sterling, or the white journalist Skaggs. Such decentering clearly departs from the disciplined and linear narrative of *The Uncalled*; it simultaneously echoes mulatta melodrama's multicharacter structure and foreshadows the modernist novel. *The Sport of the Gods* thus aptly exemplifies Pizer's argument that, formally, the "naturalistic novel stands on the threshold of the modern novel" (*Realism* 39), which is additionally emphasized by its metropolitan setting, typical for modernism.

Exiled from their hometown after the father is wrongfully accused of theft and imprisoned, the Hamiltons move to New York's Tenderloin, and despite their successful attempts to find employment, their life in the city is shaped by the "increase[d] seductiveness of moral/sexual license" (Ross 145), and in the case of the young male protagonist, it leads to a tragic ending. As a result of his intemperance and frustration, in an attack of drunken fury, Joe kills his beloved, Hattie Sterling, and "the stroke that took her life kill[s] him too" (97). The mother's plot ends on a more ambivalent note: she unknowingly enters into a bigamous union with an abusive racehorse man who is melodramatically and conveniently killed a few days after her first husband's discharge. The father, Berry Hamilton, is released from prison after a melodramatic plot twist, yet instead of a traditional soothing resolution and happy family reunion, the reader finds the old Hamiltons in their southern cabin living a life that is "not happy" (118). Their return is predominantly read as univocally tragic and largely comparable to Joe's decline: "the implied author sees no hope for blacks," argues Bernard Bell, and most critics follow his suit (73; cf. Tsemo 25–26). Yet as Bridget Tsemo convincingly argues, rather than serve as a submission to the plantation tradition and its subservient blackness, the couple's trajectory embodies "the possibilities of social uplift because of their transformative, personal experiences in the North" (26). Whereas it is true that the novel represents both the "good" and the "evil" side of urban reality, and that Dunbar's journalistic texts about the North such as "The Negroes of the Tenderloin" assume a paternalistic racial uplift perspective toward the naïve migrants and their children, whose fate is painted in bleak shades, Thomas L. Morgan correctly argues that the "desire to make Dunbar a 'city-phobic' writer ... misses [the] use of the city" in his complete oeuvre (233).

A Mulatta in Melodrama

The critics' forceful, centripetal imposition of the plot of decline and glaring critique of northern migration onto the entire novel and its intensely centrifugal form is best visible in a closer look at the dominant interpretations of the young female protagonist, Kitty Hamilton. Significantly, she is referred to as "that little *light* girl," whose "hair was very *black and wavy*, and some strain of the *South's chivalric blood*, which is so curiously mingled with the African in the veins of most coloured people, had tinged her skin to *an olive hue*" (45, 47; emphasis added). She echoes the African American mulatta trope, and just like Brown, Harper, Hopkins, and Chesnutt's young protagonists, she is melodramatically juxtaposed with her mother, Fannie. Nevertheless, Dunbar's account significantly recasts the matrilineal oppositions outlined in chapter 2 of part 1. In contrast to the mulatta melodrama characters who go back to the South and to her own mother's homecoming trajectory, Kitty is most likely the first New Negro woman in African American fiction who decides to migrate and remain in the North rather than stay in or return to the South. Although the mulattas discussed earlier are represented as vehicles of inescapable modern mobility and nondomestic femininity, the closures find them safely anchored in their new homes in the reconstructed South (Iola and Mary/Clotelle from Brown's 1867 version of the novel) or buried next to their white fathers' homes (Hagar and Rena). Kitty, closely echoing Dreiser's Carrie, does not choose to get married or settle down, and she does not die at the end of the text. In this way, she foreshadows the female characters facing the dilemmas of metropolitan modernity in the later works by Jessie Fauset, Nella Larsen, Wallace Thurman, or Ann Petry. Although it is clear that Dunbar does not construct her plotline as unequivocally euphoric, neither is it as decidedly dysphoric as the critics tend to argue.

She does not join Crane's Maggie (cf. DuRose 144; S. Wilson 130), who dies in the industrial "oily" waters of the East River after having possibly prostituted with "a huge fat man in torn and greasy garments," with "great rolls of red fat," and "brown, disordered teeth, gleaming under a grey, grizzled moustache from which beer-drops dripped" (197). In contrast to the bleakest of Crane's narratives, Kitty's story is much more ambivalent and bears a much stronger resemblance to Dreiser's *Sister Carrie*. As Robert M. Dowling correctly suggests, "Kitty finds she has a talent for the stage in the mode of Theodore Dreiser's Carrie Meeber" (87). As will be shown, Dunbar signifies on Dreiser's masterpiece in even more revealing and particular ways. Critics have recently rescued *Sister Carrie* from the limitations imposed by clichéd understandings of naturalism, such as the reductive plot of decline and the lost lady trope (Den Tandt 101), and some have argued for the protagonist's "ontological"—rather than materialist—"desire" and for her "spiritual"—rather than simply economic—"upward mobility" (Leypoldt 122–133). The open ending of Kitty's plotline, with its minor but indicative portents of decline—her "voice . . . not as good as it used to be" and "beauty . . . aided by cosmetics" (100)—is no more hopeless than the last tableaux in *Sister Carrie*, depicting the eponymous character "sitting alone," driven by "the pursuit of beauty," and filled with an indefinite longing destined to remain unsatisfied. As will be demonstrated, Kitty's plot can also be read in an empowering way that appreciates her artistic endeavors. This optimistic potential becomes especially visible when *The Sport of the Gods* is juxtaposed with Dunbar's other writings, accounts of the theater authored by his contemporary and collaborator James Weldon Johnson, and the parallels with *Sister Carrie*.

The strong parallel between Dunbar's and Dreiser's texts is suggested in the metaphor-packed epigraphs that represent the city's influence on the small-town migrant. Both authors focus on the dangerous aesthetic appeal of the urban landscape. In *Sister Carrie*, the metropolitan "beauty, like music, too often relaxes, then weakens, then perverts the simpler human perceptions," and in *The Sport of the Gods*, if the migrant has "any eye at all for the beautiful, he cannot help experiencing a thrill as he crosses the ferry over the river filled with plying craft and catches the first sight of the spires and buildings of New York" (37). In Dreiser's novel, Carrie is tempted by the city's "cunning wiles" that a few lines later find their personification in "the infinitely smaller and more human tempter" Charles Drouet (4). Introduced as the "masher," his "dress or manners are calculated to elicit the admiration of susceptible young women" (5). Akin to the "always 'bejeweled'" seductress from temperance fiction, represented, for example, by Aurelia from Hopkins's *Hagar's Daughter* (Parsons 110), he has "large, gold plate buttons, set with the common yellow agates known as 'cat's-eyes,'" "several rings—one, the ever-enduring heavy seal—and from his vest dangle[s] a neat gold watch chain" (6). Dreiser hence gender-bends the Victorian cliché of the "bejeweled" attractive *temptress* armed with feminine wiles into a masculine dandyist "*tempter*" with "a strong physical nature" (4, 6; emphasis added).

Significantly, Drouet is a salesman, and his wiles, just like Carrie's desires, blend the sexual and the commercial.

Whereas, in his depiction of the urban forces, Dreiser recasts the seduction narrative frequently incorporated in temperance literature, Dunbar more explicitly draws on the drunkard story and the intemperate's insatiable appetite for stimulants to represent the process of urbanization: "a something will take possession of him that will grip him again every time he returns to the scene and will make him *long and hunger* for the place when he is away from it.... The subtle, *insidious wine* of New York will begin to *intoxicate* him" (37; emphasis added). Dunbar's metaphors, although they refer to all the migrant Hamiltons, strictly follow the gender pattern of the male drunkard's seduction plot (Parsons 110), and ultimately they apply only to Joe Hamilton's drunken fall, which is discussed in the latter part of this chapter.

In contrast to Joe, Kitty does not accept beer from their New York hostess (42), and she does not enjoy the beer served to her by Hattie Sterling (74), who notices that and herself ceases to "drink anymore" during the meeting (76). Although they are frequently paired in critical accounts of the novel, Kitty's response to the city's "insidious wine" varies from Joe's, and the difference goes beyond Dunbar's adherence to the traditional gender binaries of the drunkard story as introduced by Parsons. Their differing attitudes are explicitly stated in the novel:

> Joe and Kit were differently affected by what they saw about them. The boy was wild with enthusiasm and with a desire to be a part of all that the metropolis meant.... No such radical emotions, however, troubled Kit's mind. She too stood at the windows and looked down into the street. There was a sort of complacent calm in the manner in which she viewed the girls' hats and dresses. Many of them were really pretty, she told herself, but for the most part they were not better than what she had had down home. There was a sound quality in the girl's make-up that helped her to see through the glamour of mere place and recognise worth for itself. Or it may have been the critical faculty, which is prominent in most women, that kept her from thinking a five-cent cheese-cloth any better in New York than it was at home. She had a certain self-respect which made her value herself and her own traditions higher than her brother did his. (39–40)

This difference in their reactions echoes the way the two are subtly contrasted at the novel's opening: Kitty is simply "pretty," "cheery," and can "sing like a lark," whereas Joe "from scraping the chins of aristocrats came to imbibe some of their ideas, and rather too early in life bid fair to be a dandy" (2). His dandyist aspirations are reminiscent of Charles Drouet's, whereas the tragic closure of his gradually declining plotline echoes the criminality and suicide of Charles Hurstwood. Unlike Joe, who is city-struck with the "spruce clothes" of "red-cravated, patent leathered" "young fellows" in general and William Thomas—their first guide to black Tenderloin—in particular (39–41), Kitty keeps her "coolness" and is hardly impressed with this "loquacious little man," "the idol of a number of servant-girls' hearts, and altogether a decidedly dashing back-area-way Don Juan," and she leaves him a "disappointed suitor" (40, 49). She is "sure she [finds] the young man 'fresh'" (41). The epithet—when juxtaposed with *The Uncalled*'s Hester Prime's accusations that Freddie's "a-gittin' too fresh" and "a-getting' mannish," whose meanings "crush" the "manly" protagonist of Dunbar's first novel (78)—takes on decidedly negative connotations and demonstrates that Kit is looking for a disciplined and "manly," not "mannish," partner. Characteristically, both in Dreiser and in Dunbar, the city's wiles are metonymically represented through male dandyist self-fashionings of swaggering young men rather than seductive women, which will be relevant in my later discussion of the black bohemia.

As Jonathan Daigle rightly observes, "Before the Hamiltons unpack at their West Twenty-seventh Street apartment, [they] already identify their new home with 'coon' shows," and their guide, Mr. Thomas, "defines the Tenderloin in terms of the theater" (644). The theater's impact on the characters serves as a hyperbole for their citification: Fannie Hamilton is ambivalently "divided between shame at the clothes of some of the women and delight with the music" (47), whereas Joe, unsurprisingly, is "lost, transfixed," completely "intoxicated"; his nerves tingle and his hands twitch. DuRose suggests that Kitty's reaction is identical: "here all of Kit's rationality and clear-sightedness fail" (381). It must be admitted that whereas "[t]he cheap dresses on the street had not fooled Kitty for an instant," "the same cheesecloth" in the "glare of the footlights" deceives as "chiffon" (47).[3] Yet she ultimately keeps her cool and some critical distance much more successfully than Joe. She breaks away from the spell of the performance to nod to her brother, who, completely mesmerized, does "not see her." Eventually, Mr. Thomas's scheme to use the show's glamour to impress her fails: she refuses to go out with him and parts with the "decidedly dashing back-area-way Don Juan" "as if he had been one of her mother's old friends" (40, 49).

Joe tells himself that "Kitty [is] the biggest fool that it [has] ever been his lot to meet" (49). Kitty's enchantment with the stage results in her desire "to be an actress and be up there!" but it does not blur her critical judgment of Mr. Thomas (47). When they meet after her successful debut, "the look she gave him stopped him, and he let her pass without a word. 'Who'd 'a' thought,' he mused, 'that the kid had that much nerve?'" (81).

There is no denying that Kitty is fascinated by the black show. She is awed by "the mystery and glamour that envelops the home of the drama. There was something weird to her in the *alternate spaces of light and shade*" (45; emphasis added). The last part of the passage, with its highlighting of the chiaroscuro aesthetic, might be read as specifically pointing to the melodramatic tradition with its "polarization of good and evil" (Brooks 13). As the chorus consists of famously, or rather infamously, light-complexioned girls (Robinson 152), Kitty is possibly fascinated by an actual mulatta melodrama on stage. As a result, she consistently strives to become a singer and an actress. She practices the urban songs "which the stage demand[s]" and is "radiant," when Joe arranges an interview for her with Hattie, who promises to "get her a place on the stage" (60, 73). Hattie, who, as one critic points out, is one of Dunbar's most sympathetic characters, warns Kit honestly that her romantic notions about the theater as "a fairyland" are mistaken (46): we "don't last long in this life: It soon wears us out, and when we're worn out and sung out, danced out and played out, the manager has no further use for us" (75). Thus the young Hamilton girl enters the vaudeville industry aware of its exploitative practices and is not a naïve victim seduced by scheming theater people. Her "grit" and "spirit" are praised by the manager of her theater company, which further highlights the agency of her character (80–81). In the last pages of the novel, Kitty is represented as only slightly interested in her brother's tragic fate. "The greatest sign of interest she showed in her brother's affair was, at first, to offer her mother money to secure a lawyer" (99). Her cool attitude toward Joe, however, becomes clearer when it is read in the context of the history of Joe's sponging off her: during "Joe's *frequent lapses from industry* he had been prone to 'touch' his sister for the wherewithal to supply his *various wants*" (99; emphasis added).

Similar to the way that Dreiser juxtaposes Hurstwood and Carrie at the end of his novel, here Kitty's position on the stage is contrasted with—rather than made analogous to—Joe's Hurstwood-like downfall. As a result, Dunbar's novel contains the same tension between a successful woman and a begging man that, as Fleissner demonstrates, is central for

US naturalism (168–177). Just like Hurstwood, Joe functions as a specific sentimental figure that "suggest[s] the crucial role of the New Woman in producing the Old Man" (172). Such a dialectic, in turn, resonates with the fallen men and redeeming women analyzed by Parsons. Yet, whereas in temperance literature the plotline evokes both sympathy for the man and admiration for the woman, in the fin-de-siècle begging man/successful woman dichotomy it continues to sympathize with the male victim, while representing the woman's economic rise with resentment. This is especially well illustrated by the figure of the actress. As Claudia Johnson contends, the economic position of women in the nineteenth-century theater was unusual because their sumptuous incomes made them "the principal or only breadwinners in their families" (qtd. in Fleissner 180). As a result, while on one hand at the turn of the twentieth century "the actress's image began to undergo a shift from 'harlot' to 'breadwinner'" (Fleissner 181), on the other hand, such a reversal of economic roles bred deep anxieties in the collective imagination of the day. Thus the successful actress in Dreiser and in Dunbar is represented as materialistic, insensitive, and egoistic. This anxiety was even more deeply rooted. Since the majority of black men and women during the Nadir did not occupy the safe, rigidly designated spaces of domestic femininity and productive masculinity, and, at the same time, most aspired to those ideologies (as Tate illustrates in her analysis of the "domestic allegories of political desire"), a reversal of male and female roles, as evidenced by Kit and Joe, could be seen as a sign of a fixed pathology rather than desired progress. The contrast between the two characters is even more disturbing than the white begging man/successful woman dynamic, as it reminds one too closely of the minstrel stereotypes that reversed the hegemonic gender politics: the dominant Mammy figure and the submissive, childlike Sambo.

In line with the fin-de-siècle resentment for the New Woman, Kitty is represented and criticized as overtly materialistic: her "chief aim was the possession of good clothes and the ability to attract the attention which she had learned to crave" (99). Yet it is not entirely true that she "falls prey to the dazzling, if tawdry, *spectacle of consumption and glamour that the nightclubs provide*" (Dudley 152; emphasis added). To the contrary, her attachment to material objects derives from her southern upbringing and her parents' emulation of their white employers' spectacle of conspicuous consumption: Fannie "spoil[s] Kit out of all reason," and there is "nothing too good for her to wear" (3). As a result, while parading in the hand-me-downs from

Mrs. Oakley, Kitty is interested mostly in "view[ing] the finery" displayed by her employers. Similar to the way in which Harper and A. E. Johnson used temperance discourse to criticize not only the drunkard's insatiable appetite for liquor but, more generally, extravagance and intemperate desires for commodities, Dunbar's narrative hardly celebrates Kitty's preoccupation with goods and public attention. Yet in contrast to the plotlines of extravagant characters from *Sowing and Reaping* and *Clarence and Corinne*, Kitty's plot ends on an ambivalent note. The exploitative practices of show business, which Hattie mentions, do indeed take their toll on the young Hamilton girl. As a result of the "wearing out and singing out" of black actresses, her "voice [is] not as good as it used to be, and her beauty had to be aided by cosmetics" (100). Yet at the same time, the narrative also highlights the self-determined character of Kitty's choices: she lives "her own life" (99). Furthermore, when read as black-on-white signifying, her commodity fetishism is yet another element that exemplifies her similarity to Carrie, who, according to critics, embodies the eternally deferred satisfaction of consumer desire (Howard 41). At the same time, as Fleissner astutely argues, turn-of-the-twentieth-century representations of modern femininity tended to represent women as "emblematizations of the consumer's desire" and consumption and ignored their labor and production. And critics today still "borrow from the 1890s . . . a tendency to subsume the working woman . . . into the figure of the deluded consumer" (188, 191).

The passages informing the reader that Kitty has "grown secretive and sly" and "dropped the simple old songs she knew to practice the detestable coon ditties which the stage demanded" are frequently cited as objective evidence, or at least the narrator's judgment, of her "surrender to the city," "downfall," and "moral decline" (60; DuRose 383–384; Bell 73; Rodgers 54).[4] Yet it needs to be clarified that these opinions are expressed in the first paragraphs of a chapter that opens with Fannie's internal monologue, and as such, they need to be seen as either her subjective assessments or at least as marked by her perspective. In the same paragraph, for example, Kitty complains to Fannie that she is "housed up like a prisoner," which is interpreted by her mother as a sign of dangerous "wistfulness" and "rebellion" (59). Fannie's identity, deeply rooted in the ideology of true womanhood and feminine domesticity (Tsemo 28), is incompatible with the notions of modern femininity that drove Kitty. That her city-phobic assessments cannot be read as the opinion of the author is evidenced when the narrative voice corrects her statement that "there could not be so many people together without a deal of wickedness," following it with "[s]he did not argue the complement of this, that the amount of good would also be increased" (39). Hence it is possible—as Tsemo correctly suggests (33–34)—to read Kitty's career in a less pessimistic way than her mother, especially when it is positioned in the context of Dunbar's texts on African American musical tradition and his own presence in the Tenderloin theater district.

According to Joe, Kitty's career in the musical theater positions her "up in the world" (99); in her father's eyes, she is simply "on the road" (117); whereas for her mother she "dances on de stage fu' a livin'" and "ain't de gal she ust to be," which does seem to suggest that she is as good as "daid" (115). Although she tries to convince her mother that "nowadays everybody thinks stage people respectable up here," Fannie consistently reiterates the ideology of true womanhood: "I can't believe in any ooman's ladyship when she shows herse'f lak dem gals does" (77). Despite such a novelistic polyphony of voices, according to a number of critics Kitty's participation in vaudeville culture transforms her "from a stock plantation figure into the novel's northern minstrel reenactment of the same emblem" (Rodgers 54). Putting the novel in the context of the black fin-de-siècle New York theater culture and Dunbar's own creative maneuvers "within and against white expectations" (637), Daigle warns against such simplistic readings and states that Dunbar's representation of vaudeville gestures beyond the limits of racist minstrel stereotyping and that it metonymically represents the more diverse black theater and musical expression, which is characterized by "artistic and political complexity" (644–645). His analysis can be further supported by Dunbar's essayistic commentary on the African American musical tradition in his essay "Negro Music" (1899). Writing already as a collaborator of what Daigle refers to as "the Marshall circle" and the creative theater community, including such famous performers as Bert Williams and George Walker, Dunbar contends in his 1899 text that black people should not be "ashamed of [their] music" and calls on "black composers—and there are such—[to] weave those melodies into their compositions" (185). Even though he most explicitly writes about "the old plantation music" (183), as Robert Toll argues, it is precisely "with the introduction of Afro-American religious songs, [that] black culture revitalized minstrelsy" (238). Drawing on Toll and other cultural historians, Cedric Robinson adds that the significance of later black minstrels—including the Marshall circle—had an "even more subversive significance" (149).

Furthermore, Dunbar's characterization of the "negro ashamed of his music" is uncannily echoed in the memories of his collaborator (185), one of the black composers whose existence Dunbar underlines with his line "and there are such" in his "Negro Music," namely Will Marion Cook. When Cook plays "coon songs" from his and Dunbar's musical *Clorindy: The Origin of the Cakewalk* (1898) to a nice black girl who only sings classics, she is deeply affected. "My soul was in my eyes, in my heart, in my voice," she remembers, to which Cook allegedly responds: "That's the kind of music you should sing, that's Negro music, and you're ashamed of it" (qtd. in Sotiropoulos 81). Furthermore, as Daigle observes, ragtime songs, and the postblackface, early all-black-cast Broadway musicals—most famously *Clorindy* and *In Dahomey* (1903)—are more complex than many critics assume and were perceived as such even by the black elites. For example, he shows that the poet's wife—the elitist Alice Moore Dunbar—and other respectable women in his circle, despite some critics' claims to the contrary, actually praised the "coon songs" from *Clorindy* (639). Another contemporaneous appreciation for the shows can be found in James Weldon Johnson's *Black Manhattan* (1930). Writing as an insider of the black Tenderloin theater district, Johnson claims that musical comedies such as *Clorindy* constituted "a complete break from the minstrel pattern," and Cook and Dunbar's "simply breath-taking" drama "was the first demonstration of the possibilities of syncopated Negro music," which "took what was then known as ragtime and work[ed] it out in a musicianly way" (102–103). Overall, when read in the context of the novel's multivocal narration, Dunbar's larger oeuvre, and contemporaneous reviews of the vaudeville stage from the fin-de-siècle black elite, Fannie's assessment of her daughter's career does not necessarily reflect either the narrator's or Dunbar's own attitude. The postblackface shows that Kit participates in cannot be reductively read as "detestable coon ditties" (*Sport* 60).

When one takes such a corrective approach to Fannie's attitudes to the stage, and especially toward women's presence on it, the novel suggests the possibilities of black cultural expression that are contained in vaudeville and ragtime. The actors in the first Tenderloin show that the Hamiltons attend "could sing, and they did sing, with *their voices, their bodies, their souls*. They threw themselves into it because they enjoyed and felt what they were doing, and they gave almost a semblance of dignity to the tawdry music and inane words" (46; emphasis added). Challenging the oppositions of body/

soul, North/South, and "simple old songs"/ "detestable coon ditties" neatly drawn by critics (Morgan 220), the fragment links the material and the spiritual in black musical expression. Moreover, it uncannily recalls contemporaneous accounts of Dunbar's own performative persona during recitals, according to which "his whole being responded to the music of the orchestra" (qtd. in G. Jones 205). An analogous power of expression is suggested in a passage about ragtime. In the novel's black and tan club, someone is "playing ragtime on the piano, and the dancers [are] wheeling in time to the music" (93). A white journalist is affected by the spectacle, which reminds him of a lost love he is still mourning over, and claims that "dancing is the poetry of motion." The black cynical bohemian, Sadness Williams, responds that "dancing in ragtime is the dialect poetry," which the journalist finds too sassy. In his bon-mot reply, Sadness—who, as Bernard Bell argues, is "the first blues figure in the Afro-American novel" (71; see also 73–74) and, as Daigle shows, can be read as a tribute to Bert Williams (646–647)—highlights the significance of specifically black musical expression and points to the interracial dynamics of blackface, dialect literature, and white theft. The parasitical nature of white cultural producers, subtly expressed in the words of Sadness and all too familiar to Dunbar, is all the more explicit when read in the context of the last lines of his "Negro Music": it "has been recently demonstrated," Dunbar declares, "that what [the black artist] refuses to accept as a gift, *others will steal*" (185; emphasis added). Such theft may point to both white blackface minstrel shows as well as the ragtime craze, whose interracial dynamic is metatextually commented on in Dunbar's song lyrics from *Jes Lak White Fo'ks*, a one-act libretto written at the same time as the essay on music. Foreshadowing the frequently quoted line from *In Dahomey*'s "On Emancipation Day" (1903), in which ragtime makes "[w]hite folks try to pass fo' coons," the musical produced in 1900 ends with a song celebrating a specifically black cultural form—the cakewalk—as an interracial entertainment:

> White folks and black folks all join the craze
> Nothin but cak walks can be seen these days. (114)

The message of the play clearly challenges the eponymous black desire to be "jes lak white fo'ks," but the final song additionally suggests that the cross-racial longing is not a one-way street. To the contrary, the white desire "to pass fo' coons" is at the center of the ragtime/coon song, and more generally, the fin-de-siècle national dance craze, which revolutionized entertainment patterns not only in terms of their racial boundaries but, equally significantly, delivered a fatal blow to the separate-sphere leisure of the homosocial saloons for men and drawing rooms for women. The latter aspect of ragtime culture will be especially relevant in the second part of this chapter, devoted to the tropes of temperance and representations of male intemperance in *The Sport of the Gods*.

Another cultural and political significance of the vaudeville in Dunbar's oeuvre, quite central from the point of view of this book, is discussed by Robinson in his study of race in American theater and film before World War II (2007). Referring to the shows that include Dunbar's *Clorindy* (154–160) and *Jes Lak White Fo'ks* (158), he argues that black minstrels "reclaimed the mulatta as an antiracist agent" (153). Not only did they "[employ] the mulatta as a means of exhibiting and marketing the Black musical" "from the still new Black colleges and the older conservatories," but the exhibition of these black women challenged "the desperate racist construction of Black women as unattractive" and thus "undermined a major ideological support for the antimiscegenation rationale for the lynching of Black men" (151–152). "The Black chorus girls who first appeared to white audiences on the burlesque stage and eventually graduated to Broadway tended by their light complexions to implode the binaries" of racial segregation during the Nadir (152). Such implosion of racial binaries is explicitly suggested in Dunbar's depictions of chorus girls in *The Sport of the Gods*, who go beyond exhibiting their light complexions—they use greasepaint to represent multiple ethnicities, which meaningfully signifies on white blackface minstrelsy: "the men discarded the greasepaint, but the women under their makeups ranged from pure white, pale yellow, and sickly greens to brick reds and slate grays" (46).

As Robert W. Snyder argues in his study of the New York vaudeville stage of the day, according to "the conventions of the period, anyone could play any nationality. All that was needed was a convincing presentation of stock traits (down to skin color: sallow greasepaint for Jews, red for Irishmen, and olive for Sicilians)" (111). Hence, Dunbar's multicolored yet harmonious chorus girls' performances challenged Jim Crow segregation, with its polar oppositions of whiteness and blackness. The shows discussed by Robinson are also assessed by J. W. Johnson as "the first successful departure made by the Negro from strict minstrelsy," whose "minstrel part" differed "from the regular minstrel show in that the girls were in the centre of the line, with a female interlocutor, and the men on the ends" (95). Thus the shows not only "glorified the coloured girl," but, more importantly, it was the women's presence and central position in the dramas that helped revise the minstrel paradigm, in which, as Eric Lott states, "there were very rarely [any] female performers" and the shows' audiences were "largely white and male" (6, 9). Whereas from today's perspective "a chorus of the sixteen most beautiful [light-skinned] coloured girls" (J. W. Johnson, *Black Manhattan* 95) could be perceived as dangerously pandering to white beauty standards, at the time, it constituted a revolutionary break from the minstrel show's "grotesque transmutations of its [black] female figures" (Lott 27). In light of Robinson's and J. W. Johnson's generous reading of the mulatta in vaudeville and on the black melodrama stage, Kitty's theater career very closely parallels the significance of the mixed-race characters in African American mulatta melodrama of the Nadir and the New Negro woman, as discussed in the first part of this book.

As has been mentioned, yet another way in which the popularity of black musicals—with the mulatta at their center and with the ragtime craze in proximity—contributed to significant shifts in the gender politics of the day was their challenge to the homosocial leisure that characterized Victorian culture. Instead of the saloon's male-only space and patterns of sociality—whose "sexual apartheid" and close masculine-only intimacy is conspicuously evidenced by the "indelicate bar accessories," such as the spittoons that sometimes lined the bar and were regularly used as urinals (Powers 20)—black migration to the very center of New York led to the rise of black clubs and honky-tonks, where "both sexes met to drink, dance, and have a good time" (J. W. Johnson, *Black Manhattan* 74). This, in turn, was one of the key factors behind the US fin-de-siècle dance craze, which is reflected in the scenes of dancing in *The Sport of the Gods* and in their contemporary black musicals' finales, with their reconciliatory and comedic, frequently cakewalk, dances as well as their metatextual song lyrics:

> White folks and black folks join the craze
> Nothin but cake walks can be seen these days.
> (*Jes Lak White Fo'ks* 144)

In the context of the Nadir and the still-dominant Victorian ideology of separate spheres, such interracial and heterosocial mixing—even despite the oppressive power dynamics of white slumming—was not only a joyous but also a politically meaningful act.

Kitty's subplot does not contain any romantic attachments apart from her "falling desperately in love with Hattie Sterling" and her craving for "possession of good clothes" and "attention" (74, 99), and as such she foreshadows, as I have mentioned, modern urban femininity in the fiction of the New Negro Renaissance. The fact that she is an olive-skinned mulatta, a chorus girl, and later a lead singer makes Robinson's arguments regarding the political significance of such figures relevant for her character. Moreover, when one analyzes the representations of the near-white mulatta in Dunbar's librettos of *Uncle Eph's Christmas* and *Jes Lak White Fo'ks*, the subversive potential of his recasting of mulatta melodrama becomes clearly visible. As Daigle points out, the former musical's "New Negro heroine," Parthenia Jenkins, is modeled on the historical Anita Florence Hemmings, who passed as white at Vassar College in 1897 (640), and whose story has been recently fictionalized in Karin Tanabe's novel *The Gilded Years* (2016). Daigle points out that Dunbar's portrayal of Parthenia Jenkins—an educated, respectable black woman—enjoying "the kind of spontaneous cultural expression that New Negroes supposedly demurred" "sends up class-based distinctions" (640). Read in the context of mulatta melodrama, the character of Jenkins, as well as her mirror image, Mandy Pompous, from *Jes Lak White Fo'ks*, interestingly recasts the New Negro daughter analyzed in the first two chapters of part 1. Whereas the postbellum characters I discussed in "The Excess of Mulatta Melodrama" either pass unconsciously as whites or decide not to since it would constitute race treason, Dunbar's recasting of Hemmings as Parthenia/Mandy openly celebrates her passing for white as tricksterism. In *Jes Lak White Fo'ks*, Mandy has "played her part so well" and "played an awful little girl" (141). She is adored by white suitors—she's "got a stock in store of their billet doux as yet" (138), yet ultimately, just like the New Negro women in mulatta melodrama, she returns to the black community. Both Mandy and Parthenia participate in the final scenes of "fun," "enjoyment," and the cakewalk "craze" (*Uncle Eph's Christmas* 127–128; *Jes Lak White Fo'ks* 144).

Interestingly, in *Uncle Eph's Christmas* it is the men that "prance" for Parthenia and not the other way around, which echoes the notion of dandyist self-display and Dreiser's "masher" figures. The libretto further complicates the traditional white romantic triangles of melodrama and their polarized images of forcefully handsome masculinity and fragilely beautiful femininity, as the winner of the "prancing" competition is not the young and dashing "Darky Dan," who has displayed his "dress" and "royal manners" especially for Parthenia to "note" (122), but the old and drunken Uncle Eph. Just as Chesnutt undercuts George Tryon's heroism and positions the black

Frank Fowler as the heroic savior in *The House behind the Cedars*, here Dunbar makes the subaltern and unmasculine drunken black man the hero who gets the girl, at least "f'r de week" (132). The dandyist self-creations of both Uncle Eph and Darky Dan echo George Walker's use of "the white dandy as a vehicle for self-assertive urban blackness" as well as Dunbar's own self-fashioning (Daigle 638; cf. Webb 7–24). However, before discussing Dunbar's own dandyism, I focus on the central dandy figure in *The Sport of the Gods*, Joe Hamilton.

The Black Drunken Dandy

The complex and interrelated notions of dandyism, decadence, aestheticism, and bohemia were, as many critics have shown, present in US public discourse at least since the Philadelphia Centennial Exposition of 1876 (Mendelssohn 29–31).[5] In the 1890s, *Harper's* published Arthur Symons's article "The Decadent Movement in Literature" and serialized George du Maurier's *Trilby*. That immensely popular novel, inspired by du Maurier's own memories of the 1850s Latin Quarter and echoing Henri Murger's *Scènes de la Vie de Bohème* (1851), immortalized the romanticized image of Parisian bohemia with its American expatriates at the center. Among its minor characters, the novel includes a thinly veiled portrayal of James McNeill Whistler, caricatured as an "idle apprentice" (Berman 103). The novel's female protagonist is, like Kitty, a successful singer, although in contrast to Kit's self-determined choice of a stage career, Trilby O'Ferrall is unaware of her talent as she sings only when hypnotized. Dunbar's own interest in visiting Paris, and possibly its bohemian milieu, is signaled in an 1897 letter to his wife, in which he states: "I had expected to go to Paris in June, but shall be detained unfortunately in London as it is the height of the London season."[6] The significance of decadent, dandyist masculinity in fin-de-siècle American culture has already been mentioned with a reference to Dreiser's introduction of "the masher," a new term that "had sprung into general use among Americans in 1880, and which concisely expressed the thought of one whose dress or manners are calculated to elicit the admiration of susceptible young women" (*Sister Carrie* 5). Whereas Dreiser's Drouet and other mashers, such as Connie Almerting from his "The Old Rogaum and His Theresa" or Pete from Crane's *Maggie*, are firmly rooted in the US metropolitan context, Dunbar's dandies have a more complex genealogy.

As I mentioned when reading Joe as Kitty's foil, the young Hamilton boy "from scraping the chins of aristocrats came to imbibe some of their ideas, and rather too early in life bid fair to be a dandy" (2). Many critics have pointed out that the novel's dysphoric drive is fueled to a large extent by the Hamiltons' "disastrous ... dependency on southern white generosity and imitation of the white race," which reiterates the master-slave paradigm (Murphy 133; Morgan 219; De Santis; Daigle 643). Dunbar undeniably criticizes the Hamiltons' slavish mimicry, in which the Oakleys' aristocratic whiteness is recast into the black tropes of subservience: "Berry ... gorgeous in his evening suit with the *white waistcoat*" directing waiters and Fannie serving "in the *whitest of white aprons*" (3; emphasis added). As Murphy astutely points out, "The setting's idyllic landscape simultaneously reflects the Hamiltons' attachment to the South and also the obsequious submission of the slave" (133). The link between the pastoral "bower of peace and comfort" of the Hamiltons' household and their dependence on the Oakleys is metaphorically depicted in the image in which, over "the door of the little house a fine Virginia creeper bent and fell in graceful curves, and a cluster of insistent morning-glories clung in summer about its stalwart stock" (2). The novel's image of the southern rural idyll with its fatal, slavery-like dependence resonates with the pastoral settings that were discussed in chapter 2. Both the mulatta mothers and the slavishly dependent Hamiltons, lulled by a false sense of security, are completely unprepared for the melodramatic peripeteia and imminent disasters and displacements that await them. Interestingly, the Hamiltons' short-lived bucolic "bower of peace" resonates with the foil of Harper's model protagonist from *Sowing and Reaping*. Unlike the self-disciplined and disciplining Belle, Jeanette would rather

> be a butterfly born in a bower
> kissing every rose that is pleasant and sweet. (103)

In both texts, the image of a garden arbor gives a false sense of security and fails to shelter either the Hamiltons or Jeanette. The former are evicted from their country cottage, whereas the latter becomes a miserable wife of a drunkard. This similarity is yet another detail in the corpus of black Nadir fiction that underlines its antipastoral sentiment.

Although the family is exiled from their hometown as a result of Berry's alleged theft, the underlying reason is their alienation from the town's black community as a result of their "cultural theft" of white conspicuous-consumption patterns: "what the less fortunate Negroes ... said of [the Hamiltons] and their offspring is really not worthwhile. Envy has a sharp tongue, and when has not the aristocrat been the target for the plebeian's sneers?" (3). As Candela points out, the sympathy for the protagonists in the passage cannot be taken at face value and is an open mockery of Berry's "aping the white man in the big house" (65). Few readers have noticed, however, that—just as was the case in the farcical treatment of slavish mimicry in *Jes Lak White Fo'ks*—the narrative in this way also criticizes and exposes the failures of white conspicuous consumption and aristocratic aspirations. In order to show such a critical edge of the novel, Tsemo quotes Dunbar's statement, which is packed with temperance tropes: "I do not want [black people] to *imbibe the dangerous draught* which has *intoxicated* their white brothers of this Western world and sent them *raving madmen*, struggling for life *at the expense of their fellows* in the stockmarkets and wheat-pits of our great cities" (qtd. in Tsemo 21; emphasis added).

Literal representations of intemperance as a habit that blacks developed under the influence of whites are found in Dunbar's *Uncle Eph's Christmas*. The characters of this farce refer to the antebellum New Year's customs famously depicted by Frederick Douglass, who poignantly undermines the illusion of "the benevolence of the slaveholders," who, during the holiday season, "plung[e] [their slaves] into the lowest depths of dissipation" with enormous amounts of alcohol. As Douglass argues, using the key temperance trope, "many of us were led to think that there was little to choose between liberty and slavery. We felt, and very properly too, that we had almost as well be slaves to man as to rum" (69–70).[7] Dunbar—who was Douglass's clerk in 1893—playfully alludes to those slavery-era origins of black drinking. Uncle Eph in an irreverentl way signifies on a Christmas song sung by the chorus and states that "in de old times, I allus hyeahed it said the immoral Shakespoke writ 'Christmas comes but once a year. Let us have our gin and beer.' White folks pour your whiskey in. Give us colored folks our gin" (120). The ironic edge of the passage, whose source has been read as belonging to "the plantation tradition with its 'black stereotypes'" (Morgan 217; see also G. Jones 187), targets the artistic pretensions of white culture embodied by the immoral/immortal Shakespoke/Shakespeare. It is a unique example of what could be called a reversal of Alan Trachtenberg's "discourse of respectability." Trachtenberg introduces this term to denote "a mode of writing which takes as its own the speech and social perspective of its 'grammatical' characters." In such texts, central for US local color tradition, "dialect either appeared within a grammatical framework or otherwise made clear it was intended for a grammatically proper reader" (Trachtenberg 189). In Dunbar's comedy, the "framework" of Uncle Eph's utterance, as well as the entire musical, is not "grammatical" but delivered in black vernacular, whereas the standard idiom—which Uncle Eph "cites" from the immoral/immortal Shakespoke/Shakespeare, exhibiting his own fluency of educated language—is the speech subordinated to "the social perspective of . . . [the text's] characters" (i.e., the black community), which evidently prefer their dialect to the "immoral Shakespoke's" English. Hence, a more thorough reading of Dunbar's subtle technique of black-on-white signifying suggests that his texts are permeated with implicit criticism of white cultural norms, pretensions, and their supremacy.

Further evidence for this can be found in the very text of *The Sport of the Gods* when one focuses on the character that frames the novel's plots: Francis (Frank) Oakley. Most likely the original dandy that Joe imitates and an expatriate US artist sojourning in Paris, Frank is the actual perpetrator of the theft that leads to the disintegration of the Hamilton family and their forced migration to the North. Apart from serving as the trigger of the novel's action, Frank's trajectory meaningfully resonates with Joe's story. As a result, the differences in the fates of the two dandies expose the race and class dynamics that lie beneath them. Whereas Joe is drawn to the "alluring" sound of "New York" and its black bohemia, Frank migrates to Paris, whose artistic community, interestingly, was also referred to as "the black Bohemia" due to its "idleness and desperation" (Seigel 220). Whereas for the Hamiltons New York is "a place vague and far away, a city that, like heaven, to them had existed by faith alone" (35), Paris's artistic allure at the time was similarly widespread, especially after it had been immortalized in Giacomo Puccini's *La Bohème*. This popular opera, inspired by Murger's romanticized vignettes in *Scènes de la vie de Bohème*, premiered in 1897 in the United States. Frank evidences the cultural aspirations of the Oakley family, which are visible also in their French rather than Anglo-American names—"Francis" and "Maurice"—as well as their choice of alcohol: French old wine and brandy (8, 13). According to Candela, "the profit-seeker Maurice depends heavily on his half-brother, Frank, to fill the artistic gap in the family image" (67), and the older man spares no expense so that the "delicate, artistic nature" of his sibling can thrive in a suitable atmosphere in the European metropolis. Frank joins the postbellum "invasion of Americans in Paris" (Burns 101). As Emily Burns states, "thousands of American artists traveled to Paris for study between the end of the Civil War and the beginning of World War I" (99). Although the American artistic presence in the French capital is primarily associated with the Lost Generation and Gertrude Stein's salon, their fin-de-siècle predecessors formed a large and well-integrated community, which even published its own journal, *The Quartier Latin* (1896–99). Burns shows that the identity of the expatriates was deeply troubled, and many distanced themselves from the French artistic community. Americans were not at ease with what they perceived as a "bohemian environment characterized by non-productivity and laziness" (Burns 99). As Jerrold Seigel argues in his study of Parisian bohemia, its members "were those for whom art meant living the life, not doing the work" (58). As a result, the "Bohemian artist represented the counter-figure to the Selfmademan, who continues to be the core of the American myth" (Frohne 82).

American discontent with the French bohemia is subtly but clearly expressed in the novel from Maurice and Leslie Oakley's perspective, who observe "that life in the Latin Quarter" and state that they "did not believe that it was a bad life or a dissipated one, but from the little that they had seen of it when they were in Paris, it was at least a bit too free and unconventional for their traditions. There were, too, *temptations* which must assail any man of Francis's looks and talents" (6; emphasis added). Even though the Oakleys deny any suspicions of evil or dissipation in Frank's long sojourns in the Latin Quarter, in the fragment they are presented as presuppositions in their internal monologue. Characteristically, the decadent artists of fin-de-siècle Paris openly declared that their bohemian attitudes were rooted in "*moeurs débraillés* [dirty mores] and laziness" (qtd. in Seigel 262). The life of Henri Murger—the prototypical bohemian on whom the opera *La Bohème* is based—was summarized in bleak words by the Goncourt brothers as "debauchery of night work, periods of poverty and periods of excess, venereal diseases not attended to, the hot and cold of the homeless life, eating one meal and skipping the next, glasses of absinthe as consolation for the pawn shop" (qtd. in Seigel 162). Such a representation of bohemia was cemented after Edgar Degas's *L'Absinthe*—a painting depicting a dejected and worn-out woman who vacantly stares into the air in a Parisian café—was exhibited in 1893 in London and sparked scandal and controversy.

Frank makes a brief but central return toward the end of Dunbar's novel. In a letter in which he pleads guilty to the theft and which ultimately helps release Barry from prison, he reveals the glimpses of his bohemian life. He writes under the influence of absinthe, which "give[s] him [an] emotional point of view"; he "can think clearly and write clearly, but [his] emotions are extremely active" (87). He confirms the anxieties that troubled the Oakleys regarding the "*temptations* which must assail any man of Francis's looks and talents"—there is a "dark-eyed mademoiselle" that he has not dared to tell his brother about (87; emphasis added). "I loved this girl," he confesses, "and she both inspired and hindered my work.... I love her too well to marry her and make of our devotion a stale, prosy thing of duty and compulsion. When a man does not marry a woman, he must keep her better than he would a wife" (88). The arrangement that he outlines fits the bohemian lifestyle and its performative challenges to bourgeois respectability. The main romantic affair in *La Bohème* is similarly lived "without the benefit of the clergy"; moreover, its protagonist's true love is evidenced in his encouragement for his beloved to find a wealthier suitor, who would help her recover from tuberculosis. Yet the representation of Frank's lover also strongly reminds one of a kept woman, which uncannily echoes the central presence of prostitution in the Parisian artistic districts. As Zoë Marie Jones claims, "known as a hot spot for prostitution, drugs, and other illicit activities," "Montmartre had taken over as the seat of artistic culture" by the 1880s (243). Similarly, Seigel argues that "the quarter was already known as a hangout of prostitutes," and the artists living there frequently depicted them, producing "high-class pornography" (233). From the perspective of this book, Frank and the mysterious, unnamed "dark-eyed mademoiselle" he financially supports also remind one of Clotel and Horatio's "marriage sanctioned by heaven, although unrecognised on earth"—the ur-interracial union of mulatta melodrama (Brown 65).[8] Whether read in the context of Brown's narrative or in the context of prostitution and the Parisian artistic district, the dandy Frank, the "great favorite both with men and women," is seduced by French bohemia, symbolized by both the dark eyes of his muse and the intoxicating absinthe.

Frank's mention of absinthe is especially telling. It echoes Degas's bleak painting as well as a depiction of the archetypal fin-de-siècle bohemian, Paul Verlaine, for whom, as Seigel claims in naturalist terms, bohemia was "an irresistible fatality" "imposed by a near-biological compulsion, deserving comparison with the Darwinian nature" (259). An analogous lack of volition is suggested in Frank's declaration that he "can never persuade [Maurice] to forgive *her* [the dark-eyed mademoiselle] *for taking me from you*" (87; emphasis added). The nameless woman is rendered as an active participant—almost kidnapping Frank from his family. That the young American is depicted as "full of romance and fire and *passion*" further emphasizes his lack of control over his bodily appetites and what was contemporaneously referred to as "lowly" desires (8). Even though the Oakleys are convinced about "the *strength* of his manhood" (6; emphasis added), when depicting Frank on the preceding pages the narrator gives the reader information that suggests quite the contrary: "There was a touch of *weakness* in his mouth," a "palpable lack in the man"; "the *weakness* of his [mouth and chin]" (5–6; emphasis added). Formally, this fragment evinces how one can easily get lost in the ironic use of different diegetic perspectives in the novel. Thematically, the depiction of unmanly weakness foreshadows not only Frank's seduction in Paris but also the theft it motivates, as well as the gambling he engages in only to lose all his money. As Nancy Cott argues, the "ideal of male continence, of virtuous and willed repression of existing carnal desires, . . . figures in nineteenth-century directions for men's respectability and achievement in the bustling new world of industrial capitalism" (235), and it is melodramatically contrasted with "aristocratic pretension, vanity, and libertinism" as well as "sexual promiscuity as one of those aristocratic excesses that threatened middle-class virtue and domestic security" (223). The aristocratic pretensions of the Oakleys, reinforced by the European setting chosen by Frank, make him an apt representative of the decayed aristocratic masculinity depicted in American nineteenth-century reform discourse. Even more significantly, his depiction as addicted to drink and gambling, and easily seduced, strongly echoes the failed white southern manhood discussed in chapter 3.

Although it does not end in murder and imprisonment, as is the case with Joe, Frank's narrative trajectory is also far from optimistic. His last words in the novel—"do not seek to find me. . . . I shall be as one who has perished from the earth; I shall be no more"—are ambiguous, and while most likely they signal separation from his family, his message can also be interpreted as a portent of death, or at least of social death, which stands in opposition to the publicity that would surround an eminent artist such as the one he went to Paris to become. Frank's "artistic ability" is the reason Maurice sends him to Paris, but his "promise never [comes] to entire fulfillment. He [is] always on the verge of a great success without quite plunging into it" (5). His paintings are not mentioned in the novel, and the fact that his dark-eyed muse "both inspire[s] and hinder[s his] work" and that it is possible that "without her [he] would be successful" further reinforces his image as a nonproductive bohemian "for whom art meant living the life, not doing the work" (88; Seigel 58).

Joe's plotline largely parallels Frank's trajectory in the novel. In his dandyist self-fashionings—"from *scraping the chins of aristocrats* [he] came to imbibe some of their ideas, and rather too early in life bid fair to be a *dandy*" (2; see also 27)—the young Hamilton mimics Frank's own imitations of white aristocracy and European bohemia already before he is exposed to American metropolitan dandyism. Such experiences significantly shape Joe's perception of urban reality. "The boy was wild with enthusiasm and with a desire to be a part of all that the metropolis meant" (39). The process of urbanization, according to Joe, meant becoming like "the young fellows passing by dressed in their spruce clothes," whom he admires with jealousy. Already on the next day after his arrival in New York, his envy is replaced with affirmative interpellation: "He looked with a new feeling at the swaggering, sporty young negroes. His attitude towards them was not one of humble self-depreciation any more. Since last night he had grown, and felt that he might, that he would, be like them, and it put a sort of chuckling glee into his heart" (45). Joe's "citification" or, as Fannie calls it, "foppery" is clearly visible in the way he is depicted by a new female migrant from his hometown, Minty Brown, who upon meeting him in New York exclaims, "[a]n' jes' look at the boy! Ef he ain't got the impidence to be waihin' a mustache too. You must 'a' been lettin' the cats lick yo' upper lip" (62, 61). The description suggests that Joe's grooming mimics the "Vandyke beard" that he sees in the Banner club on the first night (56). Such stylization was popular among black dandies of the Tenderloin and was worn, among others, by J. W. Johnson, Dunbar's contemporary and another writer related to the Marshall circle (Miller 195).

Johnson's fascination with the glamorous and dandyist side of New York's black bohemia can be found in the most significant works of his multigeneric yet thematically related oeuvre: the novel *The Autobiography of an Ex-Colored Man* (1912/1927), the study *Black Manhattan* (1930), and *Along This Way: The Autobiography of James Weldon Johnson* (1933/37). After the narrator of *The Autobiography of an Ex-Colored Man* unpacks in the lodging-house on 27th Street—the very same place where the Hamiltons' gaudily furnished lodging house is located—he admires "a half dozen or so of well-dressed men" in a black club (42). In *Black Manhattan*, Johnson the historian is fascinated with "the crowds of well-dressed people" (119). Finally, he reiterates the same image in *Along This Way*: the Tenderloin's "crowds of well-dressed colored men and women lounging and chatting" make him move to the Marshall hotel (171), a place which, as Daigle astutely argues, was also centrally important for Dunbar. Daigle points to the significance of the dandy figure in reclaiming the black coon stereotype in the black theater milieu. He exemplifies it with George Walker's self-fashioning: the famous black performer "reconstituted the white dandy as a vehicle for self-assertive urban blackness. Walker's signature character resembles the white class-crosser Beau Brummell" (639).

The import of fashion among the Tenderloin bohemians is also pointed out by one of the most powerful figures in *The Sport of the Gods*, the Bert Williams–like blues philosopher and nihilist who talks in witticisms, Sadness Williams. Echoing the anaphoric structure and paradoxical messages of Wildean maxims, such as the "only thing that can console one for being poor is extravagance. The only thing that can console one for being rich is economy" (187), Sadness peppers his monologues with statements such as "[o]nly the rich are lonesome. It's only the independent who depend upon others" or "It's a pity you weren't born older. It's a pity most men aren't" (69, 68). He talks about the "fine, rich life" of black bohemians, who "live, eat, drink and sleep at the expense of others," predicting that "[Joe]'ll like it" (69). At one point, Sadness openly declares that he will not pay for his drinks as he "can't screw [his] courage up to the point of doing so unnatural a thing" (67). At the same time, he deeply cares about his looks and appurtenances. When the reader meets him, he is concerned that his "hat . . . [is] getting decidedly shabby" (51), which perfectly embodies the idea of "well-dressed idleness" in the novel (69). In another conversation, possibly alluding to *À rebours* (*Against Nature*), Huysmans's bible of dandyism and decadence, he refuses to do anything but act his part since "it's *against nature*" (51; emphasis added). Overall, the narrator in *The Sport of the Gods* depicts black bohemia with explicitly less enthusiasm than J. W. Johnson. This "peculiar class," as she or he states, "lives, like the leech, upon the blood of others—that draws its life from the veins of foolish men and immoral women" (69), which strongly resonates with the vampiric images of drunkards, liquor traffic, and the extravagance of the rich in Harper's *Sowing and Reaping*. Yet, in contrast to the classes criticized by Harper, the fin-de-siècle bohemia, this "great hulking, *fashionably uniformed* fraternity of indolence," "prides itself upon its *well-dressed* idleness" (69; emphasis added).

The bleak portrayal of the black Tenderloin bohemians as "leeches" seems curious, given Dunbar's own willing participation in the Marshall circle and his self-fashioning as the black dandy. The newspapers reported his fashionable and showy paraphernalia in detail, listing his "gorgeous new suit," "$150 diamond ring," "gold watch and chain," and "gold toothpick" (qtd. in Daigle 641). Critics also show that the novel's original dandy—Frank—"actually shares physical qualities with Dunbar," which include "the face ... of a poet" and a "tall, slender, graceful" figure (Daigle 643; *Sport* 5). The significance of stylized self-fashioning and self-aware performance is also visible in contemporary reviews of Dunbar's recitals. For example, Lida Keck Wiggins claims that his "lithe form, graceful as a gazelle, glided about the stage when he gave his recitations with a rhythm of movement which showed that his whole being responded to the music" (qtd. in G. Jones 205).

The narrator's distancing from the black bohemia might be read either as a result of the publisher's pressure or as a sign of his anxiety stemming from the analogies between bohemian indolence and the retrogressionist mythology of blackness (Dowling 87). Interestingly, and again similar to Harper's repeated allusions to the verse "you shall reap as you sow," Dunbar refers to the Bible and concludes the passage on the "leeches" with the image of "the lilies of the field" (70), which "toil not, neither do they spin," and "even Solomon in all his glory was not *arrayed* like one of these" (Matthew 6:28–29; emphasis added). Although in the novel the lines appear to criticize the idleness of the rich, their significance in the biblical context is quite to the contrary. Jesus praises the lilies' lack of concern with material needs and thus allegorically calls on his disciples to put spiritual concerns over materialism. Furthermore, the meaning of the passage is uncannily parallel to the line repeatedly quoted in A. E. Johnson's *Clarence and Corinne*: "Casting all your cares upon him; for he careth for you" (65, 73, 109). If we read "the lilies of the field" according to the biblical context, the narrator's bleak assessment of bohemia becomes more heteroglot and gains a more ironic dimension, one that well fits the overall tone of the text. Moreover, as Daigle shows, the colonial mimicry involved in black dandyism was perceived as a threat by whites, which manifests its overt political significance. Such a reaction to black self-stylization is visible in the newspaper reports about the 1900 theater-district riot. For example, one journalist states that "'sassy, chesty coons' ... make enemies on sight." The man depicted in the account evokes violence because he is "flashily dressed" in a "white fedora hat with a red scarf," and he "waltze[s] down ... with a cigar at an angle of 45 degrees in his mouth" (qtd. in Daigle 641). The description strongly resonates with the "red-cravated" swaggering black youths admired by Joe. Such positioning of the black dandy at the center of fin-de-siècle mob violence and near-lynchings shows the militant face of black urban self-assertion and self-fashioning. Rather than represent white privileged men as lazy and lustful and hence resembling the minstrel coon stereotype—the strategy applied by mulatta melodrama novels—Dunbar reclaims and recasts the black coon as a debonair and sassy black dandy, foreshadowing the famous black dandies of the 1920s such as Bruce Nugent or Wallace Thurman.

Apart from its political potential, the black "fashionably uniformed fraternity of indolence" provides a support network for black migrants in the metropolis. "The Banner [club] was only one of a kind. It stood to the stranger and the man and woman without connections for the whole social life. It was a substitute—poor, it must be confessed—to many youths for the home life which is so lacking among certain classes in New York" (53). As Sadness states, such life "has plenty of stir in it, and a man never gets lonesome" (69). In talking about the men that live supported by others, he continues with the earlier-mentioned maxim that "[o]nly the rich are lonesome. It's only the independent who depend upon others." While his tone is deeply sarcastic, nevertheless the narrator confirms that "[t]here was not a lie in all that Sadness had said" (69), and despite its being completely at odds with the US work ethic and laissez-faire ideology of economic self-reliance, there is a powerful potential in the solidarity stemming from shared vulnerability that Dunbar depicts as central to black bohemia. The bohemian helping hand toward its members in precarious positions is illustrated when Minty Brown, a migrant from Joe's hometown, tries to drive a wedge between him and the Banner club circle by telling them about the imprisonment of Joe's father. Attacked in this way, Joe can "relieve his heart" in a conversation with Sadness, who comforts him by saying that his "case isn't half as bad as that of nine-tenths of the fellows that hang around here" (68). Hattie is even more explicit in her support: "Do you think I'd throw a friend because somebody else talked about him?" she asks in an indignant way. "I ain't an angel," she adds, "but I do try to be square, and whenever I find a friend of mine down on his luck, in his pocket-book or his feelings, why, I give him my flipper" (71). Together with other Banner club bohemians, she makes it clear to Minty that she is not welcome: she "mustn't touch one of the fraternity" (72). Although they are not able to prevent Joe from murdering Hattie in a drunken rage and are to an extent responsible for it happening since it was in their company that he became a habitual drinker, the Banner club community is shocked and moved by his fate. Sadness visits Joe in prison—which itself is meaningful, especially when juxtaposed with Joe's sister's refusal to do so and also with Sadness's blues figure never losing his cool (100). Even though when listening to stories others find shocking Sadness does not move a muscle (67), after his visit to prison he is "torn and unnerved by the sight" (97), and he declares that "it'll take more whiskey than Jack can give me in a year to wash the memory of him" (98). The scene ends in a naturalist way that dismisses Joe as "[o]nly one more who had got into the whirlpool, enjoyed the sensation for a moment, and then swept dizzily down," yet in Sadness's loss of composure, especially when read in the light of Dunbar's ironic, distanced narration, there is a visible trace of compassion and solidarity.

The ironic depictions of the "fashionably uniformed fraternity of indolence" and "well-dressed idleness" assume even more affirmative meanings when read in the context of nineteenth-century European dandyism. As Balzac puts it in *Théorie de la démarche*: "In order to be fashionable, one must enjoy rest without having experienced work," and this is not a negligible issue since an "elegant life is tied to the perfection of all human society" (qtd. in Garelick 16). Analogously, Wilde, the most influential of the fin-de-siècle dandies, expressed in one of his maxims the idea that "one should either be a work of art, or wear a work of art." These dandyist bons mots are strongly echoed in the earlier-discussed ideology of bohemians "for whom art meant living the life, not doing the work" (Seigel 58). Turning oneself and one's life into a work of art and blurring the boundary between the two is reflected in the close and complex relationship between bohemia and the theater. The Tenderloin neighborhood, also referred to as the black theater district and located one block from Broadway, perfectly represents this aspect. Apart from its structural relation to the black theater, the bohemian life in the novel is marked with theatricality in a parallel way to its French equivalent. As Seigel points out, "Bohemia was literally turned into theater, acting out its estrangement from ordinary life" (221). Similarly, the "fashionably uniformed fraternity" in *The Sport of the Gods* clearly engages in self-display and actively participates in performances in the club. Yet as Seigel shows, bohemian theatricality also "channel[s] its energy to appeal to the bourgeoisie as patrons and consumers of literary and artistic work" (221).

The bohemian acts and songs in the Banner club are similarly entangled in the dynamics of patronage, slumming, and sponging. When, to his delight, Joe is introduced to the club's fraternity, at first it seems to the reader that the patrons just want to exploit him and their performance is simply some conmen's scam. As Joe's guide, Mr. Thomas, tells Sadness, a "smart man don't need to show nothin'. All he's got to do is to act," to which the witty dandy responds "[o]h, I'll act; we'll all act," and the proprietor confirms that he can trust "old Sadness to do his part" (51). On that evening they do take advantage of Joe, but he quickly sees through the deception and still continues to enjoy life among the witty, well-dressed "leeches." When asked by Sadness if he is sore because the black dandy "invited [him] self to take a drink with" him, the young Hamilton responds, "I know you fellows now well enough to know how many drinks to pay for. It ain't that" (67). The playful performances, "highly flavored stories," and outright lies he listens to and later participates in are clearly a source of pleasure for Joe (54). When he is informed that Skaggs "is a monumental liar" and his melodramatic story is not true, he is shocked, but he does not thank Mr. Thomas "for destroying his romance" (55–56). The permeability of the boundaries between life and theater, as well as between acting and dishonesty, is exposed when the narrator points out that Skaggs "calmly believed his own lies while he was telling them, so no one was hurt, for the deceiver was as much a victim as the deceived" (55). Hence the bohemian circle of the Banner club challenges the lines between life and theater, lies and performance, the deceiver and the deceived, and the actor and the audience.

Apart from the bohemian theatricality, the significance of actual theaters in the novel is unquestionable. I have already pointed out the way the structural relationship between the theater crowd and the bohemian clubs and hotels of the district is outlined in J. W. Johnson's oeuvre and analyzed by Daigle. I have also shown that, despite Fannie's disapproving perspective, the novel's representations of vaudeville, ragtime, coon songs, and black musicals with their mulatta choruses can be read as an appreciation of the black postminstrel cultural expression. This artistic productivity is organically and structurally related to the black bohemian environment. The patrons of the Banner club are both entertained by and take part in the performances of black musicians, singers, and actors (53–56, 93). This link is explicitly pointed out in J. W. Johnson's account of the fin-de-siècle black theater district: "New York's black Bohemia constituted a part of the famous old Tenderloin; and, naturally, it nourished a number of the ever present vices; chief among them, gambling and prostitution. But it nourished other things; and one of these things was artistic effort" (*Black Manhattan* 74). As Daigle argues, Joe's "archly naturalist dive into the Tenderloin 'cesspool'" serves as "a foil to the Marshall Circle; his metamorphosis is a debased version of the performers' cultural and aesthetic transformation" (645).

Significantly, among the characters from the Banner club milieu in Dunbar's novel, only women—Hattie and Kit—engage in cultural efforts (with all their discomforts), whereas the male characters, such as Sadness or, later, Joe, remain "parasites" and "leeches." Even though Joe does not have the artistic pretensions that Frank exhibits, his fate is actually similar—he becomes a "debased version" of the Marshall Circle artists, a representative of the dandyist, "fashionably uniformed" bohemia, whose idleness precludes any productivity. As Burns argues, for Americans the bohemian lifestyle was antithetical to the ideology of the US work ethic, which became a source of discontent for the expatriates in Paris (100). Thus at the center of Dunbar's novel is a dialectic between Gilded Age laissez-faire capitalism and the *countercultural* and *counterproductive* bohemian lifestyle. Overall, in its assaults on the ideologies of laissez-faire and self-sufficiency, *The Sport of the Gods* is parallel to, yet more radical than, Harper in *Sowing and Reaping*. Whereas the empathetic reformers in her novel were to inspire self-reliance in their protégées, Dunbar's Banner club circle finds no "shame in voluntary pauperism" (69). Yet ultimately both authors, in their differing social visions, underline the interdependence, dependence, and significance of embracing the vulnerable and the oppressed.

Despite the militant potential of black dandyism, the solidarity and fraternity in the Banner club community, and its nourishing of black cultural expression, the ending of Joe's subplot in the novel is unambiguously dysphoric. Unlike the inebriate characters in Dunbar's farcical musicals, such as Uncle Eph, the young Hamilton's drinking does not end in joyous prancing meant to impress the ladies (*Uncle Eph's Christmas* 132), but at least up to a point it follows the drunkard narrative as outlined by Parsons. Like the sympathetic drunkard in temperance literature, Joe is seduced by the allure of the city, his male peers, and the wiles of Hattie, who drinks "whiskey in its unreformed state" (and possibly, as a result, her face—in a dramatic contrast to Harper's pale drunkards—is reddened; the narrator ironically comments that "with her complexion," she should not "run to silk waists in magenta" [57]). On the other hand, the violent rage and sexually charged murder of his lover—when Hattie's gown "fall[s] away from her breast and show[s] the convulsive fluttering of her heart" and Joe's "fingers close[] over her throat just where the gown had left it temptingly bare" (96)—and his complete lack of control over his desires and emotions dangerously resonate with the retrogressionist imagery of liquor-crazed, lustful black men. In the murder scene, however, Dunbar does not allude to the protagonists' race in any way: he does not mention the yellow-skinned complexion of Hattie (56), visibly lighter than Joe's "light brown face" (33). When read in the context of the whole novel, in contrast to other passages that highlight the plurality of the characters' skin tones ranging from brown, to light brown, to olive, to yellow, the most violent passage in the narrative is as racially ambiguous as the works discussed in the previous three chapters.

Whereas Frank's decline in the French metropolis is only subtly related to his absinthe drinking and its possible deteriorating effects (87; cf. Lanier), Joe's sojourn in the city is washed down with an array of liquors. In every scene where we encounter him, he drinks. In the beginning, he uses alcohol to awkwardly mask his greenhorn insecurity. On his first evening in the city, he gulps a glass of beer, defiantly opposing his mother to impress Mr. Thomas. Similarly, on his first night at the Banner club, "to cover his own embarrassment, he did what he thought the only correct and manly thing to do—he ordered a drink" (51). These passages strongly remind one of Jack London's autobiographical *John Barleycorn* (1913), where drink is a badge of manhood, and whose narrator escapes "the narrowness of woman's influence into the wide free world of men" (937) to cherish "the spirit of comradeship of drinking together" (977). Analogously for Joe, alcohol begins his process of Oedipal disidentification from his mother and his eventual move to another "lodging house" (65). The course of such whiskey-soaked maturation and citification is at first a cycle of ups and downs. Such a fluctuating trajectory has a considerable significance, as it reminds one of the movement of the Ferris wheel and the rocking chair, or the ascending and descending movements of the boat in Crane's classic short story, which according to critics were central metaphors of US naturalist plots. Threatened by Hattie with "the severance of their relations," he "went back to work he had neglected, drank moderately, and acted in most things as a sound, sensible being. Then, all of a sudden, he went down again, and went down badly. . . . For almost four years this had happened intermittently" (92). Hence, Joe's trajectory is more representative of US naturalism with its cyclic and repetitive pattern than of European fictions with their steady decline.

Nevertheless, Joe ultimately does fall. Evincing the contradictory relationship between alcohol and manhood at the time (Parsons 53–74), whiskey stops being an attribute of independent masculinity and starts to emasculate Joe. His collapse is depicted literally when the helpless protagonist cries in front of Hattie with "an expression of a whipped dog on his face"

(92). "A drunken man is always disarmed," the narrator comments, and as a result, Joe is struck by Hattie "full in the face with the flat of her hand." "He was too weak to resist the blow, and, tumbling from the chair, fell limply on the floor, where he lay at her feet, alternately weeping aloud and quivering with drunken, hic-coughing sobs" (93). In contrast to the redeeming women discussed by Parsons, here Hattie is neither brutalized by the inebriate, nor, having lost hope for his recovery, does she attend to him as a caregiver and comforter. To the contrary, she vents her disgust and anger with physical violence. Just like Kit, she represents the naturalist "New Woman" who is successful and insensitive toward male weakness. Together, Kit and Hattie are foils that make Joe the sentimental figure of the begging man as discussed by Fleissner (172).

Hattie's self-assertion and physical violence against Joe also remind one of the drunken Johnsons in *Maggie*, where the neighbor is unsure whether it is Maggie's "fader beatin' [her] mudder, or [her] mudder beatin' [her] fader" (143). Yet whereas in Crane's narrative the father dies and the mother is the survivor, in *The Sport of the Gods* Hattie is brutally murdered and "the stroke that took her life [kills Joe] too" (97). Among other naturalist murders, Hattie's death most powerfully evokes Norris's *McTeague*. Treated worse than a "dog" and turned out of doors—just like Joe—by his wife, Trina, the eponymous character kills her in a drunken rage. McTeague regularly drinks "a good deal of whiskey," which "increase[s] the viciousness and bad temper that had developed in him since the beginning of his misfortunes" and "pirouette[s] in his brain" (367, 370). Coming to Trina, he is "drunk; not with that drunkenness which is stupid, maudlin, wavering on its feet, but with that which is alert, unnaturally intelligent, vicious, perfectly steady, deadly wicked" (373), which again echoes Joe's state of mind: when "[a] part of the helplessness of his intoxication [is] gone," he abruptly leaves the bar and heads for Hattie's door (95). Whereas McTeague's violence is juxtaposed with the stray cat that listens "to the sounds of stamping and struggling and the muffled noise of blows, wildly terrified, his [cat's] eyes bulging like brass knobs" (375), Joe, after the murder, is paired with a canine. Sobered up, he channels his mourning for Hattie into her "little pet dog" (97). "He would sit for hours with the little animal in his lap, caressing it dumbly. . . . [T]hey seemed to take comfort in each other's presence. There was no need of any sign between them. They had both loved her." The similarity between Joe and the dog is highlighted in the previous chapter of the novel, in which he is "put . . . out like a dog" and compared to a "whipped dog," "drunken dog," and "lucky dog" by the chums that try to comfort him (92–95). Additionally, his drinking whiskey while already heavily intoxicated is referred to by Sadness as "a hair of the dog"—an alcoholic drink consumed as a remedy for a hangover (94). This idiom, as Madelon Powers explains, is derived from the saying that one needs "a hair from the dog that had bitten them" for the wound to heal (87). Thus, echoing naturalism's emphasis on the animalism of human beings, Joe is linked to a dog in the novels' ending, which also dangerously flirts with postbellum images of black bestiality. Yet Hattie's dog is a little lap pet and is depicted as full of selfless love, mute sorrow, and understanding for the man rather than a bloodthirsty dog-eat-dog beast (97), such as the slave-hunting bloodhounds of the US South alluded to in the opening and closing chapters of the novel (25, 102–103). Just like the stray cat that is shocked and terrified by McTeague's battering of Trina, the lap dog's devotion is ironically juxtaposed with the "inhumanity" of interhuman violence.

Thus, in contrast to the racial ambiguity of Harper's *Sowing and Reaping*, A. E. Johnson's *Clarence and Corinne*, and Dunbar's debut novel, *The Uncalled*, *The Sport of the Gods* represents intemperance as clearly racialized and firmly set in the black community of the Tenderloin. Moreover, the murder scene—with its detailed description and sexually charged details that make the reader imagine an unrobed Hattie—is more drastic than the images of drunken violence represented in the earlier, racially indeterminate African American texts. Harper's Joe Gough does cut his wife's hair in a gothic, dark-temperance episode, but he recovers and becomes a reformed drunkard and a happy family man, thus illustrating a euphoric version of the drunkard narrative. A. E. Johnson's Mr. Burton borders on the retrogressionist drunken brute, and although his brutality is not depicted directly, his wife is portrayed as a "poor broken-spirited, abused woman," whose "swollen eye" is evidence that she has been "the victim of ill-usage" (18, 7). Yet he makes an attempt to repent and apologize, and, following the conventional ending of an unreformed drunkard, he decently dies at the end of the novel. In contrast to the hyperbolically passive Mrs. Burton in *Clarence and Corinne* and self-sacrificial wives of drunkards in *Sowing and Reaping*, in Dunbar's novels the partners of inebriates—Hattie in *The Sport of the Gods* and Mag in *The Uncalled*—seek divorce or simply part with them. It does not end euphorically for the women, but such a violation of the rules of respectability is at least entertained as a possibility, and it is excused rather than condemned in the texts. Less cautious in his distancing from retrogressionist mythology than the black Woman's Era writers, Dunbar in his last novel foreshadows the twentieth-century depictions of aggressive and sexualized black masculinity, ranging from the unapologetically gynophobic texts of Richard Wright to the proto-black-feminist works of Ann Petry.

Yet the depictions of intemperance in *The Sport of the Gods* are not identical with the ones in *The Uncalled*, and the difference is linked to the respectively black and ambiguous race of the novels' characters. Like *Clarence and Corinne*, *The Uncalled* does not directly represent the scenes of violence under the influence of liquor. Tom Brent admits that he has "ill-treated [his] wife" during his testimony at the temperance meeting (220), and the first intimation regarding his brutality that the reader gets comes from his dead wife's friends: she "had a hard time of it. [H]er husband... was a brute: sich beatin's as he used to give her when he was in liquor you never heerd tell of.... Protection is a good dish, but a beatin's a purty bitter sauce to take with it.... People thought that he was a-hangin' around tryin' to git a chance to kill Mag after she got her divorce from him" (8). Although Mag is not killed by Tom Brent, the counterfactual thread of the story—his "a-hangin' around tryin' to git a chance to kill" his wife—resonates in the story of Joe and Hattie.

On the other hand, if one focuses on the contrasting representations of urbanization in the two novels, Hattie will then be juxtaposed with Alice, the namesake of Dunbar's wife to whom *The Uncalled* was dedicated, and Joe with Fred, the namesake of Douglass. Like Joe's, Fred's Oedipal disidentification with the mother figure also coincides with his migration to the city, yet his story euphorically ends with marriage. Alice teaches her fiancé "what pleasure is," and though not as zealously religious as Freddie's stepmother, she is nevertheless compared to a prayer, though at the same time she functions as "a stimulant," echoing Victorian metaphors of alcohol use (250, 255). Overall, it seems that the racially ambiguous characters of *The Uncalled* are more likely to succeed than Joe and Hattie in the black Tenderloin. Critics who pay attention to biographical details might also list another factor to explain the difference between the two novels: namely, *The Uncalled* was written during the engagement of Dunbar and Alice Ruth Moore and published in the year they got married, whereas *The Sport of the Gods* was published in the year they officially separated (Gates, Foreword xxvii–xxviii).[9]

Finally, when compared to the absinthe-drinking Frank and his dark-eyed mademoiselle, the plotline of Joe and Hattie also exposes the differences stemming from class, race, and social context even more explicitly than the juxtaposition of *The Sport of the Gods* and *The Uncalled*. The two couples are positioned in two parallel bohemian societies—the Parisian Latin Quarter and the black Tenderloin—yet the bohemian countercultural attitudes function in different ways in the two metropolises for the two men. Frank's crime is hidden by Maurice Oakley because of his desire to protect what the white bohemian ironically refers to as "that strange, ridiculous something which we misname Southern honour, that honour which strains at a gnat and swallows a camel" (88). Sponged by the woman he keeps, he could easily continue to live the bohemian life, squandering the family fortune. Maurice would have been happy to trade the fruits of his industrious productivity into the cultural capital provided by his Paris-based brother painter. Alternatively, Frank could take advantage of the "free meals and drinks" sponsored by the upper-class patrons (whose motivation largely parallels that of Maurice) that Parisian bohemians could count on (Seigel 244).

In contrast to Frank's unpunished theft that opens the novel, the police officers arrest Joe immediately after finding Hattie's body and are "irritated beyond measure" that he openly admits to everything and "there was nothing for them to *exercise their ingenuity upon*" (most likely a metaphor for police brutality), and he is ultimately sentenced to life imprisonment (97; emphasis added). The black bohemians live off others, but it is not affirmatively embraced as was the case in Paris. This breeds deep discontent, which is visible, even when treated ironically, in the comparisons of the well-dressed idlers to "leeches" and "parasites." The white patronage of black arts is only budding at the time, and interracial exchange primarily takes the form of slumming: "curious" whites, "fascinated by the bizarre" want to "see something of the other side of life" in the Banner club. During the black Nadir, the dance and ragtime crazes meaningfully change US culture, but their popularity does not translate into any visible economic improvement for the artistic or bohemian community. At the same time, the emergent black elites either are not yet financially stable enough to support black bohemians or distance themselves from them for the fear of compromising their fragile fledgling respectability. Both reasons for the relative lack of black charity are vividly evidenced in Kitty's attitude to Joe after her success and his downfall. She refuses to be "touched" and "use[d] ... for a 'soft thing'" by her brother and to share with him the money she has earned in the exploitative vaudeville industry that has diminished her voice and her looks. Later, she also declines to "see her brother" in prison. "The arrest and subsequent conviction of her brother was quite a blow. She felt the shame of it keenly, and some of the grief. To her, coming as it did just at a time when the company was being strengthened and she more importantly featured than ever, it was decidedly inopportune, for no one could help connecting her name with the affair" (99–100).

The tenuous position of the emergent black bohemia during the Nadir improved after World War I and after the movement of black social and cultural life to Harlem. The dandies of the 1920s uptown Manhattan—such as Thurman or Nugent, although their self-fashionings also were not without criticisms (Summers 149–286)[10]—could count on a much wider network of financial and social support from both white and black elites, largely driven by the white New Negro vogue and the more general embrace of countercultural attitudes that characterized the Roaring Twenties. As Summers argues, the artists, "[b]orn between 1890 and 1906, and essentially coming of age between 1910 and 1920," "were fortunate . . . in that they were in position to pursue a post-secondary education and enter a profession that either ensured social mobility or stabilized their middle-class status," and in addition, they could rely "on odd jobs, philanthropy, royalties and the help of friends" (173). Yet the "vibrant, modern Jazz Age culture" that they helped "create and maintain" would not have developed in the same way without the Tenderloin's bohemia and the ragtime era of the previous generation (Summers 289).

CONCLUSION

The Nadir & Beyond

ECHOES OF MULATTA MELODRAMA
AND THE BLACK TEMPERANCE NOVEL
IN THE EARLY TWENTIETH CENTURY

> Raymond felt nauseated. The music, the noise, the
> indiscriminate love-making, the drunken revelry began to
> sicken him. The insanity of the party, the insanity of its
> implications, threatened his own sanity. It is going to be
> necessary, he thought, to have another emancipation to
> deliver the emancipated Negro from a new kind of slavery.
>
> —WALLACE THURMAN, *Infants of the Spring*

In *The Nadir and the Zenith*, I have analyzed selected works of early African American fiction and illustrated the paradoxical position they occupy in the black canon. Despite the extensive volume of this corpus, its aesthetic complexity, and its political significance, the novels examined remain largely unread, relegated to the margins of the African American canon, and are for the most part absent from the curriculum and literary anthologies.[1] Due to the dominant twentieth-century critical perspectives, which privileged racial authenticity and eschewed the breaches of verisimilitude that characterized melodrama, sentimentalism, and naturalism, the founding works of black fiction, with their racially indefinite or white-looking protagonists and excessive aesthetics, were perceived as anomalies in the African American novelistic tradition, which until today remains considerably restricted by the monolithic myth based on authentic blackness, masculinist resistance, and literary realism.

As has been demonstrated, the novel of the Nadir is dominated by two densely interconnected figurations: mulatta melodrama and the black temperance narrative. Both forms are informed by progressive race politics, a fact that too frequently has gone unnoticed due to its subtle and implicit expression, which was required because of the antiblack offensive of the historical Nadir. More explicit and radical forms of resistance would have had significantly less impact not only on white readers but also on the black community, which in the decades following Emancipation necessarily expressed, and needed, hope for the future. Additionally, the subtle politics of the novels that have been examined, unlike the narratives of militant heroism, were more useful for the writers concerned with gender ideologies and their intersections with race and class, which is especially visible in the novels' involvement with the historical and cultural practices such as reform activism, woman's fiction, the culture of sentiment, and temperance discourse.

One of the political sentiments either implicitly or even more explicitly expressed in all the novels is their antipastoral and antinostalgic tone. As was signaled in the introduction, pastoralism and nostalgia in US literature are disturbingly correlated with racial othering, class elitism, and gender oppression. In contrast, the black novel of the Nadir does not voice an unproblematic longing for the bucolic past. Even though some novels do contain images of rural bliss, the walled gardens and vine-covered bowers do not provide shelter for the protagonists in their moments of crisis. To the contrary, they frequently begin to function as secluded prisons for the enslaved or abducted female characters. Additionally, the novels' uniform optimistic investment in the new generation of self-disciplined and self-determined young people (contrasted with their weak, indulgent, and intemperate parents) demonstrates their future-oriented direction and constitutes an interpellation of the New Negro (in most cases the New Negro woman) decades before the Harlem Renaissance.

Another politically significant strategy adopted by the black novel of the Nadir and shunned by the later generations of writers and critics holding modernist expectations for fiction is its aesthetic excess. As this book has demonstrated, the novels are informed by sentimental compassion with its heightened emotionality; radical melodramatic coincidences, revelations and oppositions, and naturalist sensationalism and implausibility. All these aesthetic modes share a powerful force of affect, which facilitates the emergence of affective attachments and intimate communities of readers. As a result, both intra- and extratextually, the black novel of the Nadir imagines and brings into being a new community, which is not rooted in phenotypical blackness but crosses the lines of race and class, the private and the public.

Although the novels do not foreground visible bodily markers of race, their narratives do emphasize the embodied nature of their characters. These representations of human embodiment are rooted in their rewriting of US reform culture. As a result, the writers devote their attention to the vulnerability and weakness stemming from lowly passions, uncontrollable appetites, sexual indulgence, and alcoholic intemperance. The black novel delivers a strong reform message and advocates self-discipline and self-control as not only ethical but pragmatically useful practices. The white features of its antagonists constitute a form of assault on the excesses of antiblack violence and the sexual exploitation of black bodies, whereas the racially indefinite or white-looking protagonists highlight the universal nature of human embodiment and vulnerability. Overall, the corpus manifests what Rosi Braidotti labels as a "desire for transformations" that would take "as its starting point the embodied and embedded, affective and relational structures of our social relations, the mixture of personal and collective, the intimate and the public" (240).

The Nadir-era writers' embrace of discipline can be seen as a desire for modern self-governance and a distancing from the ancient regime of slavery and dependence. Significantly, in contrast to the traditional perception of early black fiction as an elitist gospel of middle-class respectability (Bone 12–21), both mulatta melodrama and even more explicitly black temperance narratives are keenly aware of the significance of the environment and the economic context as well as the dark sides of patronage. Unlike some hegemonic reform works, they do not represent the enslaved, the poor, or the intemperate as undeserving and responsible for their situation. To the contrary, the novels subtly yet visibly highlight the economic exploitation of the lower classes and see it as parallel to racial oppression.

The novels' balancing between optimism toward the future and awareness of communal vulnerability is an effective response to the social conditions of the Nadir—an era that witnessed the formation of the newly freed African American community and yet was defined by historically unparalleled antiblack sentiments, violence, as well as legal and political inequities. However, the Nadir fiction's political and aesthetic formations and its deep engagement with reform discourse quickly became out of step with the early twentieth-century social and literary revolutions. New gender ideologies, the emergence of conspicuous consumption, the decline of temperance discourse, and the rise of modernism undermined ethical restraints and aesthetic minimalism: the very opposite of the earlier aesthetics of excess and ethics of temperance.

This very radical reaction against the repressions and literary excesses of Victorian culture, however, did not take total control of post–World War I fiction. The ethics of self-discipline and temperance remained residually present and can be identified in the novels of white modernism, but they are even more pronounced in the texts produced by the writers of the New Negro movement. A work that is most visibly engaged with the traditions of mulatta melodrama and temperance narratives, Nella Larsen's *Passing*, presents two albino mulatta protagonists. The central character and the eponymous passer, Clare Kendry, emerges as the polar opposite of the self-disciplined reformer of the black Woman's Era: "There had been . . . nothing sacrificial in Clare Kendry's idea of life, no allegiance beyond her own immediate desire. She was selfish, and cold, and hard. And yet she had, too, a strange capacity of transforming warmth and passion, verging sometimes almost on theatrical heroics" (5). In contrast to albino mulattas, who always ultimately identified with the black community, Clare passes for white to improve her economic standing, and when she socializes with the Harlem bohemia it is in search of excitement and not out of race loyalty. The narrative, however, does not unequivocally embrace Clare's self-abandon, indulgence, and slumming, and in this subtle way, it echoes the Nadir novel's ethics of temperance. Not only does Clare mysteriously die at the end of the novel, but she is also critically presented from the perspective of another mulatta, Irene Redfield, who shares many characteristics with the New Negro woman of the Nadir.

In contrast to Clare, Irene identifies as black despite her white looks. She marries a black man and is an active member of the Negro Welfare League (as she explains, "I'm on the ticket committee, or, rather, I *am* the committee" [123]). As Mary Wilson contends, Irene "thinks of herself as a 'race woman'" (980). Yet the polar opposition that structures the novel is not the clear-cut dichotomy of good and evil, and Irene, though her perspective is dominant, does not emerge as a sympathetic character. Her marriage and domestic respectability are far from idyllic, and the novel's presentation of the black uplift organization is parodic. Furthermore, in contrast to the Nadir-era novels, which cautioned against the hierarchies and condescension of reform activism, Irene's attitude to her black servant Zulena, "objectifying her as a part of the machinery of the modern breakfast table" demonstrates how "ideologies of middle-class domesticity intersect uncomfortably with service and servitude" (M. Wilson 979–980). Irene's elitism and condescension toward a visibly black servant is contrasted not only with temperance narratives and their concerns with the condescending reformers such as Amelia E. Johnson's Rachel Penrose or Paul Laurence Dunbar's Hester Prime, but even in Pauline Elizabeth Hopkins's *Hagar's Daughter*, a novel firmly set and largely sympathetic with the upper class, Jewel's black servant Venus is represented in a more developed way than Zulena. Venus even gets a leading role in the novel's subplot, and she saves the albino mulatta Jewel from the hands of her villainous uncle. As Hazel Carby has argued, "[T]he character of Venus . . . evolves from being a black maid to becoming a heroine of the story" (Introduction xxxix). Thus, while the ambivalent narrative of *Passing* does not embrace Clare's self-indulgence and lack of restraint, it is also critical of Irene's elitist respectability dependent on the exploitation of the black working class.

Apart from its recasting of mulatta melodrama, *Passing* also resonates with black temperance narratives of the Nadir. Clare's father is comparably represented to the failed patriarchs discussed in chapter 3 and to the violent, drunken fathers examined in part 2 of the book. The first image triggered by Clare's unexpected letter to Irene portrays "her drunken father, a tall, powerfully built man," "rag[ing] threateningly up and down the shabby room, bellowing curses and making spasmodic lunges at her" (4). The father's white identity, confirmed by Irene ("No. They weren't [passing]. They were white" [38]), is visually highlighted after his death, when she is "staring down at the familiar pasty-white face of her parent with a sort of disdain in her slanting black eyes" (6). Whereas the abusive, intemperate father, his violent death in a saloon, and her mother's premature death all strongly echo temperance narratives, the fact that Clare is analogously self-indulgent, impulsive, and aggressive implicitly supports the logic of social Darwinism and eugenics, ideologies consistently undermined in the works published during the Nadir era, in which children of drunkards became reform activists or self-disciplined citizens.

Interestingly, though writers of the New Negro Renaissance frequently depicted both black and interracial revelry, in most likely the most extensive and significant novelistic depiction of a Harlem rent party of the era, the image of a violent, drunken white (not black) man is again evoked. Wallace

Thurman devotes an entire chapter of *Infants of the Spring* (1932) to a "Donation Party" organized by the black bohemians, the Harlem descendants of Dunbar's Banner club circle. Although, at first, it seems that the "liquor, jazz music, and close physical contact had achieved what decades of propaganda had advocated with little success," as the party progresses, the main character, Thurman's literary alter ego, is gradually sickened by "the music, the noise, the indiscriminate love-making, the drunken revelry" (115). A key factor that leads to his distaste is "a scrap" between a white bohemian and two black women. Stephen, "terribly drunk and in an awful mess," hits "Janet in the face" and takes "a punch at Aline," first shouting "[y]ou goddamn sluts" at the girls (114–115). This white-male drunken violence against black female bodies powerfully resonates with mulatta melodramas' intemperate white patricians and the black female victims of their indulgence. Ultimately, however, Thurman's gaze switches back to the black community: the "insanity of the party, the insanity of its implications, threatened his own sanity. It is going to be necessary, he thought, to have another emancipation to *deliver the emancipated Negro from a new kind of slavery*" (116; emphasis added).[2]

Despite modernism's radical reactions against Victorian culture—plainly visible in Thurman, who "believes it to be the duty of those who have the will to power in artistic and intellectual fields to shake off psychological shackles, deliberately formulate an egoistic philosophy" and laments the "restraining inhibitions and complexes of Negro authors" (*Collected* 234, 252)—the anxiety over intemperance continues to recur in the works of the New Negro movement. Characteristically, Thurman's account of the rent party revelry uses the metaphor of slavery to the bottle and the notion of a second slavery, whose recastings, as *The Nadir and the Zenith* has argued, were central for temperance narratives and were also present in mulatta melodrama. When read in the context of modernism's reaction to temperance discourse, its use here is especially surprising. Whereas the literature and culture of the 1920s and 1930s are imbued with "the modernist conception of drinking as *a means of liberation* from bourgeois conventionality and a vehicle to new frontiers of personal and artistic experience" (Crowley 95; emphasis added), a black modernist, even one as scathingly critical of bourgeois respectability as Thurman, refers to drinking as *a new kind of slavery*. The fact that *Infants of the Spring* does not unproblematically share the modernist embrace of alcohol use as a liberating gesture is most likely related to the racially marked ideologies the text responds to, such as residual retrogressionism or second slavery, but also to the central significance of temperance discourse in the black letters of the Nadir, which this book has examined.

Thurman's prolific and diverse oeuvre also features a peculiar recasting of the mulatta novel: a black woman-centered melodrama, *Harlem*. The play, subtitled *A Melodrama of Negro Life in Harlem* (co-authored with the more theater-savvy William Jourdan Rapp), opened on Broadway in 1929. Doris Abramson assesses the play as an "attempt to let *sensational melodrama* grow out of the real problems of Harlem: overcrowded apartment living, prejudices among men of color, the numbers racket, transplanted and unemployed Southern Negroes" (qtd. in *Collected* 305; emphasis added). Thus Thurman consciously used the popular form of melodrama for box office purposes, but he also exposed the oppressive structural conditions of 1920s Harlem (235).[3] His 1929 melodrama significantly recasts the New Negro woman of the Nadir in several ways. First of all, the protagonist, Cordelia, "has dark brown skin and bobbed hair"; thus unlike albino mulattas, she is visibly black. Moreover, she is "an overmatured southern girl, selfish, lazy and sullen. She is inspired to activity or joy only when some erotic adventure confronts her or a good time is in view. She has no feeling for her parents or for her brothers and sisters" (316). Her character thus echoes the self-indulgent Clare Kendry, but in contrast to Larsen's white-looking passer, she does not get punished in the narrative. As the editors of his collected writings argue, "Thurman resisted moralizing about Cordelia's choices; she is a young woman in the city tantalized by its many temptations, exploring her sexual and social possibilities" (307). Hence Thurman's Cordelia (as well as several other female protagonists in his works) is, on one hand, the very opposite of the self-disciplined reformer of the Woman's Era, and, on the other, she can be read as the New Negro woman, a strong black female protagonist calibrated to the new historical context of the 1920s (see Pochmara, *Making* 155–160; 170–178). Overall, as Thurman's and Larsen's novels demonstrate, mulatta melodrama and the temperance narratives of the Nadir are residually present between the lines of modernist novels, and despite the modernists' rejection of the earlier literary conventions, they continued to exert their subtle influence also in the days of the Harlem Renaissance.

NOTES

Introduction. The Zenith & the Nadir

1. Caroline Gebhard and Barbara McCaskill, the authors of *Post-Bellum, Pre-Harlem: African American Literature and Culture, 1877–1919* (2006), make a parallel argument, contending that the field requires a new perspective. "We are required," Gebhard and McCaskill state, "to ask new questions about how to read works produced during these violent and creative decades" (7–8).

2. At the moment, the list includes William H. Anderson, Charles W. Chesnutt, Paul Laurence Dunbar, Sarah E. Farro, Sutton Griggs, Frances Ellen Watkins Harper, Pauline Elizabeth Hopkins, James H. W. Howard, Amelia E. Johnson, J. McHenry Jones, George Langhorne Pryor, Walter H. Stowers, and Katherine D. Tillman.

3. For example, Sarah E. Farro's *True Love: A Story of English Domestic Life* (1891) was recognized as a black novel only in 2016. Robert Bone, in his 1958 study of the black novel, lists only fifteen novels by ten authors released in the years 1877–1902. Not only Farro but also Amelia E. Johnson and Katherine D. Tillman are missing from his bibliography. The magazine novels by Hopkins and Harper are also absent.

4. Largely due to changes in the press industry, which led to the decline of serial novels and to the shift from realism's dominance to that of a minimalist modernist aesthetic, poets and short-story or essay writers decidedly dominate among the post–World War I authors. The following eight writers are the only ones who published at least one book-length work of fiction in the 1920s: Jessie Redmon Fauset, Rudolph Fisher, Zora Neale Hurston, Nella Larsen, Claude McKay, Jean Toomer, Wallace Thurman, Walter White, and W. E. B. Du Bois.

5. Such a critical judgment of early African American novels frequently resulted, paradoxically, from their overtly historicist readings. Even Claudia Tate—whose study sets out to construct a tradition of the black female text—argues that "[t]he aesthetic

value of these works for contemporary readers" is invisible without researching "the bases of their appeal to their first readers" (8).

6. See also A. N. Williams 7; Fabi, *Passing* 1–6; Warren, *What Was* 87. Such a critical insistence on realism dates back to the postbellum days and the contemporaneous rise of literary realism as championed by W. D. Howells, yet it was continued in the New Negro Renaissance writings of Alain Locke and was recast in the essays of Richard Wright, only to reach its high point in the 1960s Black Arts Movement, whose dominant writers and critics vocally judged the earlier black cultural productions as inauthentic and un- or even antiblack, determined by a false consciousness or white expectations. Responding to such attitudes, in 1989 Henry Louis Gates warned against reading black writers and artists according to their "fidelity to the 'Black Experience'" (*Figures* xxii), but his groundbreaking study *Figures in Black: Words, Signs, and the "Racial" Self* did not significantly enlarge or redefine the canon. Over twenty years later, in his provocatively titled *What Was African American Literature?* (2011), Kenneth Warren still felt the need to question the insistence on racial unity and the notion of racial authenticity, an insistence that continues to be relevant today (87).

7. For example, despite Caroline Gebhard and Barbara McCaskill's contention that the term "Woman's Era" adequately reflects the dominance of black female productivity, the essays collected in their anthology *Post-Bellum, Pre-Harlem: African American Literature and Culture, 1877–1919* (2006) perpetuate the dominance of the male perspective. While they revise the canon by devoting two chapters to Dunbar's anomalous and misrepresented prose, still the most frequently mentioned authors are Chesnutt (mentioned on fifty pages), Du Bois (mentioned on one hundred pages), and Washington (mentioned on seventy-six pages). Such numbers are in stark contrast with the representation of the Woman's Era novelists, none of whom receive a separate chapter. The two names that are most often cited, Hopkins and Harper, are mentioned on only twenty-two and eighteen pages respectively, and A. E. Johnson is mentioned just once and only in passing in the introduction. In a similar way, even though Gene Jarrett points out the significance of the long underappreciated and misrepresented Woman's Era novelists, who "crafted empowering iconography and narratives about black women to critique the dominance of masculine ideology" (25), nevertheless he focuses on anomalous texts that "mostly adhere to the patriarchal and masculinist conventions of their time" (26). Interestingly, Jarrett suggests that *The Uncalled* is also among those texts that reproduce the masculinist scripts, as it gives "little agency" to its female characters (*Deans and Truants* 26). But as I demonstrate in chapter 7, the novel does interrogate and twist the gender ideologies of the day. Even though it does not present the motivations behind the actions of its female characters, it does portray and advocate the ideology of compassionate masculinity, which was promoted by the women's reform movement at the time.

8. See also R. Williams 13–34; Trachtenberg 16–36, 51–59. Pastoralism, which according to Leo Marx was a central characteristic of the US canon, is defined as "a desire, in the face of the growing power and complexity of organized society, to disen-

gage from the dominant culture and to seek out the basis for a simpler, more satisfying mode of life in a realm 'closer,' as we say, to nature" (54). The historical context of the Gilded Age, a period characterized by dramatic changes, makes pastoralism especially relevant for this period. "Nostalgia inevitably reappears as a defense mechanism in a time of accelerated rhythms of life and historical upheavals," argues Svetlana Boym (16).

9. "A fascination with mixture and near-white women of color," as Suzanne Bost demonstrates in her study *Mulattas and Mestizas: Representing Mixed Identities in the Americas, 1850–2000* (2005), disturbingly permeated both US culture and academic debates at the turn of the twenty-first century (185). P. Gabrielle Foreman concurs that "the current [bi]racial vogue works as synecdoche, allowing liberal culture to express an interest in 'race' without addressing or redressing the injustices and pain experienced by communities of color as they are being targeted by the politics of poverty, police violence, and prison" ("Who's Your Mama?" 532). Such millennial fixation on biracial celebrities (Bost 16), powerfully reinforced by the election of Barack Obama as president in 2008, has frequently translated into celebrations of multiethnic identity as an ideal symbol for an allegedly postracial society.

10. Among those, the most notable studies include Karen Sánchez-Eppler's *Touching Liberty: Abolition, Feminism, and the Politics of the Body* (1997); Eve Allegra Raimon's *The "Tragic Mulatta" Revisited: Race and Nationalism in Nineteenth-Century Antislavery Fiction* (2004); and Jolie A. Sheffer's *The Romance of Race: Incest, Miscegenation, and Multiculturalism in the United States, 1880–1930* (2013).

11. Several feminist studies whose declared purpose is to examine women's fiction also include texts published by men. For example, although Tate states that "eleven extant domestic novels—about courtship, marriage, and family formation—written by African-American women during the decade of the 1890s and the first years of the twentieth century ... are the focus of this study" (4), she analyzes works by male authors not only to point to their different narratives but also to highlight similarities between them (as is the case in her reading of Charles Chesnutt's *The House behind the Cedars*). Analogously, whereas the subtitle of duCille's study is *Sex, Text, and Tradition in Black Women's Fiction*, she opens with a detailed reading of Brown's *Clotel*.

12. For example, Lauren Berlant makes a sweeping statement that the mulatta is "the most abstract and artificial of embodied citizens" in the context of US state disembodiment (*The Female Complaint* 111). Jennifer DeVere Brody introduces the term "mulattaroon" to denote the "unreal, impossible ideal" and "highly ambiguous figure" that "can be designated alternatively, as a mulatta, an octoroon, a quadroon, a mustee, mestico, griffe, or creole" (16). Such tendency to lump together different embodiments of mixed-race characters is reflected in the titles of recent scholarly works, such as Bost's *Mulattas and Mestizas*; Teresa C. Zackodnik's *Mulatta and the Politics of Race*; Emily Clark's *The Strange History of the American Quadroon*; Eve Allegra Raimon's *The "Tragic Mulatta" Revisited*; or Lisa Ze Winters's *The Mulatta Concubine*. At the same time, the works they analyze include literary and historical sources from a wide range of contexts.

13. Tate proposes that "[b]y categorizing [the postbellum domestic allegories of political desire] texts as 'female,'" she is "not referring to the female identity of the author, narrator, or principal character of the work, though female figures predominate in the female text. Rather, a female text is one in which the dominant discourses and their interpretations arise from woman-centered values, agency, indeed authority that seek distinctly female principles of narrative pleasure.... While both female and male texts inscribe racial distress and black people's desire to participate in what was then an emergent bourgeois-capitalistic society, the inscription of race in post-Reconstruction male texts, like Chesnutt's *The Marrow of Tradition* (1901), generally assumes the form of a polemical discourse of racial protest rather than one of domestic idealism" (8, 67). Although Tate argues that it is not the identity of the author that is the basis of her analysis, she does not include *The House behind the Cedars* in her corpus of "eleven extant domestic novels ... about courtship, marriage, and family formation" (4).

14. Tate's claim regarding the gender of black texts can help explain the difference in the position of Chesnutt's novels. In contrast to *The House behind the Cedars*, Chesnutt's *The Marrow of Tradition* showcases a black male heroism that matches his own identity: it is a black-male-authored "black male text." This correspondence guarantees its "realism," and hence the latter novel was not marginalized by the regime of authenticity. Paradoxically, at the time the novels were published, their popularity was reversed: "*The House Behind The Cedars* sold well enough to go through several printings," whereas "*The Marrow of Tradition* ... sold badly" (Terry 18) and was criticized by the contemporary maker or breaker of literary careers—one of the "deans" of letters analyzed by Gene Jarrett, W. D. Howells—as "bitter, bitter, ... it would be better if it was not so bitter" (882).

15. The ethics or tropes of temperance are used in, among others J. McHenry Jones's *Hearts of Gold* (1896); George Langhorne Pryor's *Neither Bond nor Free* (1902); Sutton Griggs's *Imperium in Imperio: A Political Dystopia* (1899) and *The Hindered Hand; or, The Reign of the Repressionist* (1905); Katherine Tillman's *Clancy Street* (1898–1899); and Charles W. Chesnutt's *The Marrow of Tradition* (1901) and *The Colonel's Dream* (1905). Tillman's *Clancy Street*, for example, in its opening paragraphs laments "the opportunity to satisfy the craving for strong drink which had been fostered ... by overseers and owners" (252). Yet those novels remain outside the scope of this study since temperance is not as central to their structures, in contrast to *Sowing and Reaping, Clarence and Corinne*, or *The Uncalled*, and their characters are not racially indeterminate.

Chapter 1. Mulatta Melodrama

1. For analyses of the Condict-Hopkins exchange, see Shockley 25; Wallinger 145–146; Babb 47–48.
2. Among those, the most notable accounts include Ann duCille's *The Coupling Convention: Sex, Text, and Tradition in Black Women's Fiction* (1993); Frances Smith Foster's *Written by Herself: Literary Production by African American Women, 1746–1892*

(1993); Deborah McDowell's *"The Changing Same": Black Women's Literature, Criticism, and Theory* (1995); and the previously mentioned *Domestic Allegories of Political Desire* (1992), by Claudia Tate.

3. This growing body of criticism includes Jennifer DeVere Brody's *Impossible Purities: Blackness, Femininity, and Victorian Culture* (1998); M. Giulia Fabi's *Passing and the Rise of the African American Novel* (2001); Kevin R. Johnson's *Mixed Race America and the Law: A Reader* (2003); Bost's *Mulattas and Mestizas*; Teresa C. Zackodnik's *The Mulatta and the Politics of Race* (2004); P. Gabrielle Foreman's *Activist Sentiments: Reading Black Women in the Nineteenth Century* (2009); Mary Ann Doane's *Femmes Fatales* (2013); and Lisa Ze Winters, *The Mulatta Concubine: Terror, Intimacy, Freedom, and Desire in the Black Transatlantic* (2016).

4. See also Foreman, "Who's Your Mama?" 505.

5. Probably the most renowned mulatto figure in US nineteenth-century painting is a young man from Thomas Satterwhite Noble's *The Price of Blood* (1868). This image represents a scene in which a white, rich planter is selling his mixed-race son to a slave trader. This image is an element of a series of paintings that depict race relations in the slavery era. They constitute one of the most significant visual elements of the mostly text-based US abolitionist discourse. There is a similarity between *The Price of Blood* and mulatta melodrama, yet in contrast to the casta paintings that celebrated intermarriage, Satterwhite Noble's works primarily evoke a feeling of dissent in their audience, and they do not feature mixed-race families. They fit well into the tradition of what Tate defines as the "post-Reconstruction black male text," which "assumes the form of a polemical discourse of racial protest rather than one of domestic idealism" (67).

Chapter 2. The Apple Falls Far from the Tree

1. See Fabi, *Passing* 7–28; duCille 17–26.

2. See also Tate 169; Foreman, "Who's Your Mama?" 505–539.

3. See Fisher 101; Berlant, *The Female Complaint* xii.

4. See also duCille 24; Fabi, *Passing* 5–6; Raimon 11–23.

5. They dramatically differ from the mulatta concubines analyzed by Winters, who are "free and authoritative over their bodies and sexuality" (2), and thus they enter into a dialogue with those sexualized, Jezebel-like representations of mixed-raced femininity.

6. Additionally, in subsequent versions he changes the names of characters, and the eponymous name Clotel, or more precisely "Clotelle," becomes the name of the daughter, originally called Mary in the 1853 novel.

7. The use of the term "conquest" here might be read as a residual trace of the mulatta concubine, as discussed by Winters (2–7).

8. See also Zackodnik 42–74; Berlant, "Poor" 635–664.

9. For a related analysis of Child's use of "the harmonies of nature," see Raimon 57–59.

10. Hopkins's narrator's argumentation conditionally uses the racist logic of race inferiority and argues that the intermixture of superior "blood," "the best blood," can be the source of progress through interbreeding (Hopkins, *Contending Forces* 87).

11. His gaze is interestingly charged with desire, which is nonnormative in two different ways. First, he himself acknowledges that it is incestuous. Then, as the racial secret is revealed, we may interpret it as miscegenational, since at this moment Warwick identifies as white and Rena as black. Thus the novel uses melodramatic excess to challenge the supposed opposition between incest—radical endogamy—and miscegenation—radical exogamy.

12. For an analysis of this theme in hegemonic "woman's fiction," see Baym 40.

13. Moreover, through the name of Marie, the setting in the Deep South, as well as Eugene's and St. Clare's humane but opportunistic attitude toward slavery, it is possible to see their marriage as a rewriting of the St. Clares from *Uncle Tom's Cabin*. This intertextual echo may work in two ways. It potentially racializes the passive white lady, and, on the other hand, it taints Marie Leroy with the specter of Marie St. Clare's passivity and egoism.

14. Susan Hays Bussey attributes much more self-determination to Hagar, yet she focuses almost exclusively on her actions after the jump into the Potomac, whereas I wish to highlight the parallels with the other novels, and my primary interest lies in the courtship and short-lived rural bliss (299–313). Also, the focus on the first part of *Hagar's Daughter* disproves Augusta Rohrbach's claim that "[t]he ideal of passivity and the romanticization of bondage is nowhere present in the magazine novels" (488).

15. In the 2003 edition, the original single paragraph is divided into two.

16. For a reading of this ambiguity, see Foreman, *Activist Sentiments* 75, 84–86.

17. See Gillman 21–22; McCann 806.

18. Hopkins signifies on Brown's narrative even more explicitly when she introduces elements of captivity and cross-dressed rescues. She recasts both Clotel's cross-dressing, preceding her arrest and death, as well as Mary and George's successful cross-dressing and escape. Ultimately, Jewel is saved by her maid, Venus, cross-dressed as a boy.

Chapter 3. The Fall of Man

1. For a more general historical account of southern cultural codes and masculinity, see Tindall and Shi 491–92; Fox-Genovese et al. 329–364.

2. See also Baym 26; Epstein 127–128.

3. See also R. S. Levine 93–114.

4. For a discussion of such an ambiguous meaning of "privacy," see Ph. B. Harper 1–32.

5. That the text signifies on *Huck Finn* is also clearly visible in the scene in which the visibly black Frank Fowler is taking unconscious Rena back home and, assuming an ignorant and naïve attitude, tells some white men that she has fever and it might be

contagious, tricking them into letting him pass (459). This closely parallels the scene in which Huck tells white strangers that he has a sick father on the raft to prevent them from finding Jim (90).

6. For a reading of Frank as a sexual threat to Rena and Chesnutt's insistence on the separateness of mulattoes from the rest of the black community, see Ferguson 47–53.

7. Aurelia's representation in the scene interestingly resonates with Lasiren, the figure of a mixed-race mermaid that embodied both "seductive powers and potential for violence" in Atlantic diasporic cultures (Winters 102).

8. For visual images of snakes, see the comprehensive collection of mostly British materials on temperance, *Demon Drink*, a project directed by Annemarie McAllister, www.demondrink.co.uk/picturing-temperance-archive.

9. Hopkins's uses of Afrocentrism and Pan-Africanism are more explicit in *Of One Blood*, a novel I analyze in "'In the Tangled Lily-bed': Rhizomatic Textuality and Rooted Cosmopolitanism in Pauline Hopkins's *Of One Blood*" (2019).

10. For a detailed discussion of the biblical story in nineteenth-century US fiction and Hopkins's revision of its earlier use, see Gabler-Hover 122–157.

11. It is also parallel to the way in which the novels expose the slippage between the private sphere and private property in the antebellum South after white gentlemen's children become slave chattel.

Chapter 4. The Genre Mergers of the Nadir

1. See also Koren 165, 181; Christmon 327–328.

2. Frick lists David Belasco, Augustine Daly, and Dion Boucicault as the three producers; however, he points out that Reade's venture was by far the most popular and influential (169–170).

3. See also Williamson 7; Dudley 89, 143–146; cf. Fleissner 18–21.

4. An analogous claim has been made more recently by Jennifer Fleissner, who argues that in the US naturalist tradition, sentimental faith in the power of humanity and human power is not necessarily "neutralized by the naturalist belief in random, uncaring external forces" (167).

5. In *The Social Construction of American Realism*, Kaplan focuses on the relationship between the "realism that develops in American fiction in the 1880s and 1890s," the "intense and often violent class conflicts which produced fragmented and competing social realities, and the simultaneous development of a mass culture which dictated an equally threatening homogeneous reality" (9).

6. Fleissner also rejects the tendency to see "the incursion of sentimentality into naturalist fiction" as a flaw, a problem, or an inconsistency (33). Although Fleissner's reading of Dreiser's sentimentalism might at first seem to be the opposite of Kaplan's, they can be perceived as complementary, rather than conflicting, interpretations, as their uses of the notion of sentimentality differ. *The Social Construction of American Realism* focuses on the sentimental aesthetic and its recasting in the postbellum mass culture

and consumer society, whereas in *Women, Compulsion, Modernity*, sentimentalism is primarily used as a residual ideology of domesticity.

7. Fleissner devotes her last chapter to race and motherhood in the works of Kate Chopin, Edith Wharton, and Angelina Grimke.

8. See also Lukács 110–148; Fluck 154–217.

9. The corpus analyzed in *The Nadir and the Zenith* encourages a more thorough reading from the vulnerability studies' perspective, which is, however, beyond the scope of this project. The most influential works in this burgeoning field include Martha Fineman's *The Autonomy Myth: A Theory of Dependency* (2004); *Vulnerability: Reflections on a New Ethical Foundation of Law and Ethics* (2014), edited by Fineman and Anna Grear; *Vulnerability in Resistance* (2016), edited by Judith Butler, Zeynep Gambetti, and Leticia Sabsay; and the anthology *Vulnerability: New Essays in Ethics and Feminist Philosophy* (2013), edited by Catriona Mackenzie, Wendy Rogers, Susan Dodds.

Chapter 5. Aesthetic Excess, Ethical Discipline, & Racial Indeterminacy

1. See also Bederman 28, 410–41; Luczak 1–12.

2. Characteristically, women seem to be immune to the enslaving power of drink: even though the novel presents both men and women drinking at upper-class social gatherings, only the men become drunkards. As Parsons argues, this feature of temperance fiction is a gender-inverted recasting of seduction fiction, in which the male drunkard replaces the young female victim (110).

3. For a brief discussion of the separation theme in other works by Harper, see Foster 136, 142.

4. See also Powers 80, 84; Peck 25–26, 102–103.

5. See also Fletcher 60; Rorabaugh 226; Powers 80, 84; Fuller 13–23.

6. Harper also mentions wine in *Iola Leroy*. In the first instance, its associations are largely parallel to the ones in *Sowing and Reaping* since it is served by rich planters: "Ole Cousins used to have wine at dere table ebery day, an' Marse Jim war mighty fon' ob dat wine, an' sometimes he would drink till he got quite boozy" (120). The second example is quite different. Homemade wine is offered as a refreshment by Aunt Linda, who claims that she "made myself from dat grape-vine out dere" and "dis ain' got a bit ob alcohol in it. I made it myself" (139). She is lectured by the protagonist and temperance man Robert that grape juice ferments and that "makes it alcohol" (139). In the latter scene, wine functions in a very different way from the way it does in *Sowing and Reaping*: since it is homemade it is completely severed from the liquor traffic and does not serve to enhance anyone's social status. The producer does not even see it as alcohol.

7. As Harry G. Levine demonstrates, wine cultures, in contrast to societies that are Protestant and dominated by distilled spirits, in general are "at the far non-temperance end of the spectrum" (18), which explains the relative insignificance of wine in temperance activism.

8. Such use of historical names is theorized as a strategy of "histotextuality" in Harper's other works by P. Gabrielle Foreman (76). The notion is also used by DoVeanna S. Fulton, who comments on the significance of the last name of Joe Gough, which clearly alludes to the reformed drunkard and renowned white temperance activist John Gough (211–214).

9. A similar sentiment is expressed with grim irony in Stephen Crane's *Maggie: The Girl of the Streets*: "[A]t a mission church where a man composed his sermons of 'yous,'... many of the sinners were impatient over the pictured depths of their degradation. They were waiting for soup-tickets.... 'You are damned,' said the preacher. And the reader of sounds might have seen the reply go forth from the ragged people: 'Where's our soup?'" (46).

10. The novel openly supports woman's suffrage, which positions it on the radical end of the temperance discourse spectrum, although, unfortunately, a thorough discussion of this theme is beyond the scope of this study. For a discussion of universal suffrage and temperance, see Fletcher 103–114.

Chapter 6. Tropes of Temperance, Specters of Naturalism

1. Tate also argues that despite the text's sympathy for the underprivileged, "there is virtually no interventionary discourse of direct feminine agency or female self-improvement" (98). Analogously, contrasting it with Hopkins and Harper, M. Giulia Fabi argues that "Johnson does not overtly address the power disparity between the sexes and therefore effectively effaces any demands for the societal... empowerment of women" ("Taming" 240).

2. The "Tennis Court" represented in Harper's 1876 *Trial and Triumph* (depicted in detail in two long paragraphs of the novel) is an accurate example of tenement buildings in black postbellum novels, yet since the novel is not a typical mulatta melodrama and its preoccupation with intemperance is significant but much less pronounced than that of *Sowing and Reaping*, I decided not to include it in the main corpus of this work.

3. Men opening a door for a woman to pass through first was mentioned in etiquette manuals as a taken-for-granted common courtesy for which women sometimes even forgot to thank them (Bloomfield-Moore 240).

4. This contention, repeated later by Foreman, is actually not entirely correct. Mrs. Burton does leave the chair to give bread to her children.

5. More recently, Elisabeth Wesseling refers to the image as a "rhapsody on the maternal rocking chair" (211), whereas Bärbel Tischleder claims that it is "the epitome of the ideal home" (98). For a reading that focuses on the similarity between the rocking chairs in *Uncle Tom's Cabin* and *Sister Carrie*, see Kaplan 144. The power of Stowe's image stems from the contrast between the repetitive unpleasant sound the chair makes—"'creechy crawchy,' that would have been intolerable in any other chair"—and the limitless maternal kindness of the woman in it (138). It has been insightfully read by Gregg Camfield as central to Stowe's sentimental politics and acquired, rather than

inborn, ethics and aesthetics in his "The Moral Aesthetics of Sentimentality: A Missing Key to Uncle Tom's Cabin" (319–345).

6. Many studies devoted to naturalism or to *Sister Carrie* make a reference to the significance of the rocking chair. It has been formalistically read as "a rhythmic symbol," a fractal metaphor of cyclic, unprogressive narratives dominating the naturalist aesthetic. As Pizer argues, it is the central symbol in *Sister Carrie*, which "functions ironically within the structure of [the] novel.... Carrie looks out over the teeming streets on her first night in Chicago and rocks and dreams of a happiness which consists of smart clothes, flashy men, and evenings at the vaudeville theatre. Eight years later, at the close of the novel, she is a famous New York musical comedy actress and has acquired all of these and more, but she still rocks and dreams of a happiness which might be hers if only she could devote herself to the art of dramatic expression" (Pizer, *Realism* 21). When read as a symbol of immobility from the Marxist and new historicist perspectives, it signifies the ceaselessly deferred satisfaction of consumerism and paralysis (Fleissner 188; Howard 43, 99–102). See also Fisher 154–156.

7. The image of a rocking woman is also evoked for a brief moment in *Maggie*. Mary Johnson, drunk and vulgar, rocks "to and fro upon a chair, shedding tears and crooning miserably to the two children about their 'poor mother' and 'yer fader, damn 'is soul'" (142). Since here the mother is the drunkard and an emblem of hypocrisy, she is an ironic parody of Mrs. Burton.

8. The process of imagining and managing the reality of the urban poor and their rented spaces was most vividly represented in the photographic practice of Jacob Riis, who portrayed the tenements of New York's Lower East Side and used selected pictures in his *How the Other Half Lives: Studies among the Tenements of New York*, coincidentally published in the same year as *Clarence and Corinne* (1890).

9. Parsons argues that temperance rhetoric markedly differed from the critical representations of patriarchy in texts by Charlotte Perkins Gillman or Kate Chopin, yet she admits that temperance activists, "who aimed ambiguously at the drunken husband, may well have done more to advance women's rights than those who set their sights, through the sober patriarch, on patriarchy itself" (172).

10. See, for example, Jacobs 19.

Chapter 7. Enslavement to Philanthropy, Freedom from Heredity

1. In one of the few recent scholarly analyses of the novel, Gene Jarrett positions it within the American canon of naturalism as an important text that "probes the issues of spirituality, heritage, destiny, and the environment to explain social marginality and moral turpitude" ("Second-Generation Realist" 290).

2. I will further elaborate on Dunbar's alleged city-phobia in my analysis of *The Sport of the Gods* in chapter 8.

3. For more on the relationship between non-Anglo-Saxon ethnicities, eugenics, and the notion of "shiftlessness," see J. C. Wilson 199–201.

Chapter 8. Metropolitan Possibilities & Compulsions

1. For generous analyses of Dunbar, see among others Candela 60–72; G. Jones 182–208; Jarrett, "We Must Write" 303–325; Jarrett, *Deans and Truants* 52–70; Jarrett, "Second-Generation Realist" 289–294; Tsemo 21–37, and Daigle 633–654.

2. Already in 1959, Eugene Arden labels *The Sport of the Gods* as a "naturalistic novel," in which the "treacherous New York environment... deterministically produces [the Hamiltons'] degeneration and disaster" (25). Over half a century later, Lisa DuRose argues that the novel is an "attack on popular entertainment" as corrupting "young women and exploiting the working class," which follows the "fallen woman" pattern in which a "working-class girl with all the best intentions meets a smooth-talking urban man who introduces her to city life by way of the magical vaudeville stage only in an attempt to seduce and, in some cases, 'ruin' her" (377–378). Her analysis completely ignores Dunbar's participation in the New York vaudeville scene and the drama and musical lyrics he produced at the time he was writing the novel, which necessarily problematize such a reading. John Dudley also emphasizes the bleakness of the text: "As with Maggie and Hurstwood in those novels, Berry Hamilton's children, Joe and Kitty, succumb to the temptations of the city and are ultimately *destroyed* by them" (144). Also, although he does appreciate Dunbar's conscious use of melodrama and takes into account that Dunbar's text reflects some white publishers' anxieties, Robert M. Dowling argues that—in contrast to James Weldon Johnson's texts—*The Sport of the Gods* represents migrant protagonists as "caricatures of insider urbanity" that "*fail disastrously*" (86–87). According to Lawrence R. Rodgers, "One by one the family succumbs to conventional temptations of city life" (45). In her interesting application of attachment theory to the novel, Jillmarie Murphy states that this "decidedly naturalist work of fiction" "follows the *downfall* of the Hamilton family," and despite the open ending of the female protagonist's plot, she claims that both "Joe and Kitty end their days ravaged by the 'subtle insidious wine of New York'" (168). "Kitty will *fail*—of that Dunbar makes sure" (150, 166). While taking a more balanced approach, Thomas L. Morgan nevertheless does write about "the fall that each of the characters experiences" (220). See also Hurd 90–100.

3. A comparable reaction of a woman to vaudeville is depicted in Crane's classic. His protagonist "reappeared amidst the half-suppressed cheering of the tipsy men. The orchestra plunged into dance music and the laces of the dancer fluttered and flew in the glare of gas jets. She divulged the fact that she was attired in some half dozen skirts. It was patent that any one of them would have proved adequate for the purpose for which skirts are intended. An occasional man bent forward, intent upon the pink stockings. Maggie wondered at the splendor of the costume and lost herself in calculations of the cost of the silks and laces" (*Maggie*).

4. See also Cataliotti 46; Rodgers 53–53; Murphy 166.

5. See also Stein 23–51; Freedman 385–399.

6. As Gene Jarrett states, Dunbar was "less connected to French intellectual culture

than his wife, Alice, due to her background in New Orleans, which had French historical resonances" (personal interview), yet her interest in it is a factor that might have contributed to Dunbar's own interest in and possibly fascination with French culture and fin-de-siècle Paris.

7. An analogous statement is expressed during the Nadir by the narrator of Katherine Tillman's *Clancy Street*, who argues that "the craving for strong drink ... had been fostered on the plantations by overseers and owners" (252).

8. The vision of such an unrecognized marriage in Brown might be myopic, but it is much more romantic: "If the mutual love we have for each other and the dictates of your own conscience do not cause you to remain my husband and your affections fall from me," claims Clotel, "I would not, if I could, hold you by a single fetter" (64–65).

9. Many critics point out that Dunbar himself was a habitual drinker or an alcoholic (Crowley 38; Alexander 166–170), frequently explaining that at the time alcohol was used in the treatment of tuberculosis, from which Dunbar suffered and ultimately died of at the age of thirty-three (Carey 252; Gates, Foreword xiii). Dunbar's drinking problem is suggestively alluded to by William Pickens in his 1923 autobiography, in which he states that Dunbar mentored him in his letters and warned him about the ways in which the social world of the city can "destroy [a black boy's] health and injure his morals." It is specifically linked by Pickens to "Dunbar's constant praise of the fact that he [Pickens] did not touch any kind of strong drink nor any form of tobacco" (36). One of the most drastic narratives of Dunbar's drinking problem is written by Eleanor Alexander in *Lyrics of Sunshine and Shadow: The Tragic Courtship and Marriage of Paul Laurence Dunbar and Alice Ruth Moore* (165–171). Yet the figures she cites to prove his high consumption (eight to thirteen quarts of beer monthly) are very close to the average consumption of beer by an adult US citizen at the beginning of the twentieth century, which, according to Powers, reached 29.7 gallons in 1915 (83). Hence, although Dunbar definitely did not abstain from alcohol, it is difficult to definitively confirm that Joe's drinking is an autobiographical narration.

10. See also Pochmara, *Making* 113–189; Miller 176–290.

Conclusion. The Nadir & Beyond

1. With the notable exception of *African American Literature beyond Race: An Alternative Reader* (2006), edited by Gene Andrew Jarrett.

2. Analogous sentiments are expressed in his 1930 letter to Harold Jackman: "Perhaps, after all, these past four hectic years in Harlem have not left me in a rut. I may still have my former capacity for experiencing sea changes. In which case, there is no telling what might happen next. Liquor I will always like, but my motto now is civilized tippling. Jeanette and I went to Bunnie's for dinner the other night when I was in town. The four of us, his sister made the fourth, had a glorious time, all out of three drinks each, my first in three months. I experienced that glorious mental stimulation, which liquor alone can provide, without going native, and it appealed to me so much, that except for rare occasions I never expect to gorge myself again" (*Collected* 168).

3. In a letter to Rapp, he talks about his choice not to adapt Dunbar's *The Sport of the Gods* for the musical stage and expresses his personal distaste for the popular melodrama: "these people [the producers] are soaked in the ordinary stock melodrama, and already have suggested that I make the play as syrupy and happy endingish as possible" (*Collected* 141). Thus his choice of genre for the play *Harlem*—explicitly highlighted in the subtitle *A Melodrama of Negro Life in Harlem*—evinces Thurman's strategic approach to his dramatic writings.

WORKS CITED

Ammons, Elizabeth. Introduction. *Short Fiction by Black Women, 1900–1920*. Oxford UP, 1991.
Arden, Eugene. "The Early Harlem Novel." *Phylon Quarterly*, vol. 20, no. 1, 1959, pp. 25–31. *JSTOR*, doi:10.2307/273150.
Aristotle. *Poetics*. Translated and edited by Richard Janko, Hackett Publishing, 1987.
Arthur, T. S. *Ten Nights in a Bar-Room and What I Saw There*. 1854. Applewood Books, 2000.
Ashby, William M. *Redder Blood*. Cosmopolitan Press, 1915.
Babb, Valerie. *A History of the African American Novel*. Cambridge UP, 2017.
Baguley, David. *Emile Zola: L'Assommoir*. Cambridge UP, 1992.
Bailey, Fred Arthur. "Thomas Nelson Page and the Patrician Cult of the Old South." *International Social Science Review*, vol. 72, nos. 3/4, 1997, pp. 110–121. *JSTOR*, www.jstor.org/stable/41882242.
Baker, Houston A., Jr. *Workings of the Spirit: The Poetics of Afro-American Women's Writing*. U of Chicago P, 1991.
Baker, Lee D. *From Savage to Negro: Anthropology and the Construction of Race, 1896–1954*. U of California P, 1998.
Banerjee, Mita. *Color Me White: Naturalism/Naturalization in American Literature*. Universitätsverlag Winter, 2013.
Baym, Nina. *Woman's Fiction: A Guide to Novels by and about Women in America, 1820–70*. U of Illinois P, 1978.
Bederman, Gail. *Manliness and Civilization: A Cultural History of Gender and Race in the United States, 1880–1917*. U of Chicago P, 1996.
Bell, Bernard W. *The Afro-American Novel and Its Tradition*. U of Massachusetts P, 1989.

Berlant, Lauren. *The Female Complaint: The Unfinished Business of Sentimentality in American Culture*. Duke UP, 2008.

———. "Poor Eliza." *American Literature*, vol. 70, no. 3, 1998, pp. 635–668. *JSTOR*, doi:10.2307/2902712.

Berman, Avis. "George du Maurier's *Trilby* Whipped Up a Worldwide Storm." *Smithsonian Magazine*, vol. 24, no. 9, 1993, pp. 110–116.

Berthold, Michael. "Cross-Dressing and Forgetfulness of Self in William Wells Brown's *Clotel*." *College Literature*, vol. 20, no. 3, 1993, pp. 19–29. *JSTOR*, www.jstor.org/stable/25112055.

Bloomfield-Moore, Clara Sophia Jessup. *Sensible Etiquette of the Best Society, Customs, Manners, Morals, and Home Culture*. Porter and Coates, 1878.

Bone, Robert. *The Negro Novel in America*. Yale UP, 1958.

Born, Georgina. "Mediation Theory." *The Routledge Reader on the Sociology of Music*, edited by John Shepherd and Kyle, Routledge, 2015, pp. 359–367.

Bost, Suzanne. *Mulattas and Mestizas: Representing Mixed Identities in the Americas, 1850–2000*. U of Georgia P, 2005.

Boym, Svetlana. *The Future of Nostalgia*. Basic Books, 2001.

Braidotti, Rosi. "Punk Women and Riot Grrls." *Performance Philosophy*, vol. 1, no. 1, 2015, pp. 239–254. *Performance Philosophy*, doi:10.21476/PP.2015.1132.

Branch, Enobong Hannah, and Melissa E. Wooten. "Suited for Service: Racialized Rationalizations for the Ideal Domestic Servant from the Nineteenth to the Early Twentieth Century." *Social Science History*, vol. 36, no. 2, 2012, pp. 169–189. *JSTOR*, doi:10.2307/23258091.

Broder, Sherri. *Tramps, Unfit Mothers, and Neglected Children: Negotiating the Family in Nineteenth-Century Philadelphia*. U of Pennsylvania P, 2010.

Brody, Jennifer DeVere. *Impossible Purities: Blackness, Femininity, and Victorian Culture*. Duke UP, 1998.

Brooks, Peter. *The Melodramatic Imagination: Balzac, Henry James, Melodrama, and the Mode of Excess*. 1976. Yale UP, 1995.

Brown, Lois. *Pauline Elizabeth Hopkins: Black Daughter of the Revolution*. U of North Carolina P, 2008.

Brown, William Wells. *Clotel; or, The President's Daughter*. 1853, edited, annotated, and with an introduction by M. Giulia Fabi, Penguin, 2003.

———. *Clotelle; or, The Colored Heroine; A Tale of the Southern States*. Lee & Shepard, 1867.

Brox, Ali. "'Every Age Has the Vampire It Needs': Octavia Butler's Vampiric Vision in *Fledgling*." *Utopian Studies*, vol. 19, no. 3, 2008, pp. 391–409. *JSTOR*, www.jstor.org/stable/20719918.

Burns, Emily. "Revising Bohemia: The American Artist Colony in Paris, 1890–1914." *Foreign Artists and Communities in Modern Paris, 1870–1914: Strangers in Paradise*, edited by Karen L. Carter and Susan Waller, Routledge, 2017, pp. 97–110.

Bussey, Susan Hays. "Whose Will Be Done? Self-determination in Pauline Hopkins's *Hagar's Daughter.*" *African American Review*, vol. 39, no. 3, 2005, pp. 299–313. *JSTOR*, www.jstor.org/stable/40033665.

Butler, Judith, et al., editors. *Vulnerability in Resistance*. Duke UP, 2016.

Byron, George. *The Poetical Works of Lord Byron*. W. T. Amies, 1878.

Camfield, Gregg. "The Moral Aesthetics of Sentimentality: A Missing Key to *Uncle Tom's Cabin*." *Nineteenth-Century Literature*, vol. 43, no. 3, 1988, pp. 319–345. *JSTOR*, www.jstor.org/stable/3044896.

Campbell, Joseph. *The Hero with a Thousand Faces*. New World Library, 2008.

Candela, Gregory L. "We Wear the Mask: Irony in Dunbar's *The Sport of the Gods*." *American Literature*, vol. 48, no. 1, 1976, pp. 60–72. *JSTOR*, www.jstor.org/stable/2925314.

Carby, Hazel V. Introduction. *The Magazine Novels of Pauline Hopkins: (Including Hagar's Daughter, Winona, and Of One Blood)*, by Pauline E. Hopkins, edited by Hazel V. Carby, Oxford UP, 1990, pp. xxix–l.

———. "'On the Threshold of Woman's Era': Lynching, Empire, and Sexuality in Black Feminist Theory." *Critical Inquiry*, vol. 12, no. 1, 1985, pp. 262–277. *JSTOR*, www.jstor.org/stable/1343470.

———. *Reconstructing Womanhood: The Emergence of the Afro-American Woman Novelist*. Oxford UP, 1987.

Cataliotti, Robert H. *The Music in African American Fiction*. Taylor & Francis, 1995.

Cave, Terence. *Recognitions: A Study in Poetics*. Clarendon Press, 1990.

Chase, Richard Volney. *The American Novel and Its Tradition*. Johns Hopkins UP, 1986.

Chase-Riboud, Barbara. "The Albino." *From Memphis and Peking*. Random House, 1974, pp. 19–21.

Chesnutt, Charles W. *The Colonel's Dream*. Doubley Page, 1905.

———. "Her Virginia Mammy." 1899. *The Northern Stories of Charles W. Chesnutt*, edited by Charles Duncan, Ohio UP, 2004, pp. 76–95.

———. "The Future American." 1900. *Charles W. Chesnutt: Essays and Speeches*, edited by Joseph R. McElrath Jr. et al., Stanford UP, 2001, pp. 121–136.

———. *The House behind the Cedars*. 1900. *Stories, Novels, and Essays*. Library of America, 2002, pp. 267–462.

———. *The Journals of Charles W. Chesnutt*, edited by Richard H. Brodhead, Duke UP, 1993.

———. *The Marrow of Tradition*. 1901. *Stories, Novels, and Essays*. Library of America, 2002, pp. 463–720.

———. "The Passing of Grandison." 1899. *The Northern Stories of Charles W. Chesnutt*, edited by Charles Duncan, Ohio UP, 2004, pp. 1–21.

Child, Lydia Maria. "The Quadroons." 1842. *The Children of Mount Ida and Other Stories*. Charles S. Francis, 1871, pp. 61–77.

Christian, Barbara. Introduction. *The Hazeley Family*, by Amelia E. Johnson. Oxford UP, 1988, pp. xxvii–xxxvii.

Christmon, Kenneth. "Historical Overview of Alcohol in the African American Community." *Journal of Black Studies*, vol. 25, no. 3, 1995, pp. 318–330. *JSTOR*, www.jstor.org/stable/2784640.

Clark, Emily. *The Strange History of the American Quadroon: Free Women of Color in the Revolutionary Atlantic World*. UNC Press Books, 2013.

Collins, Julia C. *The Curse of Caste; or The Slave Bride : A Rediscovered African American Novel by Julia C. Collins*. 1865, edited by William L. Andrews and Mitch Kachun, Oxford UP, 2006.

Cott, Nancy F. "Passionlessness: An Interpretation of Victorian Sexual Ideology, 1790–1850." *Signs*, vol. 4, no. 2, 1978, pp. 219–236. *JSTOR*, www.jstor.org/stable/3173022.

Crane, Stephen. *George's Mother*. Edward Arnold, 1896. *Project Gutenberg*, gutenberg.net.au/ebooks07/0700031h.html.

———. *The Open Boat and Other Stories*. Courier Corporation, 2012.

———. *The Red Badge of Courage. Maggie: A Girl of the Streets*. Borders, 2003.

Crowley, John William. *The White Logic: Alcoholism and Gender in American Modernist Fiction*. U of Massachusetts P, 1994.

Cummins, Anthony. "From 'L'Assommoir' to 'Let's Ha' Some More': Émile Zola's Early Circulation on the Late-Victorian Stage." *Victorian Review*, vol. 34, no. 1, 2008, pp. 155–170. *JSTOR*, www.jstor.org/stable/41220408.

Daigle, Jonathan. "Paul Laurence Dunbar and the Marshall Circle: Racial Representation from Blackface to Black Naturalism." *African American Review*, vol. 43, no. 4, 2009, pp. 633–654. *JSTOR*, www.jstor.org/stable/41328662.

Dannenberg, Hilary P. *Coincidence and Counterfactuality: Plotting Time and Space in Narrative Fiction*. U of Nebraska P, 2008.

De Santis, Christopher C. "The Dangerous Marrow of Southern Tradition: Charles W. Chesnutt, Paul Laurence Dunbar, and the Paternalist Ethos at the Turn of the Century." *Southern Quarterly*, vol. 38, no. 2, 2000, pp. 79–97.

Deans-Smith, Susan. "Creating the Colonial Subject: Casta Paintings, Collectors, and Critics in Eighteenth-Century Mexico and Spain." *Colonial Latin American Review*, vol. 14, no. 2, 2005, pp. 169–204. *Taylor & Francis*, doi:10.1080/10609160500314980.

Decker, Jeffrey Louis. "Dis-Assembling the Machine in the Garden: Antihumanism and the Critique of American Studies." *New Literary History*, vol. 23, no. 2, 1992, pp. 281–306. *JSTOR*, doi:10.2307/469235.

Den Tandt, Christophe. "American Literary Naturalism." *American Fiction, 1865–1914*, edited by Robert Paul Lamb and G. R. Thompson, Blackwell, 2005, pp. 96–118.

Dixon, Thomas. *The Leopard's Spots: A Romance of the White Man's Burden, 1865–1900*. 1902. Gregg Press, 1967.

Doane, Mary Ann. *Femmes Fatales: Feminism, Film Theory, Psychoanalysis*. Routledge, 2013.

Dobson, Joanne. "The Hidden Hand: Subversion of Cultural Ideology in Three Mid-Nineteenth-Century American Women's Novels." *American Quarterly*, vol. 38, no. 2, 1986, pp. 223–242. *JSTOR*, www.jstor.org/stable/2712851.

Dorsey, Bruce. *Reforming Men and Women: Gender in the Antebellum City*. Cornell UP, 2002.

Douglas, Ann. *The Feminization of American Culture*. Knopf, 1977.

Dowling, Robert M. *Slumming in New York: From the Waterfront to Mythic Harlem*. U of Illinois P, 2008.

Dreiser, Theodore. *Sister Carrie*. 1900. Pocket Books, 2010.

———. *Political Writings*. U of Illinois P, 2010.

———. *Short Stories*. Courier Corporation, 2012.

Du Bois, W. E. B. *The Souls of Black Folk*. 1903. Library of America, 1990.

duCille, Ann. *The Coupling Convention: Sex, Text, and Tradition in Black Women's Fiction*. Oxford UP, 1993.

Dudley, John. *A Man's Game: Masculinity and the Anti-Aesthetics of American Literary Naturalism*. U of Alabama P, 2004.

Dunbar, Paul Laurence. *The Fanatics*. Dodd Mead, 1901.

———. *In His Own Voice: The Dramatic and Other Uncollected Works of Paul Laurence Dunbar*. Ohio UP, 2002.

———. *Jes Lak White Fo'ks*. 1900. *In His Own Voice: The Dramatic and Other Uncollected Works of Paul Laurence Dunbar*. Ohio UP, 2002, pp. 133–144.

———. *The Love of Landry*. Dodd Mead, 1900.

———. *Lyrics of Lowly Life*. Dodd Mead, 1896.

———. *Oak and Ivy*. Press of United Brethren, 1893.

———. *The Sport of the Gods*. 1903. Dover, 2013.

———. *The Uncalled: A Novel*. Dodd Mead, 1901.

———. *Uncle Eph's Christmas*. 1899. *In His Own Voice: The Dramatic and Other Uncollected Works of Paul Laurence Dunbar*. Ohio UP, 2002, pp. 115–132.

DuPlessis, Rachel Blau. *Writing beyond the Ending: Narrative Strategies of Twentieth-Century Women Writers*. Indiana UP, 1985.

DuRose, Lisa. "How to Seduce a Working Girl: Vaudevillian Entertainment in American Working-Class Fiction, 1890–1925." *Prospects*, vol. 24, 1999, pp. 377–391. *Cambridge Core*, doi:10.1017/S0361233300000429.

"Editorial." *Colored American Magazine*, vol. 6, no. 5, March 1903, pp. 397–400.

Epstein, Barbara Leslie. *The Politics of Domesticity: Women, Evangelism, and Temperance in Nineteenth-Century America*. Wesleyan UP, 1981.

Fabi, M. Giulia. *Passing and the Rise of the African American Novel*. U of Illinois P, 2001.

———. "Taming the Amazon? The Price of Survival in Turn-of-the-Century African American Women's Fiction." *The Insular Dream: Obsession and Resistance*, edited by Kristiaan Versluys, Amsterdam UP, 1995, pp. 228–241.

———. "White Lies: Amelia E. Johnson's Sunday School Fiction and the Politics of Racelessness." *Comparative American Studies*, vol. 5, no. 1, 2007, pp. 7–35. Taylor & Francis, doi:10.1179/147757007X204097.

Fanon, Frantz. *Black Skin White Masks*. Translated by Charles Lam Markmann, Pluto Press, 1986.

Farro, Sarah E. *True Love: A Story of English Domestic Life*. Donohue & Henneberry, 1891.

Ferguson, Sally Ann H. "'Frank Fowler': A Chesnutt Racial Pun." *South Atlantic Review*, vol. 50, no. 2, 1985, pp. 47–53.

Fineman, Martha. *The Autonomy Myth: A Theory of Dependency*. New Press, 2004.

Fineman, Martha Albertson, and Anna Grear. *Vulnerability: Reflections on a New Ethical Foundation for Law and Politics*. Routledge, 2016.

Fisher, Philip. *Hard Facts: Setting and Form in the American Novel*. Oxford UP, 1985.

Fleissner, Jennifer L. *Women, Compulsion, Modernity: The Moment of American Naturalism*. U of Chicago P, 2004.

Fleming, Walter L. "The Servant Problem in a Black Belt Village." *Sewanee Review*, vol. 13, no. 1, 1905, pp. 1–17. *JSTOR*, www.jstor.org/stable/27530662.

Fletcher, Holly Berkley. *Gender and the American Temperance Movement of the Nineteenth Century*. Routledge, 2007.

Fluck, Winfried. "Realismus, Naturalismus, Vormoderne." *Amerikanische Literaturgeschichte*, edited by Hubert Zapf, Metzler, 1996, pp. 154–217.

Foner, Eric. *Reconstruction: America's Unfinished Revolution, 1863–1877*. 1988. Harper & Row, 2010.

Foreman, P. Gabrielle. *Activist Sentiments: Reading Black Women in the Nineteenth Century*. U of Illinois P, 2009.

———. "Who's Your Mama?'White' Mulatta Genealogies, Early Photography, and Anti-Passing Narratives of Slavery and Freedom." *American Literary History*, vol. 14, no. 3, 2002, pp. 505–539. *JSTOR*, www.jstor.org/stable/3054582.

Foster, Frances Smith. Introduction. *Minnie's Sacrifice, Sowing and Reaping, Trial and Triumph: Three Rediscovered Novels*, by Frances Ellen Watkins Harper, edited by Frances Smith Foster, Beacon Press, 1994, pp. xi–xxxvii.

———. *Written by Herself: Literary Production by African American Women, 1746–1892*. Indiana UP, 1993.

Foucault, Michel. *Discipline and Punish: The Birth of the Prison*. Translated by Alan Sheridan, Vintage Books, 1995.

———. "Of Other Spaces: Utopias and Heterotopias." Translated by Jay Miskowiec, *Diacritics*, vol. 16, 1986, pp. 22–27.

Fox-Genovese, Elizabeth, and Eugene D. Genovese. *The Mind of the Master Class: History and Faith in the Southern Slaveholders' Worldview*. Cambridge UP, 2005.

Freedman, Jonathan. "An Aestheticism of Our Own: American Writers and the Aesthetic Movement." *In Pursuit of Beauty: Americans and the Aesthetic Movement*, edited by Doreen Bolger Burke, Rizzoli, 1986, pp. 385–399.

Freud, Sigmund. *Beyond the Pleasure Principle*. Translated by C. J. M. Hubback, International Psycho-Analytical Press, 1922.

Frick, John W. *Theatre, Culture, and Temperance Reform in Nineteenth-Century America*. Cambridge UP, 2003.

Frith, Simon. "Mood Music: An Inquiry into Narrative Film." *Screen*, vol. 25, no. 3, 1984, pp. 78–88.

Frohne, Ursula. "'A Kind of Teutonic Florence': Cultural and Professional Aspirations of American Artists in Munich." *American Artists in Munich: Artistic Migration and Cultural Exchange Processes*, edited by Christian Fuhrmeister et al., Deutscher Kunstverlag, 2009, pp. 73–86.

Fuller, Robert C. *Religion and Wine: A Cultural History of Wine Drinking in the United States*. U of Tennessee P, 1996.

Fulton, DoVeanna S. "Sowing Seeds in an Untilled Field: Temperance and Race, Indeterminacy and Recovery in Frances E. W. Harper's *Sowing and Reaping*." *Legacy*, vol. 24, no. 2, 2007, pp. 207–224. *Project MUSE*, doi:10.1353/leg.2007.0035.

Gabler-Hover, Janet. *Dreaming Black / Writing White: The Hagar Myth in American Cultural History*. UP of Kentucky, 2000.

Garelick, Rhonda K. *Rising Star: Dandyism, Gender, and Performance in the Fin de Siècle*. Princeton UP, 1999.

Gates, Henry Louis. *Figures in Black: Words, Signs, and the "Racial" Self*. Oxford UP, 1989.

———. Foreword. *In His Own Voice: The Dramatic and Other Uncollected Works*, by Paul Laurence Dunbar. Ohio UP, 2002.

Genette, Gérard. *Narrative Discourse: An Essay in Method*. Translated by Jane E. Lewin, Cornell UP, 1983.

Gillman, Susan. *Blood Talk: American Race Melodrama and the Culture of the Occult*. U of Chicago P, 2003.

Ginsberg, Elaine K., and Donald E. Pease, editors. *Passing and the Fictions of Identity*. Duke UP, 1996.

Gledhill, Christine, editor. *Home Is Where the Heart Is: Studies in Melodrama and the Woman's Film*. British Film Institute, 1987.

Goddu, Teresa A. "Vampire Gothic." *American Literary History*, vol. 11, no. 1, 1999, pp. 125–141. *Oxford Academic*, doi:10.1093/alh/11.1.125.

Gramsci, Antonio. "The Intellectuals." Translated by Quintin Hoare and Geoffrey Nowell Smith, *The Continental Philosophy Reader*, edited by Richard Kearney and Mara Rainwater, Routledge, 1996, pp. 181–193.

Griggs, Sutton. *The Hindered Hand; or, The Reign of the Repressionist*. Orion, 1905.

———. *Imperium in Imperio: A Political Dystopia*. Editor Publishing, 1899.

———. *Unfettered*. Orion, 1902.

Grimsted, David. *Melodrama Unveiled: American Theater and Culture, 1800–1850*. U of California P, 1968.

Hack, Daniel. *Reaping Something New: African American Transformations of Victorian Literature*. Princeton UP, 2016.

Hadley, Elaine. "The Old Price Wars: Melodramatizing the Public Sphere in Early-Nineteenth-Century England." *PMLA*, vol. 107, no. 3, 1992, pp. 524–537. *JSTOR*, www.jstor.org/stable/462759.

Harper, Frances Ellen Watkins. "On Free Produce." 1854. *A Brighter Coming Day*, pp. 44–45.

Harper, Frances Ellen Watkins. *A Brighter Coming Day: A Frances Ellen Watkins Harper Reader*, edited by Frances Smith Foster, Feminist Press at CUNY, 1990.

———. *Iola Leroy; or, Shadows Uplifted*. 1893. Book Jungle, 2008.

———. *Minnie's Sacrifice, Sowing and Reaping, Trial and Triumph: Three Rediscovered Novels*, edited by Frances Smith Foster, Beacon Press, 1994.

———. "Signing the Pledge." 1886. *A Brighter Coming Day*, pp. 254–255.

———. "Something and Nothing." 1866. *A Brighter Coming Day*, p. 251.

———. "We Are All Bound Up Together." 1866. *The Black Past: Remembered and Reclaimed*, www.blackpast.org/1866-frances-ellen-watkins-harper-we-are-all-bound-together-0.

———. "The Woman's Christian Temperance Union and the Colored Woman." 1888. *A Brighter Coming Day*, pp. 281–284.

Harper, Phillip Brian. *Private Affairs: Critical Ventures in the Culture of Social Relations*. New York UP, 1999.

Heermance, J. Noel, and William Wells Brown. *William Wells Brown and Clotelle: A Portrait of the Artist in the First Negro Novel*. Archon Books, 1969.

Herd, Denise. "Ambiguity in Black Drinking Norms: An Ethnohistorical Interpretation." *The American Experience with Alcohol: Contrasting Cultural Perspectives*, edited by Linda Bennett and Genevieve M. Ames, Springer, 1985, pp. 149–170.

———. "Prohibition, Racism and Class Politics in the Post-Reconstruction South." *Journal of Drug Issues*, vol. 13, no. 1, 1983, pp. 77–94. *SAGE*, doi:10.1177/002204268301300105.

Holmes, Katie. "'Spinsters Indispensable': Feminists, Single Women and the Critique of Marriage, 1890–1920." *Australian Historical Studies*, vol. 29, no. 110, 1998, pp. 68–90. *Taylor & Francis*, doi:10.1080/10314619808596061.

Holton, Milne. *Cylinder of Vision: The Fiction and Journalistic Writing of Stephen Crane*. Louisiana State UP, 1972.

Hopkins, Pauline Elizabeth. *Contending Forces: A Romance Illustrative of Negro Life North and South*. 1900. With an introduction by Richard Yarborough, Oxford UP, 1991.

———. *Daughter of the Revolution: The Major Nonfiction Works of Pauline E. Hopkins*, edited by Ira Dworkin, Rutgers UP, 2007.

———. "The Evils of Intemperance and Their Remedies." 1874. *Daughter of the Revolution*, pp. 3–6.

———. "Famous Men of the Negro Race: Hon. Frederick Douglass." 1901. *Daughter of the Revolution*, pp. 23–33.

———. *The Magazine Novels of Pauline Hopkins: (Including Hagar's Daughter, Winona, and Of One Blood)*, edited by Hazel V. Carby, Oxford UP, 1990.

Horn, Katrin. *Women, Camp, and Popular Culture: Serious Excess*. Palgrave Macmillan, 2019.

Howard, June. *Form and History in American Literary Naturalism*. U of North Carolina P, 1985.

Howells, William Dean. "A Psychological Counter-Current in Recent Fiction." *North American Review*, vol. 173, 1901, pp. 872–888.

Hurd, Myles. "Blackness and Borrowed Obscurity: Another Look at Dunbar's *The Sport of the Gods*." *Callaloo*, vol. 4, nos. 1–3, 1981, pp. 90–100. *JSTOR*, www.jstor.org/stable/3043833.

Jacobs, Harriet Ann. *Incidents in the Life of a Slave Girl*. 1861. Signet Classics, 2010.

James, Henry. *Daisy Miller*. 1878. Aerie Books, 1988.

Jarrett, Gene Andrew, editor. *African American Literature beyond Race: An Alternative Reader*. New York UP, 2006.

———. *Deans and Truants: Race and Realism in African American Literature*. U of Pennsylvania P, 2007.

———. "'Entirely Black Verse from Him Would Succeed': Minstrel Realism and William Dean Howells." *Nineteenth-Century Literature*, vol. 59, no. 4, 2004, pp. 494–535. *JSTOR*, www.jstor.org/stable/10.1525/ncl.2005.59.4.494.

———. Personal email. July 6, 2018.

———. "Second-Generation Realist; or, Dunbar the Naturalist." *African American Review*, vol. 41, no. 2, 2007, pp. 289–294. *JSTOR*, www.jstor.org/stable/40027062.

———. "'We Must Write Like the White Men': Race, Realism, and Dunbar's Anomalous First Novel." *Novel: A Forum on Fiction*, vol. 37, no. 3, 2004, pp. 303–325. *JSTOR*, www.jstor.org/stable/40267597.

Johnson, Amelia E. *Clarence and Corinne; or, God's Way*. With an introduction by Hortense J. Spillers, Oxford UP, 1988.

———. *The Hazeley Family*. With an introduction by Barbara Christian, Oxford UP, 1988.

———. *Martina Meriden*. American Baptist Publication Society, 1901.

Johnson, James Weldon. *Along This Way: The Autobiography of James Weldon Johnson*. Viking Press, 1933.

———. *The Autobiography of an Ex-Colored Man*. 1912. Courier Corporation, 2012.

———. *Black Manhattan*. Perseus Books Group, 1930.

Johnson, Kevin R., editor. *Mixed Race America and the Law: A Reader*. New York UP, 2003.

Johnson, Lorenzo D. *Martha Washingtonianism; or, A History of the Ladies Temperance Benevolent Societies*. Saxton & Miles, 1843.

Jones, Gavin. *Strange Talk: The Politics of Dialect Literature in Gilded Age America*. U of California P, 1999.

Jones, Zoë Marie. "Gino Severini's Bohemian Paris: Integrating the Italian Artist, 1906–1914." *Foreign Artists and Communities in Modern Paris, 1870–1914: Strangers in Paradise*, edited by Karen L. Carter and Susan Waller, Routledge, 2017, pp. 239–252.

Kaplan, Amy. *The Social Construction of American Realism*. U of Chicago P, 1992.

Kelley, Robin D. G. *Race Rebels: Culture, Politics, and the Black Working Class*. Free Press, 1994.

Kimmel, Michael S. *Manhood in America: A Cultural History*. Free Press, 1996.

Koren, John. *Economic Aspects of the Liquor Problem*. Houghton Mifflin, 1899. *Internet Archive*, archive.org/details/economicaspects00farngoog.

Lanier, Doris. *Absinthe: The Cocaine of the Nineteenth Century: A History of the Hallucinogenic Drug and Its Effect on Artists and Writers in Europe and the United States*. McFarland, 2016.

Larsen, Nella. *Passing*. A. A. Knopf, 1929.

———. *Quicksand*. 1928. Courier, 2012.

Lepine, Anna. *The Old Maid in the Garret: Representations of the Spinster in Victorian Culture*. PhD diss., University of Ottawa, 2007, doi:10.20381/ruor-19750.

Leverenz, David. *Manhood and the American Renaissance*. Cornell UP, 1989.

Levine, Harry G. "Temperance Cultures: Alcohol as a Problem in Nordic and English-Speaking Cultures." *The Nature of Alcohol and Drug-Related Problems*, edited by Malcolm Lader et al., Oxford UP, 1993, pp. 16–36.

Levine, Robert S. "'Whiskey, Blacking, and All': Temperance and Race in William Wells Brown's *Clotel*." Reynolds and Rosenthal, *The Serpent in the Cup*, pp. 93–114.

Leypoldt, Günter. "1890s Middlebrow: *Sister Carrie* as an Artist Novel." *Revisionist Approaches to American Realism and Naturalism*, edited by Jutta Ernst and Sabina Matter-Seibelpp, Universitätsverlag Winter, 2018, pp. 117–142.

Lipiński, Filip. Personal email. July 12, 2018.

Loewen, James W. *Sundown Towns: A Hidden Dimension of American Racism*. New Press, 2005.

Logan, Rayford W. *The Negro in American Life and Thought: The Nadir, 1877–1901*. Dial Press, 1954.

London, Jack. *John Barleycorn; or, Alcoholic Memoirs*. 1913. *Novels and Social Writings*. Library of America, 1982, pp. 933–1112.

Lott, Eric. *Love and Theft: Blackface Minstrelsy and the American Working Class*. Oxford UP, 1993.

Luczak, Ewa Barbara. *Breeding and Eugenics in the American Literary Imagination: Heredity Rules in the Twentieth Century*. Springer, 2016.

Lukács, György. "Narrate or Describe?" *Writer and Critic and Other Essays*, translated by Arthur David Kahn, Merlin Press, 1970, pp. 110–148.

Mackenzie, Catriona, et al., editors. *Vulnerability: New Essays in Ethics and Feminist Philosophy*. Oxford UP, 2014.
MacKethan, Lucinda Hardwick. *The Dream of Arcady: Place and Time in Southern Literature*. LSU Press, 1999.
Marx, Leo. *The Machine in the Garden: Technology and the Pastoral Ideal in America*. 1964. Oxford UP, 2000.
Mattingly, Carol. *Well-Tempered Women: Nineteenth-Century Temperance Rhetoric*. Southern Illinois UP, 2000.
Mayfield, John. *Counterfeit Gentlemen: Manhood and Humor in the Old South*. UP of Florida, 2011.
———. "'The Soul of a Man!': William Gilmore Simms and the Myths of Southern Manhood." *Journal of the Early Republic*, vol. 15, no. 3, 1995, pp. 477–500. *JSTOR*, www.jstor.org/stable/3124119.
McCann, Sean. "'Bonds of Brotherhood': Pauline Hopkins and the Work of Melodrama." *ELH*, vol. 64, no. 3, 1997, pp. 789–822. *Project Muse*, doi:10.1353/elh.1997.0025.
McCaskill, Barbara, and Caroline Gebhard, editors. *Post-Bellum, Pre-Harlem: African American Literature and Culture, 1877–1919*. New York UP, 2006.
McDowell, Deborah E. *"The Changing Same": Black Women's Literature, Criticism, and Theory*. Indiana UP, 1995.
McElrath, Joseph R. "The Comedy of Frank Norris's 'McTeague.'" *Studies in American Humor*, vol. 2, no. 2, 1975, pp. 88–95. *JSTOR*, www.jstor.org/stable/42573074.
McHenry Jones, J. *Hearts of Gold*. Daily Intelligencer Steam Job Press, 1896.
Mendelssohn, Michele. *Henry James, Oscar Wilde and Aesthetic Culture*. Edinburgh UP, 2014.
Miller, Monica L. *Slaves to Fashion: Black Dandyism and the Styling of Black Diasporic Identity*. Duke UP, 2010.
Modleski, Tania. *Loving with a Vengeance: Mass-Produced Fantasies for Women*. Archon Books, 1982.
Morgan, Thomas L. "The City as Refuge: Constructing Urban Blackness in Paul Laurence Dunbar's *The Sport of the Gods* and James Weldon Johnson's *The Autobiography of an Ex-Coloured Man*." *African American Review*, vol. 38, no. 2, 2004, pp. 213–237. *JSTOR*, www.jstor.org/stable/1512287.
Murdock, Catherine Gilbert. *Domesticating Drink: Women, Men, and Alcohol in America, 1870–1940*. Johns Hopkins UP, 2001.
Murphy, Jillmarie. *Attachment, Place, and Otherness in Nineteenth-Century American Literature: New Materialist Representations*. Routledge, 2018.
Newton, Richard. *The Giants and How to Fight Them*. James Nisbet, 1861.
Norris, Frank. *McTeague: A Story of San Francisco*. Doubleday & McClure, 1899.
North, Michael. *The Dialect of Modernism: Race, Language and Twentieth-Century Literature*. Oxford UP, 1998.

Page, Thomas Nelson. *In Ole Virginia; or Marse Chan and Other Stories*. Charles Scribner's Sons, 1895.

Parsons, Elaine Frantz. *Manhood Lost: Fallen Drunkards and Redeeming Women in the Nineteenth-Century United States*. Johns Hopkins UP, 2003.

Pavletich, JoAnn. "Pauline Hopkins and the Death of the Tragic Mulatta." *Callaloo*, vol. 38, no. 3, 2015, pp. 647–663. *JSTOR*, doi:10.1353/cal.2015.0103.

Peck, Garrett. *The Prohibition Hangover: Alcohol in America from Demon Rum to Cult Cabernet*. Rutgers UP, 2009.

Peterson, L. Carla. "Frances Harper, Charlotte Forten, and African American Literary Reconstruction." *Challenging Boundaries: Gender and Periodization*, edited by Joyce Warren and Margaret Dickie, U of Georgia P, 2000, pp. 39–61.

Pickens, William. *Bursting Bonds. The Heir of Slaves: The Autobiography of a "New Negro,"* edited by William L. Andrews, U of Notre Dame P, 2005.

Pizer, Donald. *Realism and Naturalism in Nineteenth-Century American Literature*. Southern Illinois UP, 1984.

———. "Theodore Dreiser's 'Nigger Jeff': The Development of an Aesthetic." *American Literature*, vol. 41, no. 3, 1969, pp. 331–341. *JSTOR*, doi:10.2307/2923993.

Pochmara, Anna. "'In the Tangled Lily-bed': Rhizomatic Textuality and Rooted Cosmopolitanism in Pauline Hopkins's *Of One Blood*." *New Cosmopolitanisms, Race, and Ethnicity: Cultural Perspectives*, edited by Ewa Łuczak, Anna Pochmara, and Samir Dayal, De Gruyter, 2019, pp. 43–58.

———. *The Making of the New Negro: Black Authorship, Masculinity, and Sexuality in the Harlem Renaissance*. Amsterdam UP, 2011.

Powers, Madelon. *Faces along the Bar: Lore and Order in the Workingman's Saloon, 1870–1920*. U of Chicago P, 1998.

Pryor, George Langhorne. *Neither Bond nor Free*. J. S. Ogilvie, 1902.

Punter, David, and Glennis Byron. *The Gothic*. Blackwell, 2004.

Raimon, Eve Allegra. *The "Tragic Mulatta" Revisited: Race and Nationalism in Nineteenth-Century Antislavery Fiction*. Rutgers UP, 2004.

Reynolds, David S. *Beneath the American Renaissance: The Subversive Imagination in the Age of Emerson and Melville*. Oxford UP, 1988.

Reynolds, David S., and Debra J. Rosenthal, editors. *The Serpent in the Cup: Temperance in American Literature*. U of Massachusetts P, 1997.

Riis, Jacob A. *How the Other Half Lives*. Scribner, 1890.

Robinson, Cedric J. *Forgeries of Memory and Meaning: Blacks and the Regimes of Race in American Theater and Film before World War II*. U of North Carolina P, 2011.

Rodgers, Lawrence R. "Paul Laurence Dunbar's *The Sport of the Gods*: The Doubly Conscious World of Plantation Fiction, Migration, and Ascent." *American Literary Realism*, vol. 24, no. 3, 1992, pp. 42–57. *JSTOR*, www.jstor.org/stable/27746503.

Rohrbach, Augusta. "To Be Continued: Double Identity, Multiplicity and Antigenealogy as Narrative Strategies in Pauline Hopkins' Magazine Fiction." *Callaloo*, vol. 22, no. 2, 1999, pp. 483–498. *Project Muse*, doi:10.1353/cal.1999.0095.

Romero, Lora. *Home Fronts: Domesticity and Its Critics in the Antebellum United States.* Duke UP, 1997.
Rorabaugh, W. J. *The Alcoholic Republic: An American Tradition.* Oxford UP, 1979.
Rosenthal, Debra J. "Deracialized Discourse: Temperance and Racial Ambiguity in Harper's 'The Two Offers' and *Sowing and Reaping*." Reynolds and Rosenthal, *The Serpent in the Cup*, pp. 153–164.
Ross, Marlon Bryan. *Manning the Race: Reforming Black Men in the Jim Crow Era.* New York UP, 2004.
Rousseau, Jean-Jacques. *Rousseau's Emile; or, Treatise on Education.* Translated by William H. Payne, D. Appleton, 1892. *Internet Archive*, archive.org/details/rousseausemileor00rousiala.
Saks, Eva. "Representing Miscegenation Law." *Raritan*, vol. 8, 1988, pp. 39–69.
Sánchez-Eppler, Karen. "Bodily Bonds: The Intersecting Rhetorics of Feminism and Abolition." *Representations*, no. 24, 1988, pp. 28–59. *JSTOR*, www.jstor.org/stable/2928475.
———. "Temperance in the Bed of a Child: Incest and Social Order in Nineteenth-Century America." *American Quarterly*, vol. 47, no. 1, 1995, pp. 1–33. *JSTOR*, doi:10.2307/2713323.
———. *Touching Liberty: Abolition, Feminism, and the Politics of the Body.* U of California P, 1997.
Seigel, Jerrold. *Bohemian Paris: Culture, Politics, and the Boundaries of Bourgeois Life, 1830–1930.* Johns Hopkins UP, 1986.
Sheffer, Jolie A. *The Romance of Race: Incest, Miscegenation, and Multiculturalism in the United States, 1880–1930.* Rutgers UP, 2013.
Shockley, Ann Allen. "Pauline Elizabeth Hopkins: A Biographical Excursion into Obscurity." *Phylon*, vol. 33, no. 1, 1972, pp. 22–26. *JSTOR*, doi:10.2307/273429.
Shufeldt, Robert W. *The Negro: A Menace to American Civilization.* R. G. Badger, 1907.
Smith, Valerie. *Self-Discovery and Authority in Afro-American Narrative.* Harvard UP, 1987.
Snyder, Robert W. *The Voice of the City: Vaudeville and Popular Culture in New York.* 1989. 2nd ed., I. R. Dee, 2000.
Sollors, Werner. *Neither Black nor White yet Both: Thematic Explorations of Interracial Literature.* Harvard UP, 1997.
Sotiropoulos, Karen. *Staging Race: Black Performers in Turn of the Century America.* Harvard UP, 2009.
Spillers, Hortense J. Introduction. *Clarence and Corinne; or, God's Way*, by Amelia E. Johnson. Oxford UP, 1988, pp. xxvii–xxxviii.
Stancliff, Michael. *Frances Ellen Watkins Harper: African American Reform Rhetoric and the Rise of a Modern Nation State.* Routledge, 2010.
Stebbins, Jane E. *Fifty Years History of the Temperance Cause: Intemperance the Great National Curse.* J. P. Fitch, 1874.

Stein, Roger B. "Artifact as Ideology: The Aesthetic Movement in Its American Cultural Context." *In Pursuit of Beauty: Americans and the Aesthetic Movement*, edited by Doreen Bolger Burke, Rizzoli, 1986, pp. 23–51.
Stowe, Harriet Elisabeth Beecher. *Uncle Tom's Cabin; or, Negro Life in the Slave States of America*. Robert Bentley, 1852.
Summers, Martin. *Manliness and Its Discontents: The Black Middle Class and the Transformation of Masculinity, 1900–1930*. U of North Carolina P, 2004.
Sumner, William G. *What Social Classes Owe to Each Other*. 1883. Ludwig von Mises Institute, 1954.
Tanabe, Karin. *The Gilded Years: A Novel*. Washington Square Press, 2016.
Tate, Claudia. *Domestic Allegories of Political Desire: The Black Heroine's Text at the Turn of the Century*. Oxford UP, 1996.
Terry, Eugene. "Charles W. Chesnutt: Victim of the Color Line." *Contributions in Black Studies*, vol. 1, 1977, pp. 15–44.
Thurman, Wallace. *The Collected Writings of Wallace Thurman: A Harlem Renaissance Reader*, edited by Amritjit Singh and Daniel M. Scott, Rutgers UP, 2003.
———. *Infants of the Spring*. 1932. Modern Library, 1999.
Tillman, Katherine Davis Chapman. *The Works of Katherine Davis Chapman Tillman*, edited by Claudia Tate, Oxford UP, 1991.
Tindall, George Brown, and David Emory Shi. *America: A Narrative History*. 9th ed., Norton, 2013.
Tischleder, Bärbel. "Literary Interiors, Cherished Things, and Feminine Subjectivity in the Gilded Age." *English Studies in Canada*, vol. 1, no. 1, 2005, pp. 96–117.
Toll, Robert C. *Blacking Up: The Minstrel Show in Nineteenth Century America*. Oxford UP, 1974.
Tompkins, Jane. *Sensational Designs: The Cultural Work of American Fiction, 1790–1860*. Oxford UP, 1985.
Trachtenberg, Alan. *The Incorporation of America: Culture and Society in the Gilded Age*. Hill & Wang, 2007.
Tsemo, Bridget Harris. "The Politics of Self-Identity in Paul Laurence Dunbar's *The Sport of the Gods*." *Southern Literary Journal*, vol. 41, no. 2, May 2009, pp. 21–37. *Semantic Scholar*, doi:10.1353/slj.0.0042.
Twain, Mark. *Adventures of Huckleberry Finn*. Charles L. Webster, 1884.
———. *Life on the Mississippi*. Dawson Brothers, 1883.
Walker, Alice. *In Search of Our Mothers' Gardens: Womanist Prose*. Harcourt Brace, 1983.
Wallinger, Hanna. *Pauline E. Hopkins: A Literary Biography*. U of Georgia P, 2012.
Warren, Kenneth W. *Black and White Strangers: Race and American Literary Realism*. U of Chicago P, 1995.
———. *What Was African American Literature?* Harvard UP, 2012.
Washington, Booker T. *Up from Slavery*. 1901. Courier, 2012.

Webb, Barbara. "The Black Dandyism of George Walker: A Case Study in Genealogical Method." *Drama Review*, vol. 45, no. 4, 2001, pp. 7–24. *JSTOR*, www.jstor.org/stable/1146926.

Wesseling, Elisabeth. "'Like Topsy, We Grow': The Legacy of the Sentimental Domestic Novel in Adoption Memoirs from Fifties America." *Neo-Victorian Studies*, vol. 1, 2012, pp. 202–233.

White, Charles. *An Account of the Regular Gradation in Man, and in Different Animals and Vegetables*. C. Dilly, 1799. *Internet Archive*, archive.org/details/b24924507.

Wilde, Oscar. *Epigrams of Oscar Wilde*. Wordsworth Editions, 2007.

Williams, Andreá N. *Dividing Lines: Class Anxiety and Postbellum Black Fiction*. U of Michigan P, 2013.

Williams, Raymond. *The Country and the City*. Oxford UP, 1975.

Williamson, Jennifer A. *Twentieth-Century Sentimentalism: Narrative Appropriation in American Literature*. Rutgers UP, 2013.

Wilson, James C. "Evolving Metaphors of Disease in Postgenomic Science: Stigmatizing Disability." *Rhetoric Review*, vol. 22, no. 2, 2003, pp. 197–202. *JSTOR*, www.jstor.org/stable/3093041.

Wilson, Mary. "'Working Like a Colored Person': Race, Service, and Identity in Nella Larsen's *Passing*." *Women's Studies*, vol. 42, no. 8, 2013, pp. 979–1009. *Taylor & Francis*, doi:10.1080/00497878.2013.830541.

Wilson, Sarah. "New York and the Novel of Manners." *The Cambridge Companion to the Literature of New York*, edited by Cyrus R. K. Patell and Bryan Waterman, Cambridge UP, 2010, pp. 121–133.

Winter, Kari J. *Subjects of Slavery, Agents of Change: Women and Power in Gothic Novels and Slave Narratives, 1790–1865*. U of Georgia P, 2010.

Winters, Lisa Ze. *The Mulatta Concubine: Terror, Intimacy, Freedom, and Desire in the Black Transatlantic*. U of Georgia P, 2016.

Wollstonecraft, Mary. *A Vindication of the Rights of Woman with Strictures on Political and Moral Subjects*. 1792. Edited by Amy E. Zelmer et al., 2002. *Project Gutenberg*, www.gutenberg.org/cache/epub/3420/pg3420-images.html.

Wyatt-Brown, Bertram. *Southern Honor: Ethics and Behavior in the Old South*. Oxford UP, 1982.

Zackodnik, Teresa C. *The Mulatta and the Politics of Race*. UP of Mississippi, 2010.

Zola, Émile. *L'Assommoir*. Translated by Margaret Mauldon, edited by Robert Lethbridge, Oxford UP, 2009.

INDEX

abolitionism, 31, 46–47, 62, 75–78, 80, 104–105, 127, 152, 160. *See also* Emancipation; reform activism; reform discourse; slavery as a metaphor; slavery era
Alexander, Eleanor, 222n9
American Baptist Publication Society, 131, 161
anagnorisis, 13, 45, 47, 52, 75, 82, 132, 144; definitions of, 23–25, 56. *See also* Cave, Terence
Anderson, William H., 211n2
antebellum era. *See* slavery era
Anzaldúa, Gloria E., 20
Arden, Eugene, 221n2
Aristotle, 56
Arthur, Timothy Shay, 105, 125, 139, 154

Baker, Houston, 18
Balzac, Honoré de, 193
Baym, Nina: on "the passive woman" in literature, 33–34; on pastoralism, 5; on the seduction novel, 36; on the temperance novel, 111; on woman's fiction, 22, 46, 49–50, 52, 63–64, 66, 71, 132, 140
Belasco, David, 217n2
Bell, Bernard, 168, 175, 178
Berlant, Lauren, 6–7, 8, 83–84, 213n12, 215n3, 215n8
Black Arts Movement, 212n6
black temperance narratives, 112, 132, 139, 167, 179, 204–205, 207; definitions of, 12–14, 104–108, 110–111, 148–150; and mulatta melodrama, 9, 13, 23, 36, 71, 88, 91, 99. *See also* drunkard narrative; temperance movements
Bone, Robert, 2, 4–5, 11, 205, 211n3
Bost, Suzanne, 7–8, 20, 213n9, 213n11, 215n3
Boucicault, Dion, 217n2
Bradky, Nellie H., 27, 95
Braidotti, Rosi, 205
Broadway musicals. *See* musicals
Broder, Sherri, 151, 158
Brody, Jennifer DeVere, 213n11, 215n3
Brooks, Peter, 7, 22–24, 26, 110, 173
Brown, William Wells, 8–10, 21–22, 27, 31–32, 36–40, 42–43, 46–48, 56–57, 64–66, 92–95. Works: *Clotel; or, The President's Daughter*, 9–10, 17, 18, 22, 31–32, 36–40, 42–43, 46–48, 57, 64–66, 72, 77, 85–86, 90, 92–95, 117, 167, 187, 213n11, 215n6, 216n18, 222n8; *Clotelle; or, The Colored Heroine; A Tale of the Southern States*, 10, 32, 48, 72, 169, 215n6
brownness, 9, 20
Brummell, Beau, 190
Burns, Emily, 185–186, 195
Bussey, Susan Hays, 216n12
Butler, Judith, 20, 218
Byron, George Gordon, Lord, 122

Cabrera, Miguel, 28–29
Candela, Gregory L., 184–185, 221n1
Carby, Hazel V., vii, 3, 20, 34, 35
casta paintings, 27–30
Cave, Terence, 23–25, 35, 58
Chase, Richard, 12, 107
Chase-Riboud, Barbara, 22
Chatman, Seymour, 63
Chesnutt, Charles W., 8–9, 27, 39, 85, 95, 98, 181; on mulattoes, 20–22. Works: "Her Virginia Mammy," 17, 21; *The House behind the Cedars*, 9, 10, 13, 17, 18, 32, 36, 39–43, 51–53, 57–58, 70, 72–77, 85, 95, 114, 181–182; *Journals*, 27; *The Marrow of Tradition*, 10, 214n13, 214n14, 214n15; "The Passing of Grandison," 75–76
Child, Maria Lydia, 32, 38–39, 66
Chopin, Kate, 218n7, 220n9
Christian Recorder, 112, 128, 161
Civil War, 4, 10, 48, 61, 104, 106, 151, 186
Collins, Julia C., 144
Colored American, The, 18
compassionate manhood. *See* ideologies of masculinity
Condict, Cornelia A., 19, 24, 214n1
Confederacy, 61, 87, 90, 95, 146. *See also* Civil War
Cook, Will Marion, 177
Cott, Nancy, 65, 188
Crane, Stephen, 75, 96, 111, 134–135, 154, 197, 219n9, 221n3. Works: *George's Mother*, 111, 155; *Maggie: A Girl of the Streets*, 96, 111, 134–135, 154–155, 169, 182, 197, 219n9, 220n7, 221n2, 221n3
creolization, 20, 22, 213n12
critical race theory, 9, 20

Daigle, Jonathan, 14, 172, 176–178, 181, 183, 189–191, 194, 221n1
Daly, Augustine, 217
dance craze, 178, 180, 200. *See also* ragtime
dandyism, 167, 170, 172, 181–183, 185, 187, 189–195
Dannenberg, Hillary P., 36, 57
Darwinism, social, 115, 129, 153, 187, 207
decadence, 43, 67, 182, 186, 190
Decker, Jeffrey Louis, 5
Declaration of Independence, 65

Degas, Edgar, 186
determinism, 63, 69, 99, 133, 149, 152–154, 163, 167, 221n2; biological, 114–115, 149, 153; social, 12, 106, 111, 115, 132–133, 149
discourse of respectability, 184–185
Dixon, Thomas W., 61, 151–152
Dodd Mead, 147, 150
domestic novel, 12, 22, 106, 162, 213n11, 214n13. *See also* sentimentalism; woman's fiction
Dorsey, Bruce, 60, 62, 89, 91, 119, 140, 142, 161
Douglas, Ann, 161
Douglass, Frederick, 157, 184, 199
Dreiser, Theodore, 108–109, 111, 136–137, 151–152, 167, 181–182. Works: "Nigger Jeff," 111, 151–152; "The Old Rogaum and His Theresa," 182; *Sister Carrie*, 111, 165, 169–171, 172–175, 182, 219n5, 220n6, 221n2
drunkard narrative, 139, 141–144, 152–154, 163, 195, 198. *See also* black temperance narratives; reform discourse; temperance movements
Du Bois, W. E. B., 105, 212n7
Dudley, John, 174, 217n3, 221n2
du Maurier, George, 182
Dunbar, Alice Ruth. *See* Moore, Alice Ruth
Dunbar, Paul Laurence, 8, 27, 112–113, 131, 147–164, 165–201. Works: *Clorindy: The Origin of the Cakewalk*, 177, 179; *The Fanatics*, 166; *In Dahomey*, 177–178; *Jes Lak White Fo'ks*, 21, 167, 178, 180–181, 184; *The Love of Landry*, 166; *Lyrics of Lowly Life*, 147; "Negro Music," 176–178; *Oak and Ivy*, 37; *The Sport of the Gods*, 6, 11, 14, 37, 47, 59, 97, 165–201, 208, 220n2, 221n2, 223n3; *The Uncalled*, 11, 23, 99, 130, 145–146, 147–164, 207; *Uncle Eph's Christmas*, 167, 181, 184–185, 195; "We Wear the Mask," 166
DuPlessis, Rachel, 36, 58

Emancipation, 34, 35, 42, 50–51, 57, 63, 96, 132, 152, 178, 203, 204, 208
Epstein, Barbara Leslie, 35, 139, 140
erotics of politics, 23–24, 26, 57, 72

Fabi, Giulia M., vii, 32, 47, 52, 134, 139, 142–143, 145, 212n6, 215n1, 215n3, 215n4, 219n1
Fanon, Frantz, 24
Farro, Sarah E., 211n2, 211n3

Fauset, Jessie, 169, 211n4
Felton, Rebecca Latimer, 132
femininity. *See* ideologies of femininity
Fisher, Philip, 22, 137, 142, 220n6
Fisher, Rudolph, 211n4
Fleissner, Jennifer, 109–110, 136, 173–175, 197, 217n3, 217n4, 217n6, 218n7, 220n6
Fletcher, Holly, 103–105, 111, 123, 125, 129, 218n5, 219n10
Foner, Eric, 105, 145
Foreman, P. Gabrielle, vii, 26, 33, 106, 132, 138, 142, 144. *See also* histotextuality; simultextuality
Foster, Frances Smith, 127, 129, 214n2, 218n3
Foucault, Michel, 4, 41
Fox-Genovese, Elizabeth, 5, 44, 60–61, 69, 216n1
free labor, 132, 145
Freud, Sigmund, 136–137
Fulton, DoVeanna, 126–127, 219n8
future orientation in literature, 6, 10, 13, 25, 33, 71, 114, 116, 142, 164, 204. *See also* nostalgia; pastoralism

Gates, Henry Louis, Jr., 199, 212n6, 222n9
Gebhard, Caroline, 211n1, 212n7
Genette, Gérard, 37
Genovese, Eugene D., 5, 44, 60–61, 69, 216n1
Genteel Patriarch. *See* ideologies of masculinity
George, St., 73, 80
Gilded Age, 4, 195, 216n8
Gillman, Charlotte Perkins, 220n9
Gillman, Susan, 22–23, 25, 39, 216n17
Gledhill, Christine, 23–24
Goncourt, Edmond de, 186
Goncourt, Jules de, 186
Gough, John, 153, 219n8
Graham, Sylvester, 119–120
Gramsci, Antonio, 119
Great Migration, 163
Griggs, Sutton, 211n2, 214n15
Grimke, Angelina, 218n7
Grimsted, David, 25

Hall, Stanley, 20
Haney-López, Ian, 20
Harlem, 201, 206–209

Harlem Renaissance. *See* New Negro Renaissance
Harper, Frances Ellen Watkins, 8–11, 20–21, 26–29, 105–106, 112–131, 148–153, 155, 159–164, 175; and temperance activism, 96–97. Works: *Iola Leroy; or, Shadows Uplifted*, 9, 10, 13, 18, 23, 26, 32, 35–36, 38, 43–44, 46, 48–52, 57–58, 59, 64, 66–69, 72, 77–78, 85–88, 96, 115, 117–119, 126, 128–129, 144, 169, 218n6; *Minnie's Sacrifice*, 128–129, 144; "On Free Produce," 124; "Signing the Pledge," 127; *Sketches of Southern Life*, 127; "Something and Nothing," 127; *Sowing and Reaping*, 96, 99, 106, 108, 112–130, 132, 138, 140, 146, 148, 150, 154–155, 160–161, 175, 183, 190–191, 195, 198, 218n6, 219n2; *Trial and Triumph*, 126, 219n2; "Two Offers," 127; "We Are All Bound Up Together," 128; "The Woman's Christian Temperance Union and the Colored Woman," 120, 129
Harper's Weekly, 105, 182
Harris, Joel Chandler, 5
Hartman, Saidiya, 22
Heermance, J. Noel, 32, 48, 160
Hemmings, Anita Florence, 181
Herd, Denise, 104, 125, 128
histotextuality, 26, 120, 153, 157, 219n8
Hopkins, Pauline Elizabeth, 8–10, 18–20, 27, 32–33, 53–58, 69–70, 78–90, 92, 94–95, 98; and evolution, 39; and temperance, 78. Works: *Contending Forces*, 23, 39, 45, 54, 216n10; "The Evils of Intemperance and Their Remedies," 95; "Famous Men of the Negro Race: Hon. Frederick Douglass," 78; *Hagar's Daughter*, 9–10, 13, 18, 31–33, 35–36, 44–45, 53–58, 59, 62, 69–70, 78–90, 94–95, 105, 121, 144, 169–170, 207, 216n14; *Of One Blood*, 111, 217n9
Howard, James H. W., 211n2
Howard, June, 7, 92, 109, 111, 133, 141, 148, 151, 175, 220n6
Howells, W. D., 147, 150, 212n6, 214n14
Hurston, Zora Neale, 79, 211n4
Huysmans, Joris-Karl, 190

ideologies of femininity: domestic femininity, 36, 38, 97, 104, 106, 109, 135–136, 139, 144, 157, 161–162, 174–176, 206–207, 218n6;

ideologies of femininity (*continued*)
    modern femininity, 6, 45–46, 136, 169, 175, 181. *See also* mulatta melodrama: mulatta mother in; New Negro woman
ideologies of masculinity: compassionate manhood, 60, 62–63, 82, 88, 98, 113, 119, 162, 164, 212n7; manliness, 63, 66–67, 71–72, 79, 82–83, 86, 91; marketplace manhood, 60, 71, 91; patrician masculinity, 60–63, 65, 68
intemperance: and gender, 10, 63, 98, 154, 163, 208; and heredity, 155, 160–161, 204; in mulatta melodrama, 10, 53, 58, 63, 67, 78, 79, 92–99, 103, 104, 208; and naturalism, 110–111, 148, 150; and the New Negro movement, 205–208; and racial indeterminacy in literature, 53, 106, 113, 125–130, 132, 139–143; and retrogressionist mythology, 151–152; and sentimentalism, 110–111, 148, 150; and slavery, 96–97, 105, 184. *See also* black temperance narratives; temperance movements
intersectionality, 9, 20, 167

Jacobs, Harriet, 5, 9, 43, 45, 220n10
James, Henry, 44, 84
Jarrett, Gene, vii, 2–3, 148, 153, 212n7, 214n14, 220n1, 221n1, 221n6, 222n1
Jefferson, Thomas, 25, 65–66, 90, 137
Jim Crow regime, 1, 19, 29, 53, 57, 105, 110–111, 117, 129, 150, 163, 179. *See also* segregation
Johnson, Amelia E., 112–113, 125, 131–146, 148–153, 155–164; *Clarence and Corinne*, 8, 11–13, 99, 106, 108, 111, 125, 130, 131–146, 148–153, 167, 175, 191, 198–199, 207, 220n8
Johnson, James Weldon, 170, 177, 179–180, 189–190, 194, 221n2
Jones, Gavin, 166, 178, 184, 190, 221n1
Jones, J. McHenry, 214n15

Kaplan, Amy, 108–110, 137, 217n5, 217n6, 219n5
Kimmel, Michael S., 60, 68, 98
Koren, John, 117–118, 217n1

Larsen, Nella, 21, 169, 206–207, 209, 211n4
Latin Quarter, 186, 200

Leverenz, David, 60
Levine, Robert, 92, 216n3
Lincoln, Abraham, 90
Locke, Alain, 212n6
Loewen, James, 19
Logan, Rayford, 1
London, Jack, 108, 111, 155, 196
Long, Edward, 21
Lott, Eric, 180
Lukács, György, 41, 218n8

manliness. *See* ideologies of masculinity
marketplace manhood. *See* ideologies of masculinity
Marshall circle, 176, 189–190, 194–195
Marx, Karl, 123
Marx, Leo, 4, 212n8
masculinity. *See* ideologies of masculinity
masher, 170, 181. *See also* dandyism
Mayfield, John, 61–62, 88
McAllister, Annemarie, 7, 217n8
McCaskill, Barbara, 211n1, 212n7
McDowell, Deborah, 22, 34, 215n2
McKay, Claude, 211n4
melodrama: and black temperance narratives, 13–14; definition of, 6–7, 22–24. *See also* mulatta melodrama; sentimentalism; woman's fiction
mestiza, 8, 20, 22, 29. *See also* mulatta
Modleski, Tania, 34
Moore, Alice Ruth, 149, 177, 182, 199, 222n6, 222n9
moral suasion, 77, 113, 116, 120, 124, 136, 154, 161–162
mulatta: in African American literature, 18–22; albino, 3, 17, 21–22, 24–25, 29, 33, 72, 206–207, 209
mulatta melodrama: definition of, 9–11, 24–30; and mother-daughter opposition, 32–36; mulatta mother in, 35–46; New Negro daughter in, 9, 21–22, 33, 46–58, 71–72, 119, 180; patrician father in, 63–72. *See also* melodrama; New Negro woman
Muñoz, José Esteban, 20
Murger, Henri, 182, 185–186
musicals, 14, 21, 27, 166–167, 176–181, 185, 193–195, 209, 220n6, 221n2, 223n3. *See also* melodrama; ragtime; vaudeville

Nadir era, 1, 9, 11, 18–20, 50, 57, 98, 104–105, 128–129, 133–134, 167, 179, 204–205. *See also* Jim Crow regime; segregation
naturalism, 7, 12, 63, 138, 141, 163, 167, 170, 196, 198, 203, 220n6 (chap. 6), 220n1 (chap. 7); definitions of, 107–111, 133–134, 147–150
naturalist brute, 133, 141, 143, 151. *See also* retrogressionist brute
new ethnicities, 20
New Negro, 4, 14, 204
New Negro Renaissance, 2, 201, 204, 206–209, 222n2, 222n3
New Negro woman, 9, 33, 36, 48, 54, 169, 180–181, 204, 206, 209. *See also* mulatta melodrama: New Negro daughter in
New Woman, 174
Noble, Thomas Satterwhite, 215n5
Norris, Frank, 107–109, 111, 118, 197–198
nostalgia, 4–6, 13, 25, 33, 39, 71, 109, 142, 149, 204, 213n8. *See also* pastoralism
Nugent, Bruce, 192, 201

Oedipal separation, 34, 160–161, 196, 199
Old Negro, 4. *See also* mulatta melodrama: mulatta mother in

Page, Thomas Nelson, 5, 61–62, 69
Parsons, Elaine Frantz, 91, 110, 114–116, 161, 170–171, 174; on the drunkard narrative, 103, 105, 139–143, 152–155, 195–198
pastoralism, 4–6, 25, 35, 39, 44–45, 60, 84–85, 135, 142, 149, 183, 204, 212n8. *See also* nostalgia
patrician masculinity. *See* ideologies of masculinity
performative identity, 7, 20, 187
Peterson, Carla, 115, 120, 125, 126
Petry, Ann, 169, 199
Philadelphia Centennial Exposition, 182
Pickens, William, 222n9
Pizer, Donald, 12, 107–108, 110, 138, 151, 167–168, 220n6
Plessy v. Ferguson, 19. *See also* Jim Crow era; segregation
plot of decline, 111, 115, 133, 137, 145, 148, 155, 169–170. *See also* naturalism
Powers, Madelon, 118, 180, 198, 218n4, 218n5, 222n9

Progressive Era, 103, 109
Pryor, George Langhorne, 211n2, 214n15
Puccini, Giacomo, 185

race fabrication, 20
ragtime, 167, 177–180, 194, 200–201. *See also* dance craze; musicals; vaudeville
Raimon, Eve Allegra, 22, 213n10, 213n12, 215n4, 215n9
Rapp, William Jourdan, 209, 223n3
Reade, Charles, 108, 146, 217n2
recognitions. *See* anagnorisis; Cave, Terence
reform activism, 3, 7, 106, 149; and the African American community, 26, 52, 54, 104; and class, 83–84, 121, 123, 143, 158, 207; and gender, 54, 62, 159, 204, 206. *See also* abolitionism; temperance movements; woman's suffrage
reform discourse, 29, 52, 67, 88, 91, 98, 105–111, 112–124, 140–150, 163, 195, 204–207, 209, 219n8; and abolition of slavery, 127, 152–153, 155, 160, 205; and class, 52, 119, 141, 150; and compassionate manhood, 62, 72, 79–84, 114–115, 188, 212n7; and discipline, 62, 71, 119, 140, 205, 207; and gender, 34–35, 132–133, 155, 159. *See also* black temperance narratives; drunkard narrative; slavery as a metaphor
respectability, discourse of, 184–185
retrogressionism, 84, 99, 104–106, 125, 132, 163–164, 191, 195, 198–199, 209; definitions of, 63, 73, 92, 104, 125, 151–152
retrogressionist brute, 151–152, 154, 198. *See also* naturalist brute
Reynolds, David S., 107
Riis, Jacob, 109, 220n8
Robinson, Cedric, 176, 179, 180
Rorabaugh, W. J., 117, 218n5
Rosenthal, Debra J., 107, 113, 122, 126
Rousseau, Jean-Jacques, 45

Sánchez-Eppler, Karen, 35, 37, 46, 141, 160–161, 213n10
Scott, Walter, 73, 76
segregation, 11, 19–20, 29, 32, 35, 57, 97, 117, 129, 132, 179; *Plessy v. Ferguson*, 19. *See also* Jim Crow regime; Nadir era
Seigel, Jerrold, 185–188, 193, 200

sentimentalism, 6–8, 12, 83, 107–111, 134, 136, 147–153, 163, 167, 203, 217n6. *See also* melodrama; woman's fiction
separate spheres ideology, 38, 85, 90, 135, 179–180. *See also* ideologies of femininity: domestic femininity; ideologies of masculinity: marketplace manhood
Shakespeare, William, 184–185
Shepherd, Jessie, 79–81, 105
simultextuality, 106, 127, 144
slavery as a metaphor: "a second slavery," 105, 127, 145, 208–209; "slave to the bottle," 91–92, 96–98, 105, 152, 184; "wage slavery," 91–92, 97–98; "woman as a slave," 44. *See also* abolitionism; reform discourse
slavery era, 4, 9–10, 20–22, 91, 95, 105, 119, 123–124, 127, 152, 184, 215n5, 217n11; and mulatta mother, 36, 46, 72; and patrician masculinity, 61, 62, 68–70, 86–88. *See also* abolitionism
social Darwinism, 115, 129, 153, 187, 207
Spillers, Hortense, 135, 143
Stancliff, Michael, 26, 106, 111, 120, 124, 126–127
Stebbins, Jane E., 103, 118–119, 122, 124–125
Stein, Gertrude, 186
Stewart, "Mother" Eliza Daniel, 120
Stowe, Harriet Beecher, 136–137, 219n5
suffrage movements. *See* woman's suffrage
Summers, Martin, 201
Symons, Arthur, 182

Tanabe, Karin, 181
Tate, Claudia, 9, 18, 22, 51, 54, 92, 106–107, 132, 143–144, 146
temperance crusade of 1873, 120, 124. *See also* reform activism
temperance movements, 78, 91, 95–96, 104–105, 118, 124, 133, 139, 153, 218n7, 219n8, 220n9; Washingtonian temperance movement, 123–124; Woman's Christian Temperance Union, 96, 120, 129. *See also* reform activism
temperance narratives. *See* black temperance narratives; drunkard narrative
Tenderloin district, 27, 166, 168, 172, 176–177, 189–190, 193–194, 198–201
Thompson, "Mother" Eliza Jane Trimble, 120
Thoreau, Henry David, 40–41
Thurman, Wallace, 169, 192, 201, 208–209, 211n4, 223n3
Tillman, Katherine Davis Chapman, 5–6, 211n2, 211n3, 214n15, 222n7
Tompkins, Jane, 22, 132, 136, 157, 161–162
Toomer, Jean, 211
Trachtenberg, Alan, 184–185, 212n8
true womanhood. *See* ideologies of femininity: domestic femininity
Tsemo, Bridget Harris, 168, 175, 176, 184, 221n1
Twain, Mark, 5, 73, 216n5

vaudeville, 14, 27, 167, 173, 176–180, 194, 201, 220n6, 221n2, 221n3. *See also* melodrama; musicals; ragtime
Verlaine, Paul, 187

Washingtonian temperance movement, 123–124
Woman's Christian Temperance Union, 96, 120, 129
woman's fiction, 4, 22, 35, 44, 46, 111, 132–133, 140, 204, 216n12; the heroine of, 50, 52, 64, 162; and "the passive woman," 33–34; and the termination of male control, 63–64, 66, 70–72, 86, 144; and the trial and triumph formula, 49–50, 52, 64. *See also* melodrama; sentimentalism
woman's suffrage, 37, 104, 120, 219n10

Zackodnik, Teresa C., 8, 33, 38, 215n8
Zola, Émile, 107–108, 134, 146, 155

www.ingramcontent.com/pod-product-compliance
Lightning Source LLC
Chambersburg PA
CBHW011755220426
43672CB00018B/2973